DUPED

DUPED

Double Lives, False Identities, and the Con Man I Almost Married

ABBY ELLIN

PUBLICAFFAIRS

New York

Jacket design by Pete Garceau
Jacket photograph © I Stock / Getty Images
Cover copyright © 2019 Hachette Book Group, Inc.

PublicAffairs
Hachette Book Group
1290 Avenue of the Americas
New York, NY 10104
www.publicaffairsbooks.com
@Public_Affairs

Printed in the United States of America

First Edition: January 2019

Published by PublicAffairs, an imprint of Perseus Books, LLC, a subsidiary of Hachette Book Group, Inc. The PublicAffairs name and logo is a trademark of the Hachette Book Group.

The publisher is not responsible for websites (or their content) that are not owned by the publisher.

Some names and identifying details have been changed to protect the identity of individuals.

Print book interior design by Amy Quinn.

Library of Congress Cataloging-in-Publication Data
Names: Ellin, Abby, author.
Title: Duped : double lives, false identities, and the con man I almost
    married / Abby Ellin.
Description: First edition. | New York, NY : PublicAffairs, [2019] | Includes
    bibliographical references and index.
Identifiers: LCCN 2018032057| ISBN 9781610398008 (hardcover) | ISBN
    9781610398015 (ebook)
Subjects: LCSH: Ellin, Abby. | Man-woman relationships--Psychological
    aspects. | Deception.
Classification: LCC HQ801 .E39 2019 | DDC 306.7--dc23
LC record available at https://lccn.loc.gov/2018032057

ISBNs: 978-1-61039-800-8 (hardcover); 978-1-61039-801-5 (e-book)

LSC-C

10 9 8 7 6 5 4 3 2 1

For my mother, who was right from the beginning.

CONTENTS

 **ONE**

GASLIT: A LOVE STORY

The truth will set you free, but first it will piss you off.

—Gloria Steinem (Maybe)[1]

My ex-fiancé orchestrated the raid on Osama bin Laden. He received a Purple Heart for his military service and a medal of honor from Golda Meir, which he tucked neatly away in a private vault. He thwarted a bioterrorism attack in New York City and saved the grandson of one of the world's wealthiest men from an attempted kidnapping.

That I know all this is a privilege in itself. None of it was public. He wasn't in it for glory; he made guest appearances at major events but refused the acclaim or even a paycheck. He didn't write a book about his escapades, or sell his story to Hollywood. His goal wasn't to become rich and famous but to keep his children—and all of America—safe from the "bad guys."

"I'm not going to sit by while people are in danger," he'd often say as he packed his bags for a secret mission.

It was wonderfully noble, except for one minor detail: none of it was true.

But that's getting ahead of the story.

Let's rewind to early 2006, when I was writing a newspaper article on detox diets, those lemon-and-hot-water cleanses said to eradicate toxins, inflammation, cellulite, and hangnails. I needed an expert to tell me if they were at all legitimate. Someone recommended a doctor with a posh Beverly Hills practice.

I am most comfortable interviewing people remotely, from behind the warm, safe glow of my computer screen. The roles are clear: I ask questions and the other person answers them. So it went with the doctor.

He told me that adherents of detox programs ran the risk of "hypervitaminosis." These diets were, in essence, bullshit, he said.

He had me at hypervitaminosis.

The quote made it into the story, but the article was put on indefinite hold. Nearly a year later, when the piece was finally slated to run, I called the doctor to fact-check. Had anything changed? Was he still in Los Angeles?

"No," he said. "I'm in the military now. A navy doc." He had quit his lucrative practice and moved to Jacksonville, Florida, to work at a naval hospital.

"How can you be in the military?" I teased. "You're Jewish!"

He lobbed the ball right back at me. "There are seven of us," he deadpanned.

I'd never known anyone who'd joined the military in later life. But then, I'd never known anyone in the military. The doctor told me he'd served years earlier and had reenlisted in order to open a hospital in Iraq for kids with cancer. He was a lieutenant commander. Soon, he would start a job at the Pentagon.

What a coincidence! I was planning on moving to the capital to attend graduate school at Johns Hopkins School of Advanced International Studies, for what I half-jokingly dubbed my Second Useless Master's. I wanted to write about global human rights issues, and this hospital project was a story worth pursuing.

"Keep me posted," I said.

And so he did, emailing every few months with snippets of information. His emails were laden with medical jargon and slightly odd; the language was indecipherable to me. But I was still interested in the story, so I responded enthusiastically.

In December 2009, the emails began picking up in frequency. By late January, they had blossomed into daily, almost hourly, telephone calls. Apparently he, too, had felt a connection during our initial call; he confessed to visiting my website and watching various television interviews I'd done.

"You looked great in that green dress," he said, referring to my appearance on a morning TV show. He waxed poetic on my sternal notch, the indentation in the middle of the clavicle.

We spoke deeply, honestly. The Commander, as I took to calling him, was fifty-eight, a former Navy SEAL, divorced a few years earlier. His two children, then five and twelve, lived on the West Coast with his ex-wife. It hadn't been an amicable split, but he spoke to his kids often and visited frequently.

I told him about my ambivalence toward relationships, how they were really not my area of expertise. I'd just emerged from a brief and disappointing dalliance with a guy I'd known at summer camp. I'd been trying so hard to find a good man I hadn't even cared that he was a Wall Street Republican who played fantasy football.

"I'm not going to learn anything or grow spiritually from another failed romance," I told the Commander. "I've paid my dues. It's time for something good."

"I understand," he said. "I've suffered enough, too."

The demise of his marriage had been excruciating, which was why he'd fled LA. "I couldn't stand the breakup of my family," he told me. "I couldn't bear to live in the city of my failure. The navy saved me."

Moving across the country from your adored young children didn't seem like *Father Knows Best* behavior to me, but I don't have kids and have not endured a divorce. We're all so fragile in our own unique ways. Anyway, it seemed like a good sign that his ex-wife was open to him spending so much time with his kids.

And I was impressed that he was so loyal to the country. Such passion! Such dedication! He didn't care about money. He cared about *people*.

One of the main issues in his marriage, in fact, had been that he wasn't earning enough to placate his ex. She sounded like such a diva. Both she and the other doctors in his office—he was a partner there—had pressured him to refuse Medicaid patients, but he wouldn't. "I'm not going to turn people away just because they can't afford it," he said.

On our first date, in early February 2010, he took me to the Four Seasons in Manhattan—"somewhere celebratory," as he'd put it. I wore a gray silk dress and thigh-high black suede boots; he'd just come from addressing the United Nations and was in navy whites. We embraced as if he were returning from Iwo Jima. The bartender was so moved that he plied us with free drinks (red wine for me, vodka for him). As a present, the Commander brought me a white navy cap—a "cover," in military parlance. I slipped it on, feeling like Debra Winger in *An Officer and a Gentleman.*

Granted, he was no Richard Gere. I'd only seen a few photos of him online, and most were from a distance. In person, he looked a decade younger, but his nose was beakish and he had an overbite and a mouthful of capped teeth. His shoulders hunched forward when he walked, as if he were midbow; he suffered from asthma and squirted nasal spray in public. But his smile was bright and wide, and his hair, though slightly receding, was a beautiful black and silver. He had not a centimeter of fat on his body. And he was entranced with me.

Later, over seared tuna and pinot noir, he confessed that the great trauma of his life was not becoming a brain surgeon, his true calling. He'd wanted to treat glioblastomas, one of the deadliest types of brain tumors, but he hadn't received any surgical fellowships. My grandmother had died of the same cancer. How weird.

This hospital project was his chance to "hit the reset button." "Who gets to start over at my age?" He beamed.

Then he told me that during the previous summer he'd been the medical director at Guantánamo, treating high-level terrorists. He lowered his voice. At Gitmo, a "country club for bad guys," one of his patients was a Very Important Terrorist. He gave me a rundown of the VIT's medical history: kidney trouble, diabetes, enlarged heart.

Bin Laden?

That made no sense to me. If it were true, wouldn't the president want to take credit for his capture? That would guarantee reelection. Besides, a secret that big would never remain that way.

"The president doesn't know," he said.

That seemed even more absurd. I told him that was a stupid thing to tell a journalist.

"It's not verifiable," he said. "I'd deny it. It would be my word against yours."

When I pressed further, he backpedaled: "Maybe it wasn't bin Laden. All I know is what they told me."

"You would know what he looked like! He's six foot six!"

"They all look alike," he said. His glance never wavered.

Every so often he still did undercover work, black ops, in conjunction with the CIA. He had a vault brimming with medals for operations that "did not officially exist." "I'll show you one day," he said.

That was how he had met his ex-wife twenty years earlier. It was when she was being held hostage in Iran and he swooped in like Superman to pluck her out of captivity. "In 1990?" I said. "Why was she being held hostage?"

He told me a long, involved story about her dissident Iranian uncle and the government. When I asked why I'd never read any press on it, the answer was prompt: "Secret mission."

"So, you put your life on the line and you get no public accolades?" In New York, where I live, people are reluctant to get out of bed in the morning unless there's the possibility for some kind of acclaim. But this guy was working under the radar to make the world a better place. He was like no one I'd ever known, a regular Jason Bournestein.

"I want to have an impact," he said. "As long as my kids are in danger, I'll do what I have to do to make the world safe for them."

The acid in my gut started churning a bit. Danger from what, exactly? If this had been a story, I'd have fact-checked the hell out of it. But he was right, there was no way to verify anything, since it was all sub rosa. And maybe there was something to it. *Someone* has to do these jobs in real life, don't they? Isn't that what we've learned from *Homeland* and *Zero Dark Thirty*? The Commander looked nothing like a CIA operative. But what better decoy than an asthmatic, adenoidal physician with bad posture? Such a perfect disguise! His stories were so ludicrous they had to be true.

I'm not a connoisseur of spy novels; I find the Bond movies a bit of a snooze. Nor am I a conspiracy theorist—except when I am. Let's face it: things are not always what they seem. Eleven words are still missing from the Pentagon Papers. We don't know the full story behind JFK's death, or Princess Diana's. Maybe the doctor was nuts. But maybe he wasn't. I knew a bad product when I saw one, and he wasn't it. There's a whole galaxy of unknown unknowns, and I was intrigued.

After dinner, he invited me back to his hotel for that fabled drink. I went. I didn't want the night to end. We kissed, got naked, rolled around on the bed, and then . . . nothing.

"Sometimes it doesn't work," he said. "I'll do better next time." He sounded like an overgrown five-year-old.

"It's okay," I said. "We've been drinking. It happens."

"Not with me it doesn't," he said. "I promise I'll do better next time."

He had a key-shaped scar on his abdomen. I traced it with my forefinger. "What's this?"

He sighed and took a swig of water. "I got into a pole-vaulting accident in college." He paused. "And I was shot."

Shot? That's when he told me about being held hostage in China, detained in a crawl-space room, and tortured mercilessly. Sometimes the guards beat him in the middle of the night, so he took to sleeping sitting up to remain alert. Finally—miraculously—after twenty-three days, he managed to escape. Thank God he'd been a long-distance runner in college.

He was still afraid of the dark and still slept in a reclining position, three pillows propped against the headboard, lights blazing and Food Network blaring. Sometimes he kept a tennis racket by his bed as protection.

"When was the US in China?" I asked. "What were you doing there?"

"Secret operation," he said. "You wouldn't have heard about it."

AFTER THAT NIGHT, we spoke three, four, five times a day. He was reliable and steady. He did not pull the Great American Disappearing Act, a trick perfected by many a man involving telephones, emails, texts, and a sudden inability to use them. He called when he said he would and sent generous gifts: an enormous bouquet of flowers, a strand of pearls, a replica of a Jacqueline Kennedy Onassis emerald-and-diamond necklace. They were "rehearsals" for when he could buy me the real thing. I was falling for him. And why not? It's easy to adore someone who adores you.

And he did, that was obvious. "I would support you through anything," he often said. "I would harbor you, I would protect you. You could tell me you were an ax murderer and I wouldn't care, that's how much I love you." His twelve-year-old son welcomed me into the fold with a charming and surprisingly mature email.

We saw each other every ten days or so, sharing romantic weekends in DC, Maine, and Manhattan. He always bought first-class plane tickets and put us up at five-star hotels. He sent love letters and adoring notes on slips of paper. He was good and decent and exciting and noble. Intense, for sure, but that was okay. He was so passionate about everything! And driven!

And it was so easy. There were no games. On a trip to LA to meet his kids, I decided to put it out there. My biological clock had never thrummed loudly, but adoption always appealed to me. I'd already given money to an agency and was planning to move forward on my own. I wasn't sure if I should continue as a single person or wait to see how things went with him.

"If you're in this, great," I said. "If not, that's okay, too. Just let me know. I'm not interested in any more pain in the relationship department."

"I'm mad for you," he said. "I'm crazy about you. At some point I'm going to ask you to marry me, so I'm on board with whatever you want to do."

A wave of calm washed over me, the antithesis of how I usually felt when men spoke that way. This was the first time I'd ever discussed marriage without wanting to flee. I'd been passionately in love once and "preengaged" twice, and both times a ball of rubber bands had traveled up my stomach and into my throat whenever the subject of marriage came up.

The Commander, however, was different. We were on the same page about everything: religion, career, money, family. The relationship seemed preordained, if you believe in that sort of thing. And even if you don't, there were some mighty strange coincidences.

A few months before we'd begun dating, I'd gone to see a chain-smoking Yonkers psychic named Carmella, who owned a dog the size of a small horse. While the animal lolled about, Carmella received instant messages from the Other World and doodled them on a piece of paper until her pencil tip was down to the nub. She predicted that I'd link up with a man I'd known in the past. He would be wearing a uniform, and his initials were R, P, B, or D (apparently psychics often confuse letters).

"I don't know anyone in uniform other than the FedEx guy," I said.

"Not the FedEx guy!" she rasped. "You're going to move for a man in a uniform. A professional man." A few months later, I got back in touch with the doctor. His initials did indeed include an R, P, B, or D.

I was moving to Washington for grad school; his next assignment was at the Pentagon. I wanted to write about global human rights issues; he was opening a medical facility in Afghanistan. My first book had been about food and fat and eating disorders; he had a background in nutrition. We also both had weird eating habits. I'm a Diet Coke addict; Mountain Dew was his beverage of choice. That made me happy. Nothing's worse than a sanctimonious non–soda drinker.

He led a big life of travel and adventure. I abhor routine. He talked of sailing the world, trekking Aconcagua, visiting the White House. Power! Excitement! And yes, love. Grown-up love. Not backbreaking, mind-numbing passion, which tends to induce craziness. But life-mate kind of love. The kind of love on which foundations are built.

The beauty of it was that he wasn't the sort of man I usually went for, which is to say he didn't know a Burning Man from a burning bush, nor did he care. He (non-ironically) liked the music of the 1970s Muzak band Bread. He was up at 5:00 a.m. As far as I'm concerned, nothing good happens before 10:00. I worried about our different nocturnal habits. But compromise is key, right? The person you end up with is rarely the person you thought you'd end up with. The person you have the best sex with is not necessarily the person you should marry.

(That department had cranked itself up quite nicely, by the way. He made up for that first flaccid night. The main problem now was that the sex went on and on and on. "That's what you do to me," he said. "I can't get enough of you.")

When you've been single long enough and dated everyone from hetero-questionable set designers to alcoholic chefs, you become flexible. All those years of men with empty bank accounts and woodchips under their finger-nails, and now, finally: a doctor! The Jewish Holy Grail. He was so good with my parents, listening to their medical woes and commending them for raising a terrific daughter.

For years my mother had been wishing I'd embrace a nice dentist or lawyer, and I hadn't been able to sprint fast enough in the opposite direc-tion. It pained me to admit it, but maybe all along my future had involved a mezuzah, a stethoscope, and a drawer full of medals for operations that didn't officially exist.

My mother, however, was a little confused about his job status. "It doesn't make sense," she said. "What doctor leaves a private practice in Bev-erly Hills? I wish you could call his ex-wife, but of course you can't."

I fumed. "Why do you have to question everything?" I said. "Why are you so mistrustful?"

But secretly, I wondered, too. He traveled often; for an old guy, he was in high demand. He dutifully called from Haiti, Iraq, and Afghanistan, where he was doing things he would tell me about "when there's a secure line." My friends thought it amusing: the insatiably curious journalist in-volved with someone who couldn't tell her what exactly he did for work. They knew it drove me bananas; I've been known to flip to the last page of a book, just to see how it ends.

My friend Steve suggested I reach out to a private eye he knew. It was tempting, but I didn't think spying would be a loving way to kick off a relationship. Besides, could a detective penetrate the hallowed walls of the Pentagon and the CIA?

My friend Jill suggested that this was simply The Lesson I Needed to Learn. "This is the universe's way of telling you that there are some things you're not supposed to know," she said. "You have to learn to trust."

I don't believe the universe has a personal shout-out for me, or any of us. If it does, then its priorities are totally out of whack. That's simply the excuse we use to pretend we have a modicum of control, because, let's face it: shit happens because it happens.

Except. Maybe it doesn't. Maybe Jill was right. Maybe my attitude needed a complete overhaul. Maybe I just needed to salute the sun and inhale gratitude. Trust, after all, was a choice, was it not?

As a journalist, someone whose job it is to ask questions, I pride myself on my gut, my ability to suss out deception. I'm curious about everything, even when I'm not technically on the clock. I don't even realize I'm doing it. I like to get to the bottom of things, even—especially—when the bottom is muddy and cakey and teeming with snakes.

More than one boyfriend had said that my inquisitiveness was about as pleasant as a root canal. "You interrogate," they'd say. "You should have been a trial lawyer." (A friend put it more succinctly: "You're exhausting.")

They're right. But I come from a long line of skeptics. Doubt is in my DNA. And my digging has usually uncovered good stuff: Drug addiction. Infidelities. Debt.

Maybe a state of denial is the place to live if you want to be happy, but I couldn't reside there.

Curiosity didn't kill the cat. It just left her single.

A BRIEF WORD on marriage.

I am not the sort of woman who puts all her eggs in one trousseau. They'd be cracked and runny by now, anyway, and probably all over my face.

Meeting men was never a problem. They were everywhere: on buses and planes, in offices and malls, on city streets and online. But I found it hard to meet men I liked who liked me back.

I preferred first dates, beginnings. I don't care for quotidian details. I was happiest casually dating one or two people at the same time, so I could keep both at arm's length. Abandonment issues? Fear of intimacy? Gross insecurity? Doubtless all three.

But I've never longed to be a wife. I can't even imagine uttering the words "my" and "husband" in the same sentence. I'd be lying if I didn't admit to desiring a nice big diamond, a beaded white gown, and a giant gala celebrating "me." (I mean—us.) But that's mostly about materialism and being a star, not the drudgery of long-term cohabitation, which never looked like much fun. Plus, I didn't see the point of lingering in a relationship if I knew it wasn't going to last. That's just killing time, and what good is that?

The stories in my head weren't about romance and weddings; they were about excitement. Passion.

Drama was my aphrodisiac, and it had fueled my relationship with an earlier boyfriend, Will, a luthier I'd met in Chilean Patagonia. He'd just battled Stage 4 tonsil cancer; the trip to South America had been his first hurrah since the diagnosis. We'd had one crazy romantic night together in a cabin with no electricity or hot water, and the next day I'd taken off for Machu Picchu.

Not long afterward, he'd bitten into an apple, and his jaw, already weakened from radiation, cracked in half. He'd returned to the States immediately, and we'd plunged headfirst into a relationship, commuting between New York City and the mountains of Virginia. He'd had to do a month's worth of hyperbaric oxygen treatments before he could do jaw reconstruction surgery, to try to increase the blood flow to a necrotic area. We'd trekked all over the place trying to find the best hospital—Sloan Kettering? Duke University?—and settled on Chapel Hill. I was his Do Not Resuscitate person. This was all within the first three months of knowing each other, but it had felt natural. Who had time to waste when he could be disfigured for life, or die? Oh, the plotlines!

He wasn't disfigured, and he didn't die. But the relationship did. The commute was arduous for both of us; I had a life in the city, and he had a woodworking business in the country. We loved each other, but we couldn't be together. Within two months, he met the "farm girl" he would later marry. I spent a good year on my couch, watching *Sex and the City* reruns and nursing my sorrow.

I've never understood why marching down the aisle is seen as some kind of triumph. And it is seen that way, don't let anyone tell you otherwise—especially for women. We might be shouting from rooftops and marching for equal rights (as we goddamn well should), but make no mistake: marriage is still considered a victory for women, perhaps the ultimate one. (Consider the reality show *Say Yes to the Dress*, in which future brides and their coterie vote on a gown. But is there a *Big Bucks for the Tux*? No, there is not.)

Before my maternal grandmother died of brain cancer, she said her big regret was not seeing her grandchildren marry. I was twenty-three at the time, imperious and angry. This was a woman who had been separated from my grandfather for forty years. Why didn't she regret not seeing us win Academy Awards or Pulitzers? Why was marriage such an indicator of life success?

"I don't know," my mother said. "She wants to see you settled."

How did being married "settle" you? And how did my grandmother still believe that it did? It wasn't as if my grandparents' union was happy, and neither one of them had remarried.

Both my mother's generation and my own pitied my single state. It infuriated me. An accomplished magazine editor, who'd been divorced in her twenties and was having a terrible time dating in her forties, put it to me this way: "Even if I never marry again, at least I can say I *was* married." But I'd never defined myself in those terms. While I wanted a life partner, it never seemed possible to have a relationship and also maintain the independence so critical to my sense of self. I didn't want to stay home with the kids. I wanted a big life, with options.

Even though I didn't feel bad about my frequently single status, everyone else was concerned with it: cab drivers, my parents' friends in South Florida, a former college professor *who had never been married*, my four-year-old pal Katie, the daughter of a friend.

"Do you have a husband?" she asked during her princess phase.

"No," I replied.

"You should," she said.

"Why?"

"It's just better. Don't you get lonely?"

How to tell her that yes, I'd had debilitating, aching bouts of loneliness, a hole in my chest so vast that neither food nor booze nor sex nor work could plug it? That I'd woken up every day for the past thirty-five years hoping that on *this* day the love of my life might make his entrance? How to tell her that I was most alone when in the wrong relationship—and most sure-footed when by myself? I'd mastered the art of doing anything on my own. I like my company. Being with another person? *That* was a real challenge.

Like many women who've dated extensively, I've spent godawful nights analyzing the situation. Why couldn't I find anyone right for me? Was it my physical appearance? My personality? Was I paying karmic debts from my past life as Lizzie Borden?

Though marriage was never my goal, I *did* want a playmate, a lover, someone with whom to get into benign mischief. Someone I dug who dug me too: mutual digment.

By the time the Commander entered my life, I'd been actively trying to combat my issues. I would throw my cynicism to the side, stop the Inquisition, and open my heart. So I filed away the Gitmo thing, the Chinese torture, the hidden medals and super-secret missions. Not completely away, but in a synaptic cabinet beneath my amygdala. He was the best person I knew, a grown-up whose life philosophy matched mine in so many ways.

I wanted to trust him. I wanted this relationship to work.

When the Commander proposed five months into the relationship, handing me a tiny round solitaire—"a token, I'll do better when I have more money"—I said, "Yes." Maybe it was rushed, but we weren't kids: I was forty-two and he was fifty-eight. My parents had met at a singles week in the Catskills and had been married within twelve weeks. Three kids and 18,980 days later, they're still together.

He popped the question right after we got back from a jog, with a pithy "I need a running partner for life." He held out a rust-colored box. "Will you be it?" he asked. "Will you marry me?"

Man, I thought. *He must really love me. He knows exactly what he's getting, poor guy.* Because when a man asks for your hand while you're in your sweaty sports bra and shorts, your hair matted under a Red Sox cap—that's a special man. You say "Yes!" to that man. You cherish that man. You think maybe there is a Universe, and maybe it does have your back.

I watched him dial his aunt, his late mother's sister, to share the joyous news. "She screamed, she was so happy!" he told me after hanging up.

"Did you call your son?" I asked.

"Not yet," he said. "I already told him I was going to ask you to marry me."

"What did he say?"

"He said, 'What took you so long?'"

I vaguely began planning a wedding, something I'd never imagined doing. My parents had eloped; they believed couples were better off using the money they'd waste on a wedding as a down payment for a house. I agreed.

For the past twenty years, I've contributed to the Vows column in the *New York Times*, which spotlights a euphoric couple's journey to the altar. I often refer to it as "Other People's Happiness."

I've been to beautiful weddings and fancy weddings and elaborately catered affairs and City Hall gatherings with fizzy wine in plastic cups. I've covered people whose unions were clearly written in the stars, and a couple who broke up on their honeymoon. I met a nonagenarian who married his eighty-year-old bride after their fifty-year adulterous affair. The celebrations were exultant and often beautiful, but despite my queen-for-a-day fantasies, it looked like an awful lot of work.

Nonetheless, with everyone excited for me (I got hundreds of Facebook "likes" when I announced my engagement, basically the digital equivalent of a Nobel) and my friends lobbying hard for a wedding, I decided to do it up. I *did* want a party. And a dress. I quickly settled on a strapless, bejeweled, mermaid-style gown: Rita Hayworth meets Jessica Rabbit. The Commander and I talked about having a blowout in Vegas in November. Or maybe his buddy Seth MacFarlane, creator of *Family Guy*, would throw us a shindig at his mansion.

I made a list of all the people we wanted to invite, mostly from my side. Besides his son, brother, and aunt, he didn't have anyone.

Okay. I did something else. I bought a fake ring.

I know, I know. Find the hypocrite in *that* sentence. Despite my protests, I'm as superficial as everyone else. But I hated the one he gave me; I've had larger pimples. I'd held out all those years for a Diamond as Big as a Whitehead?

So one early October afternoon I trudged over to the Indian district in New York and rummaged through racks of velvet trays. I told myself I was being protective of the Commander. He was such an important guy; I didn't want people to think he couldn't afford a nice ring.

And okay, yes, it was partly my own ego. At my advanced age, I wanted something with a little gravitas.

I settled on a 2.5-carat cubic zirconia. It cost less than $50. I told no one other than my mother and a few of my septuagenarian friends, all of whom had been married for decades. None of them thought it was a big deal. "A lot of women I know wear fake jewelry," said my friend Evelyn, a well-heeled Upper East Sider.

I also wrote an email to Bob Woletz, my editor in the *New York Times* wedding section, asking to be featured in the Vows column. I could see the headline: "Chronicler of Other People's Happiness Finally Marries!" This had Major Motion Picture all over it.

At my monthly authors' group, I casually waved my sparkling finger in the air. "I'm engaged!" I said, amusing them with anecdotes about my Jewish doctor Navy SEAL.

My friend Gretchen's eyes opened wide. "What if he's an impostor?" she asked.

"I thought of that," I said. "But I've met his friends and family. I've seen the Pentagon website. He's legit."

Ada marveled at my ring. "Look at that rock!" she said. I didn't tell her *that* was the real impostor.

IN LATE AUGUST 2010, when Washington is the tenth circle of hell, the Commander and I moved into the Watergate, ground zero for deception. We landed in one of the only rental properties amid the million-dollar condos, a 900-square-foot one-bedroom for $1,500 a month, which the navy was paying for, he said. I hadn't seen the place in advance, but I trusted his choice.

We hadn't seen each other for a while. He'd been in Afghanistan earlier in the summer and returned home with a case of asthma so incapacitating he could barely walk across the street. He didn't want me to witness that, so we were apart for almost five weeks.

During this time, he hired some interns to drive to Jacksonville, pick up his belongings, and transport them back to DC. "Why don't we drive down when you're better?" I asked. "I'd like to see where you lived."

"I'm too old for that," he said.

This bothered me. He could traipse around the Middle East and kill terrorists but was unable to reclaim his belongings? Road trips were one activity I longed to do with a partner. But I figured this was yet another relationship compromise.

Since he was so sick, he couldn't come to New York and help me move out of my place. So I arrived in Washington by train, lugging two suitcases and three shopping bags. The DC air was as thick as old oatmeal. My hair hung limp and my clothes stuck to me. I cabbed over to the Watergate, where he was waiting for me outside.

I was tickled to be living in the famed complex and eager to meet our neighbors. I hadn't gone to the board interview, but apparently Plácido Domingo and William Kennedy Smith had both been there. The Commander knew the latter, the exonerated alleged rapist, from medical school. "I told Kennedy I'd kill him if he even looked at you," he said.

"*Plácido Domingo?*" my mother said when I told her. "Don't you think he's a little too busy to go to board meetings?"

"Maybe he actually cares about where he lives," I said snottily.

My excitement evaporated when I saw the place. We were living in Watergate West, the slummy cousin of tony Watergate East. The lobby was nice—for the Ford administration. Worn carpet, ragged sofas. The floral wallpaper, marble tiles, and gold-plated mirrors were feeble attempts at elegance. We were among the youngest residents; the median age hovered between decrepit and deceased. (I once ran into a neighbor carrying an urn. "This is my landlord," he explained. Oh.)

On my first night there, the Commander set up a little mise-en-scène: a vase of irises and chilled white wine on a metal table, along with a gushy card. "I want this to be a sanctuary for us," he said. "An oasis where we can be together." We toasted our life. Our future.

Later that night, in bed, I briefed him on different wedding venues. Seth MacFarlane hadn't responded to his numerous calls, so that was out. But I had found other options.

"There's a restaurant at the Mandalay Bay in Vegas that looks great. It has a spiral staircase that I could walk down. We could hold the ceremony and reception there."

Silence.

"Or we could go to Caesar's," I continued. "They have a nice chapel. Not so expensive."

More silence.

Finally, he mumbled: "I don't think we should get married in November. Let's wait."

The air sucked out of me, and yet I wasn't surprised. "You were the one who wanted a rushed wedding!" I said. "What changed?"

Apparently his son, who'd initially been so effusive, was having a delayed response to his parents' divorce. "He's having a really hard time, and I don't think I can do it to him right now," he said.

And then he started weeping, violently, his shoulders heaving like an old Italian widow. "I'm so overwhelmed," he said, snot dripping from his nose and onto the sheets. He couldn't even speak, he was crying so hard.

What to do? Be supportive. Comfort him. Tell him I loved him and that we were a team. So I did all that. But my insides turned to water. Had he been jerking me around all this time?

Later that night, I was awakened by a piercing, shrill wail that sounded like a tortured coyote. I knew he had nightmares, remnants from being brutalized in China, but I'd never experienced them.

"It's okay, baby," I said, gently hugging him. "I'm right here."

I figured we'd eventually get separate bedrooms.

THE NEXT MORNING, he left a series of Post-its on the bathroom mirror, in the refrigerator, and on the stove, a scavenger hunt of sticky notes. He apologized for being such a disaster, telling me how lucky he was, how excited he was, to make our union official.

I brushed my hurt aside. The guy had suffered mightily.

About a week later, I borrowed his laptop to type an email while mine was being charged. A note he'd written to his ex-wife before going to Afghanistan a few months earlier popped up. "I'm sorry for all I put you through," he wrote, adding that if he survived the mission he would do his damnedest to "make things right" between them.

It felt like a Brillo Pad had scraped against my insides, leaving them bloody and raw. I called him at his Pentagon office. "Do you want to get back together with your wife?" I demanded.

He was livid that I'd read the email. "You had no business snooping around on my computer!" he said. "You don't know the context! You leap to conclusions without knowing the facts."

He was right. But all bets are off when someone's manipulating you. "So give me the facts," I said.

He told me that the military required everyone to write letters before deploying; he was simply following orders. He'd really written it to "flash" before his suffering son. He wanted to show him that he hadn't abandoned him, that he was willing to try once again with his ex-wife even though *she'd* dumped *him*. He had an answer and an excuse for everything.

I felt bad for reading it, but the whole thing gnawed at me. If he wasn't lying to me, then he was lying to his son. What good was that?

The enormity of my situation hit me: I was stuck.

I'd been the first person to point a finger at women who stayed with bad men—men who lied, men who cheated, men who drank, men who hit. I'd condemned women who stayed in abusive relationships. Why didn't she leave? I would wonder. If I were in that situation, I thought condescendingly, I'd walk away so fast they'd think I'd been a hallucination.

Now finally I understood what it was like to be trapped. My situation was minor compared to people whose lives were embroiled with children, finances, real estate. But I had nowhere to go. My New York apartment was rented, and I knew no one else in Washington.

I called my parents, sobbing. They offered to give me money to move out, but I didn't want that. I was forty-two years old! It wasn't their responsibility.

The Commander came home that night proffering a bouquet of roses. "I can't imagine what you must have felt reading that," he said, stroking my hair. "I was really just trying to help my son. I'm so sorry."

I forgave him. Sort of.

We settled into a groove: every morning he starched his uniform and shined his shoes and went to the Pentagon, where he was on a task force relating to the Middle East. His name and bio were on the website in big bold letters; I met some of the people he worked with, including the grandson of one of the richest men in America. But he would never take me to work fêtes or even the office. Every time he considered it, he would come up with a reason—security was too tight or the event was only open to employees.

I overheard him on the phone, enthusiastically, then increasingly desperately, trying to get funding for his hospital. He called former patients from Beverly Hills, including the movie producer Jerry Bruckheimer and the architect Zaha Hadid, who might design the building.

While I went to grad school, he often took off for parts unknown at a moment's notice: he was active-duty military, and we were a nation at war. Of course, he couldn't tell me the specifics of what he was doing, but he would when he returned.

Sometimes he couldn't be reached even when he was in Washington. He was off meeting with high-level officials from foreign governments, or conducting a secret military exercise in the middle of the night.

HERE WAS THE other problem, though I didn't want to admit it: he was kind of a drag. He wasn't up for sightseeing; he couldn't stay awake in movies. He liked to eat dinner around 6:00, Early Bird Special time. And even then he'd nod off, his fork poised in midair.

I was so lonely. Wasn't the whole point of having a partner to help fill the void? He canceled plans with zero awareness that his actions might affect me, or anyone else. But that seemed to fit right in with his job description: he was just someone who was not trained to emotionally engage with or worry about the impact he had on others.

I missed New York. In Washington, no one is who they seem to be. In New York, no one is who they want to be. At least in New York you knew where you stood.

Mostly, the Commander liked to lie in bed and watch TV. In addition to his asthma, he had chronic malaria, which he'd acquired years earlier in some tropical locale. Every so often the disease would attack his body and leave him itchy and shaking, wracked with diarrhea.

Still, he was loving and romantic. I often came home to a fabulous gift: A military coin he was going to get engraved with my name. A blouse from a Georgetown boutique. I tried to be happy. But I wasn't. And I hated myself for it.

I don't know if my loneliness stirred up my doubts or if my doubts ignited my loneliness, but my sense that the Commander was "truth-challenged" increased. I worried that my commitment issues were getting the best of me, and I needed to work through them. But I couldn't.

One day he showed up with a strand of creamy white pearls. "Mikimoto!" he announced proudly.

I turned them over in my hands. Not my style, but lovely, the gemstones smooth and perfectly round. I peered at the clasp. A more emotionally intelligent woman would have kept her mouth shut.

"Mikimoto? I don't think so," I said. "If they were, they would have an insignia or monogram. There's nothing."

He exploded. "What do you want from me? I don't know from pearls! The guy told me they were Mikimoto! Why can't you just take things in the spirit in which they're given?"

I realized how ungracious I sounded, the ultimate emasculator. But in what spirit were they given? "I'm just worried someone sold you a fake," I said quickly. "But maybe they don't stamp their necklaces." I apologized for doubting him.

Then there were stories that seemed to leap right off the pages of a Tom Clancy novel, which he read nightly. Hillary Clinton requested he sit next to her on a flight to New York. He had a twenty-minute audience with President Obama, who'd autographed a baseball for his son. Somewhere between their conversations about national security and the Chicago Cubs, they'd discussed the book I'd written on childhood obesity, which the president was certainly going to share with Michelle. One day soon the Obamas would invite us for a visit, the Commander was sure. But nothing ever came.

Or there was the time he was standing with a colleague, the grandson of the famous rich guy, on a DC Metro platform. Someone stuck a gun in the grandson's back. Thank God, my man was there to judo chop the assailant. I waited for news coverage of the incident, but he said no one was around to see it. Not even surveillance cameras picked it up.

"Don't mention it when you meet him," the Commander told me when we were en route to brunch with his colleagues. "His fiancée doesn't know it happened. We don't want to scare her."

EVEN THOUGH I was suspicious, no one else seemed to be. I asked his brother—the only person who knew the full scope of the Commander's antics—how best to talk to him. "He has an important job," he told me. "He's busy. You've got to go easy on him."

The Commander's adolescent son, who worshiped him, knew all about his father's work. He wanted to join the military like his dad. Once he called and asked his father if the black sedan parked outside their house was "one of his guys." Apparently, the Commander was in danger of being hurt by the "bad guys" he had foiled. Just to be safe, he and his loved ones were being followed by the Secret Service.

"I've never noticed anyone," I said, peering out the window.

"That's the point," he said.

"Really? They're spending their time watching us? In hiding?"

"Yes."

Sounded ridiculous to me, but just in case, why not put them to good use?

"Next time they're around, ask them to give me a lift," I said. "I can save money on cabs."

My sarcasm did not amuse him.

"Stop doubting me!" he said. "You're like Jekyll and Hyde. I never know which one I'm going to get. You can't have a relationship without trust."

He was right. You can't. But here's how we differed: if my partner didn't trust me, I'd do everything in my power to make him feel safe. I told him that. He told me I should believe him no matter what. Should I? Was that what people did? I didn't know.

Like my mother, I often wanted to call the bitchy ex-wife, but what would she say? In any case, he'd deny everything and spin it. As he told it, she'd never been nice to him, and then one day she'd changed the locks and that was it.

Once I joked about wanting to work for the CIA. "You couldn't do it," he said. "You're not subtle enough." Besides, he said, CIA people were scary because they were "paid liars."

Ah. So was that it? Was my fiancé a paid liar? Maybe I should never have expected him to be honest; he was trained not to be. If you're taught to compartmentalize, it becomes second nature. And that's bound to seep into every aspect of your life.

The more I pressed, the more circumspect he became. "I have no problem with my honor," he often said, thumping his fist against his heart. Semper fucking fi!

I became increasingly paranoid, questioning my own sanity. Gaslights flickered like a semaphore. I longed for some good old-fashioned infidelity; I wished he could be like other men and lie about sex with the babysitter. The questions I had about him weren't verifiable. There was no way to tell what was true and what wasn't. I worried that I was a terrible person, suspicious and unworthy of love.

AFTER FIGHTS, HE sent notes, full of lavish declarations and promises:

Dear Abby,

I write this evening to: 1) proclaim how much I love you and, 2) to try to express how it is that my feelings change, intensify and deepen with each day. . . . You are sexy and achingly beautiful and athletic. You are funny and poignant. Your intelligence is wonderful and multi-dimensional. . . . Sometimes your vulnerability is cloaked in an edginess that I mis-interpret (because of my residual insecurity). I am working on this, both at the level of my shit and at the level of my errors in perception. . . . I want to explore all the possibilities with you, from the grand dreams and romantic world capitals to the latest pizza take-out. . . . I do bring a load of shit with me but am attacking and controlling it. . . . I would love to raise a child with you. I can think of nothing more fulfilling and warm and right.

He signed his letter "Bman," as if he were the star of a *Top Gun* sequel. I read it to my friend Jamie. "What a charmer!" she said. "I've never gotten a letter like that."

"But it's meaningless," I said.

"You are so cynical! Why would he say those things if he didn't mean them?"

I didn't know. I'm a writer; I take words seriously. But I was learning not to.

Worse than not trusting him, I no longer trusted myself.

In November, I asked him to mail a birthday card for my friend's son. He swore he had sent it, but it never arrived. Finally, it came back to me. I'd forgotten to put on the stamp.

IN THE END, Brussels sprouts, not national security, were our undoing.

One night we went out to dinner with my parents. The restaurant was nothing special, but he gushed, unsolicited, about the meal—the best sprouts he'd ever eaten, the culinary love child of Mario Batali and Eric Ripert. My folks were pleased, which pleased me.

So I was dumbfounded when he told me later how much he'd hated the food. I'd had no idea—not a smidgeon of an inkling—that he'd disliked it so much. "Why did you tell them you loved it?" I asked.

"I was trying to make them feel good," he said. "I was being polite."

"There's etiquette and there's unnecessary lying!" I replied. "No one asked you what you thought. Why rave over something you hate?"

And that's when I finally got it: if he could lie so convincingly about something so inconsequential, then he could lie about anything.

I still had no idea if I was with Jason Bourne, Walter Mitty, or a psychotic combination of the two, but I couldn't live in that liminal space anymore. I decided the best thing to do was conduct my own investigative research: Nancy Drew and the Mystery of the Navy SEAL.

I began at Johns Hopkins, where I was studying with some of the greatest political thinkers and military strategists in academia, including a former deputy director of the CIA. My classmates were Army Rangers, SEALs, and Marines. On a class field trip to the Pentagon, I asked one of them if anything the Commander had told me was possible. "The guy's pulling your leg," he said.

One afternoon I bolted the apartment door. I pulled open boxes the doctor kept in the closet, in the dresser, but all I found were notes from students praising his teaching and a photo of him and his ex-wife as newlyweds. There was also a bottle of Vicodin in the medicine cabinet, but that wasn't much of a surprise. I knew he took a painkiller every so often.

Then I worked the phones. In the spring, he'd booked us a romantic weekend at the Inn at Little Washington, an elegant Virginia hotel. But the day before the trip he'd told me he'd received an "unexpected tax bill" for investments he had with his ex-father-in-law. "I can't swing the trip," he said. It was simply too much money; he'd leave the $1,000 deposit he'd already paid for another time. I called the hotel, my heart thumping as I waited, and the answer was yes, we were in the system: a nonrefundable deposit was in place to be used for a future visit. So he really had made a reservation. I was happy about that. But then, why'd he cancel the trip? Had he really been in business with his former wife's father?

What did this all amount to? I didn't know what to think. I suggested couple's therapy, but he said he was too emotionally fragile for that—they were probably the most honest words he ever uttered.

THE FINAL GASP took place over Christmas, when I overheard him and his son talking behind a closed door. We were all staying with his brother's family in Georgetown.

"What's up with the ring on Abby's finger?" his son asked. "Is that from you, Dad?"

"No, child," I felt like saying. "But the real source is a CIA secret."

I pressed my ear to the door but I couldn't make out the Commander's response. But I could imagine him denying it.

"You told me your son knew we were engaged!" I said when we were alone.

"I did!" he said. "He forgot."

"Kids don't forget that their father's getting married," I snapped.

"He's got a lot on his mind," he said. "This is a tough time for him."

That was true. His parents were recently divorced, and his mother had remarried only a few months earlier. But I didn't believe that was really the problem. "You're making a fool out of me," I said, "and I'm not sure why."

"What do you want from me?" he screamed.

"Maybe some honesty?"

Later that night, I took the train back to New York. I had no immediate plans; I just knew I had to get away from him and his family, and he didn't protest. I hugged his kids and aunt goodbye, and thanked his brother and sister-in-law for their hospitality. That was the last time I saw any of them.

Once I got to the city, I felt like I could finally breathe. I was free. But then the disorientation set in. Of *course* his son had been upset! He was a teenager! He was dealing with so much transition! I was such a bitch. I decided I would take a few days and then return to DC to spend the first day of 2011 with the Commander.

But that was not to be. He couldn't get together on New Year's Day, because his expertise was needed to deter a "bioterrorism attack" in New York.

The water supply was in danger of contamination, and only he could save the day. While thousands of people were tossing confetti in Times Square, the Commander was on a secret mission around the corner, protecting the city from dirty bombs.

I went out to dinner with friends at an Upper East Side bistro. It was no different from being single.

The next day I called him up and told him I was done. "I can't do this anymore," I said. No tears, no anger. I was too exhausted for that.

"I agree," he said, equally calmly.

And just like that, I was no longer engaged.

THE PLAN WAS for me to stay at the Watergate until I found a new apartment in Washington, while he stayed with his brother in Georgetown. And then one day in late January 2011, right before school started back up, he told me that we both had to be out of the apartment in two weeks. The navy needed the place for someone else, and he was going to move everything, the furniture and dishes, the TV and futon, into his brother's basement. I needed to vacate.

It sounded fishy to me, but I handed over my keys, and he shipped my clothes back to my parents' apartment in New York. "It's the least I can do," he said.

I commuted to DC once a week for classes—$1 each way on the Megabus! The Commander and I spoke on occasion; he was busy trying to get the clinic opened, but the project wasn't moving as fast as he wanted.

About six weeks after we broke up I passed by the Watergate in a taxi. A light glowed in the apartment. The new tenant? I emailed the Commander. He told me the navy had changed its mind and he was back in the apartment.

"It was a comedy of errors," he wrote. "I got everything out and into storage and then had to move everything back in."

Nancy Drew reared her quizzical head. I went over to do some investigating, using a lost phone bill as an excuse, but the doorman told me he'd gotten a note from the Commander saying that Abby Ellin wasn't to be let upstairs.

I called the Commander immediately. He denied leaving the note. "A woman was assaulted in the building and they're being careful about who they let in," he said. Later, I asked the building management about this. There'd been no attack.

I met him that night at the apartment. Everything was exactly as it had been when I left—right down to my cookbooks lying on the countertop and the sliver of Ivory in the soap dish.

"You never moved out," I said calmly.

"Yes, I did," he said, his eyes cold and unblinking.

"You moved everything out, the bed, the couch, all your clothes—only to bring it all back a few weeks later?"

"Yes," he said.

I think he believed it himself.

CAN YOU LOVE someone who has one foot in one world and one foot in another? I can't. And ultimately, does it make a difference if the lies are to hide an illegitimate child, a dominatrix habit, an addiction to opioids, or a Ponzi scheme? It's the same thing: a person with a hidden world, who looks you straight in the eye and vehemently denies your accusations. Who tells you the sky is plaid and makes you think there's something wrong with you for believing it's blue.

I composed one final email:

Hi there,

I've written a bunch of emails and tossed them, so I'll keep this brief. If you ever want to tell me the truth about things, I would be most happy to hear. But as it stands now, you are right—I really don't trust you, and neither one of us wants to live like that. Too many inconsistencies and fictions and unanswered questions and broken promises and impossibilities.

*I don't think you are malicious AT ALL, just emotionally unaware/
bereft. If you ever feel able to be fully honest and present, I would be
happy to hear from you.*

Take care,
Abby

His reply came swiftly:

*Some of the greatest discoveries and achievements have been made be-
cause there were a few individuals who refused to go along with what
was considered clearly impossible and unbelievable. There is no way the
earth is round, there is absolutely no way the pyramids could be built,
there is no way a man can fly or walk on the moon, or write music like
Mozart.*

You take good care too.

I wish I could say that once I was done I never looked back, but I spent
the next year and a half alternating between relief and self-flagellation. Had
I blown the best thing that ever happened to me? So he'd pretended to buy
expensive pearls. So he'd embellished his appreciation for vegetables. So
what? We all tell white lies. One study suggests that people tell two to three
lies every ten minutes, not including those we tell ourselves. Maybe I was
too quick to judge.

These feelings ate at me until one blustery March morning in 2012
when I got a call from Special Agent Dan Ryan with the U.S. Naval Criminal Investigative Service (NCIS).

A doctor who worked for the federal government had been writing
fraudulent prescriptions for Vicodin, among other drugs (including Cialis
and Viagra, which explained the marathon sex sessions). I—along with colleagues at the Pentagon, his octogenarian aunt, his former father-in-law, his
new girlfriend, and a host of fictional creations—was among the names he
used to get the goods. Did I know this man?

Why, yes, I did.

In my head, I danced a little jig. All that unnecessary angst! All that self-doubt! And all along, I was right. He was *bad*.

I automatically kicked into journalist mode, calling his ex-wife, his co-workers, his new girlfriend, Emma, whom he'd dated thirty years earlier. Each one was shocked—*devastated*—that the man they'd trusted had used them in such a way. As far as they knew, he was their nice nerdy doc who was just trying to do good in the world.

"I almost had a heart attack when I got the call," his ex-wife, Kate, told me, adding that they'd met in medical school, not Iran—she'd never set foot in the country—and that he'd actually been married once before her. He was not in the CIA, had never been a SEAL, although he was in the navy and did work at the Pentagon. Their adolescent son believed his father was a military juggernaut, which is more common than you might think.[2] Websites like Pownetwork.org and Fakewarriors.org regularly chart stories of people pretending to be fake military elite. The Stolen Valor Act, which was passed in 2013, makes "fraudulent representations about receipt of military decorations or medals" with "intent to obtain money, property, or other tangible benefit" a crime. These medals include a Congressional Medal of Honor, a Navy Cross, an Air Force Cross, and a Purple Heart, among others.[3]

Although he'd worked in the Beverly Hills doctor's office, he'd never been a partner (they'd actually wanted him out). She'd had no idea he was addicted to prescription drugs. She thought he was bipolar; I voted for psychopath. We settled on narcissist.

Kate was eighteen years younger than the Commander, petite and gorgeous, with shoulder-length black hair and thick dark eyebrows. She had remarried and was, as she put it, "living a fairy tale." A real one this time.

From Kate I learned not only that the Commander had been married once before her, but that he'd also been engaged to Eileen from Jacksonville *while we were engaged*. Kate wasn't sure why they'd split up, but everyone knew Eileen, all of his friends and family members. This explained why so many of them had looked askance at me when I'd shown up. *Who's Abby? What happened to Eileen?*

The Commander tried to worm out of it. According to the government's lawsuit against him, he'd sent an email to someone he'd worked with at the Pentagon, "P.B.," entitled "my bonehead move." In part, it said, "I am terrified about my poor judgment leading to an accusation of insurance fraud. . . . I don't want to dig myself any deeper, but I feel like I've got to be proactive to avoid disaster. I apologize for burdening you with this, but if you help me out of this one, I will happily owe you Everything."

In a call to Blue Cross Blue Shield, the Commander claimed that some of the pills were prescribed for P.B., because he suffered from injuries caused by an improvised explosive device. The remainder of the medication was "for starving adolescents" at a clinic in Afghanistan. As we all know, poverty-stricken children desperately need narcotics and pills for erectile dysfunction.

I later met with P.B. in person. A well-connected businessman, he was floored by the whole saga. He most certainly had not helped the Commander out. "He stole my identity, that motherfucker!"

The Commander was arrested and sentenced in 2012, but the navy didn't discharge him until late 2013. He voluntarily surrendered his medical license in August 2014. After plea-bargaining, he was sentenced to two years and one day, the mandatory minimum, in a minimum security prison, and ultimately he served twenty-one months. I got periodic updates from the Department of Justice; he told his son that Obama was going to give him a presidential pardon. He didn't.

"YOU'RE LUCKY," FRIENDS said when the Commander was safely ensconced in a West Virginia prison. "You dodged a bullet."

Lucky? That's like saying, "You're lucky you're only a paraplegic after the bus slammed into you." If you were truly lucky, you would never have been hit by the bus, never have been on the same street as the bus, never been in the same goddamn city.

And anyway, it was more like a Scud missile.

Others wondered why I hadn't gotten out sooner. "Weren't there red flags?" they asked. "Did you *really* think he was a war hero?"

The subtext was there in flashing neon letters: How could a professional interlocutor, someone with decades of experience separating fact from fiction, get taken for such a ride?

How to explain that, of course there were red flags, enough to decorate the United Nations, but the wind was blowing them in twelve different directions? That it's almost impossible to see red flags when you're wearing rose-colored glasses?

I felt the need to defend myself.

"Well, I didn't stick around," I pointed out. The Commander and I were only together a year. And I was most certainly not one of those vulnerable women on Dr. Phil, draining my life savings for some guy I met online. Why was everyone blaming me?

Ah, but here's the rub: I blamed me, too.

Why *hadn't* I walked out at the first sign of lunacy—which, if I were being honest with myself, I'd noticed the very first night at the Four Seasons? People show you who they are in the first two minutes you meet them: two *seconds*, if you believe Malcolm Gladwell's *Blink*.

It's not like I hadn't been cautious. But there was no reason for him to lie to me. Of all the single women in the world, why prey on a forty-something pain-in-the-ass journalist with a big mouth? Why not a supermodel or diplomat or heiress? His finances mystified me—he was broke one minute and super-extravagant the next.

But once, when he asked me if I had a trust fund, I'd replied, "Unfortunately, I do not." If it was money he was after, wouldn't he have left after discovering there was none?

I'd even called a lawyer to ask what would happen if my partner came into the marriage with debt. Would I incur it? I'd also wanted to make sure there was no way he could grasp control of my New York apartment. I'd been told that our respective assets and debts existing previously would remain our own, but I could become responsible for whatever was incurred after we wed, depending on how we set up our accounts.

Still, I ignored many other signs that he was fabricating stories. Why?

Oh, the usual reasons. Loneliness. Desire. Compromise. Love. Because he had a Big Life, and seemed more upstanding than any man I'd ever known.

No one really gets it unless they've been duped themselves. They don't understand what it's like to believe in someone and be utterly, completely mistaken. To discover that the person closest to you is actively working against you. One of the main reasons to be in a relationship is to have someone who's got your back. That was a large part of the Commander's appeal: he was on my team. Except, of course, he wasn't.

TWO

THE SECRET LIVES OF ALMOST EVERYONE

Everybody lives in some kind of condition of secrecy.

—John le Carré[1]

After learning the truth about my fiancé, I called everyone I could think of, trying to piece it all together. Very quickly, I started seeing dishonesty everywhere. And, perhaps as a way of dealing with the mess the Commander had made of my personal life, I became fascinated with the subject. Obsessed, actually.

I began noticing how little attention is granted the victims of deception, those "suckers" whose lives were upended by emotional fraud and had to rewrite their entire life histories according to a new reality. There's scant support for people who've been hoodwinked, little to reassure them—*us*—that they're not the only fool walking the earth.

Like Ingrid Bergman in the film *Gaslight*, whose husband has convinced her that she's delusional when all along he's set her up, the victims often lose faith in their ability to determine what's real and what isn't. ("Gaslight" has since become a psychological term, meaning to deliberately manipulate someone.) Being duped contaminates your entire sense of self. It throws you off-kilter, makes you question your perceptions about everything and everyone—lovers, friends, and acquaintances. Cocktail-party banter becomes a mental game of true-or-false.

And being blamed, and blaming oneself, for one's own betrayal causes even more trauma.

In July 2015, I wrote a cover story about this kind of betrayal for *Psychology Today*. I wasn't sure what kind of response I'd get, but I suspected many women would write in. And they did. I received dozens of emails from people who'd been duped. Most, but not all, were women, ranging in age from sixteen to eighty. They shared their stories with me, begging for advice. How to make sense of their lives. How to trust again. They were grateful that someone had shed light on the subject and, more importantly, not blamed them for being taken for such a ride.

But secret lives are all around us, especially in today's culture. Flip on the TV or surf the web and tales of gross betrayal will assault you: The respected Wall Street financier operating a billion-dollar Ponzi scheme. The friendly neighbor with three women imprisoned in his basement. A beloved comedian known as "America's Dad" accused of drugging and sexually assaulting dozens of women.[2] Married, anti-gay, family values–spouting politicians who solicit men in airport bathrooms. Political and environmental activists who are romantically involved with female group members, and sometimes have children with them—only to be revealed years later as undercover police officers spying for the state.[3]

While leading a double life sounds like the stomping ground of psychopaths, moles, and covert agents with indeterminate dialects, plenty of "normal" people in appearance and affect keep canyon-sized secrets from those in their immediate orbits. These untold stories lead to enormous surprises, often unpleasant ones.

In 2011, the Dutch psychologist Diederik Stapel, who published 130 well-regarded studies on human behavior, was discovered to have fabricated data for at least 55 of them.[4] A few years later he wrote an autobiographical thriller, *Derailed*, detailing how he had conned his fellow scientists. ("I opened the file that contained research data I had entered and changed an unexpected 2 into a 4.")[5] Along with some praise, there were accusations of plagiarism of James Joyce and Raymond Carver.[6]

Andrew Ingham, a British supermarket manager in Hertfordshire, England, kept two wives and twelve children who lived only ten miles apart. Three months after the families became aware of one another in early 2012, he hanged himself.[7]

These intricate tales of deception both captivate and repel us. What do we watch these days? *Big Little Lies*, *The Americans*, *The Affair*. Who do we talk about? Tony Soprano, Walter White, Francis Underwood, Carrie Mathison. People with alternate universes and closets bursting with skeletons. Thanks to individuals like these, we've normalized, and sometimes glamorized, lying, cheating, and conning. We're intrigued by these impostor stories. The media lavishes attention on them, and we, the viewers, eat it up.

Although we might find dupers' behavior morally reprehensible, in some cases we root for them. The hero of the TV show *Younger* is a forty-something woman posing as a twenty-six-year-old. *Grace and Frankie* is about two women whose husbands were cheating on them—with each other!—for twenty years. And these shows are *comedies*.

We might even fantasize about leading a similar existence, like serial impostor Frank Abagnale, whose life story spawned a cottage industry of deception: a book, *Catch Me If You Can*, a movie of the same name with Leonardo DiCaprio, and a Tony-nominated Broadway show.

Thanks to social media and the Internet, it's easier than ever to covertly straddle two (or more) worlds. With a simple mouse click, you can connect with almost anyone, anywhere, at any time.

About 15 percent of married women and 25 percent of married men have had affairs, according to the American Association for Marriage and Family Therapy. That number increases by about 20 percent if you consider emotional and sexual relationships without intercourse.[8]

More than thirty million people were signed up for Ashley Madison, a website for married people seeking extracurricular activities, in 2015. Some social scientists estimate that in the general population about four out of every one hundred people are mistaken about who their biological father is.[9] In other words: there's a whole lot of pretense taking place in households across the country.

Yes, secret lives are everywhere: men with two families unaware of one another's existence; people who fabricate entire careers or heroic exploits; women who cheat or commit fraud to a degree and for a length of time that most of us would find unbearably stressful and impossible to pull off. Yet these folks carry on with their regular lives as if everything were normal.

Of course, we all tell white lies sometimes; white lies are the lubricant of society. But there's a big difference between choosing not to inform your friend that her new haircut makes her look like Kim Jong-un and siring a child with the nanny. So why do some people lie habitually, even pathologically, while others don't?

EVEN BEFORE THE Commander, double lives had intrigued me. I was always fascinated by the idea of a life split in two, and terrified of being someone's target. I've never liked being denied information, which probably explains why I became a journalist. Magicians drive me bananas. I hate not knowing how they do their tricks.

As a precocious five-year-old, I did a stint on *Romper Room*, the now-defunct kids' TV program. At the end of each show, Miss Louise, the preternaturally merry hostess, would peer into her "magic mirror." She'd recite a spell, a psychedelic swirl would flash on the screen, and—yowza!—the mirror became translucent. She would then name the children she "saw" in "televisionland," imploring them to be "good doo-bees." (It was the 1970s—what can I say?)

Before the segment, the producers shepherded us preschoolers into the control room to see the wall of TV monitors. We were supposed to watch on the largest screen, which showed what home viewers saw. But I always opted for the smallest one in the corner, where you could see the stagehand give Miss Louise the see-through mirror.

I was thrilled with my discovery. "Look!" I said to a platinum-haired boy standing next to me.

He followed my outstretched finger and quickly looked away. "I don't want to see that!" he cried. He didn't want the illusion broken. I'd rather be disillusioned than duped.

Being lied to by someone close to me has always been one of my great fears. I never wanted to be one of those women who was shocked to discover that her husband kept his socks on during sex with prostitutes she didn't know he frequented. Or that he had a cocaine habit, or was involved in an elaborate Ponzi scheme. I would much rather have all the facts, however ugly.

In high school I was consumed by the story of a schoolmate whose father ran off with the mother's best friend while the mother was recuperating from a near-fatal car crash. It brought up so many questions. Like: To whom should you be true, yourself or your family? Where do obligations begin and end? How did the husband maintain the deception? And how could the friend do that to her best friend?

I quoted a few lyrics to "Everything," a song from the Barbra Streisand film *A Star Is Born*, in my high school yearbook: "I'd like to plan a city, and play the cello, play at Monte Carlo, play Othello, move into the White House, paint it yellow . . ." The lines that resonated with me most, however, came after: "I'd like to have the perfect twin, one who'd go out, as I came in." (I briefly considered something from *Yentl*—who, if you think about it, lived a serious double life, dutiful daughter by day, cross-dressing Talmudic scholar at night. I never said I was cool.)

Years later, I wrote a story for *Marie Claire* in which I was dressed by Tony Mendez, the former CIA agent and the hero of the film *Argo*. Tony and his wife, Jonna, who'd also worked for "The Agency," bought me a wig, fake spectacles, and tight-fitting clothes; they crafted fake teeth for me that completely changed my jawline, caked makeup onto my face, and gave me an unidentifiable accent. The idea was to see if I could fool my friends and boyfriend. I failed miserably. My walk gave me away. Apparently, I swagger like a cowboy.

AFTER COLLEGE, I moved to Manhattan with a gay college buddy named—I swear—James Bond. We were just like Will and Grace, but broke. James and I had a perfect system for figuring out whether a guy was on my team or his. We'd approach whomever caught our eye, sidle up to him, and say: "If you were going to go off with one of us—hypothetically—which one would it be?" Not subtle. But efficient.

One night James came home with a sexy bearded Scotsman from Glasgow. Ewan had only been in the country a few months. He was a writer and spoke in a gorgeous lilting brogue, and James fell wildly in love. Ewan had some family outside Boston, but he wasn't close to them. Soon, he was living with us, and I didn't mind. He made James happy, and he helped with chores. If the Con Edison bill was due, he'd volunteer to walk over to the office and pay it. All I had to do was hand him the money. He also gave me the name of a family friend who was a big shot at MTV, who would most assuredly hire me.

During the month Ewan stayed with us, things started to seem a little suspicious: Con Ed sent me a late notice, for example. How could this be, when Ewan paid the bill?

"Beats me," he shrugged. "They must have made a mistake."

I doubted it, but I was starting a new job (not at MTV, but at a women's magazine in New Jersey) and didn't have time to investigate. And James was still gaga. I didn't want to kill his buzz.

One night I found James and Ewan clutching each other on the couch, red-eyed. Ewan's brother in Boston had been admitted to the hospital; he was dying of AIDS.

A few days later, I told a friend the story. "Do you believe it?" she asked.

Until that point, it hadn't even occurred to me—not consciously, anyway—that Ewan might be lying. But no, I didn't buy it. She and I spent the next hour calling Massachusetts hospitals to see if anyone by his brother's name had been admitted. We found nothing.

I didn't have a chance to see James to tell him the news. The next day, I called home from work and checked our answering machine (this was before the iPhone took over the world). There was a message from the police, "calling about the robbery." *Robbery?*

Ewan had stolen all of our CDs—Dreamgirls! The Who!—and sold them for drug money, which was also where the Con Ed cash had gone. He was not from Scotland but Vermont. He knew no one at MTV, which explains why I never got a call back on the résumé I sent over. The accent was a hoax.

James was mortified. As the youngest of five kids, he always despaired of being the only person in a room who didn't have the same information as everyone else. He spent the next few months scouring East Village record shops and trying to buy back our lost music. He also tracked down Ewan, who was living on the streets.

James barked at me whenever I brought up Ewan's name.

"Can't you just drop it?" he'd say. "I feel like a total asshole."

"But you didn't know! He lied to you!"

"I don't care."

We never discussed it again. Twenty years later, it's still too upsetting.

IT'S EASY TO understand why the duped don't like to talk about their experiences. Over the years, Dr. Phil has featured several women who lost their savings to Nigerian scammers or whose husbands turned out to be sex addicts or gamblers or bigamists. But the audience doesn't *identify* with the victims. They're spectacles, trotted out as cautionary tales. *That would never happen to me*, the viewer thinks smugly. *How could she be so naive?*

It could happen to any of us, at any time. Duplicity is rampant and has been for eons. Literature is rife with characters who are not what they appear. So is the Bible, in story after story: God fooled Abraham into almost slaying Isaac. Rebecca coaxed poor blind Isaac into blessing her favorite, Jacob, instead of the more hirsute Esau. Laban tricked Jacob into slaving for seven years before allowing him to marry his daughter, Rachel—and then foisted the wrong daughter on him at the altar. The bride was veiled, and Jacob didn't realize he'd been tricked until the next morning.

Shakespeare often features dissemblers, periodically in a flattering light, from Falstaff (in *Henry IV* and *V*) to Viola (in *Twelfth Night*) to Rosalind

(*As You Like It*). Novels across the ages have painted meticulous portraits of
double lives: Dr. Jekyll and Mr. Hyde. Dorian Gray. Gatsby. Ripley.

Arthur Miller's lesser-known play *The Ride Down Mt. Morgan* is about a
bigamist named Lyman—Lie-man!—who's recuperating in a hospital after
a car crash. That's when his two families meet. By way of explanation, Lyman says this: "A man can be faithful to himself or to other people, but not
to both, at least not happily."[10]

The Broadway darling *Dear Evan Hansen* focused on a morose teenager who pretends to be a close friend of a classmate who committed suicide, fooling his family. The audience was supposed to sympathize with
the con man.

Of course, there have also been real-world figures leading closeted lives,
historical counterparts to our Bernie Madoffs: Thomas Jefferson (who fa-
thered six children with his slave Sally Hemings). Charles Lindbergh (who
had three separate families on two continents). J. Edgar Hoover (a racist,
cross-dressing, anti-gay gay man). Lance Armstrong. Harvey Weinstein.

Pop culture is littered with deceit: Hitchcock's films are all about deception, from *Suspicion* to *Vertigo* to *Rear Window*.

More recently there was *The Departed*, a fictionalized account of Boston
mob boss Whitey Bulger and his Winter Hill Gang. Bulger was an interesting figure. He was the dark prince of double lives, the ultimate backstabber.
The police finally arrested him in 2011 in a Santa Monica apartment complex, where he lived with his longtime girlfriend, and ultimately tried him
on multiple counts of racketeering, extortion, and other charges, including
complicity in nineteen murders. Bulger and his henchman hated tattlers, or
"rats," but Bulger was the biggest one of all: it turned out that for years, he'd
been *secretly working for the FBI*.

(Being an FBI informant isn't as rare as you might think: about 15,000
people are secretly in cahoots with the feds.[11] A *New Yorker* article noted that
in a 2013 letter, the FBI said it had authorized informants to break the law
more than 5,900 times during the previous year.[12] Rat upon rat upon rat.)

Thanks to the Internet, heavily scripted "reality" TV, social media, and
websites dedicated to adultery, the lines between fiction and reality have
blurred for all of us. Sure, digital footprints might make it easier to get

caught than in years past; so do identity verification programs like Spokeo, which claims eighteen million unique visitors per month.[13] But the opportunity for deception is just as great, if not greater.

CareerExcuse.com offers fake hotel bills, fake doctor's notes, fake reference letters from fake bosses, fake receipts for fake office furniture, and fake background noises like hacking coughs or trains taking off. For as little as $69 a month, Paladin Deception Services provides character and personal references, landlord referral, and "verification of specific skills." Ninety-nine dollars gets you verification of a white lie or "exaggeration," along with voice mail, a dedicated phone line in the city of your choosing, and your choice of male or female operator.

For romantic deceivers, there's broapp.net, a virtual wingman that sends automated sweet nothings to your lover, so you can spend more time with your mates while remaining in good standing with your beloved.

But you don't have to have broapp. Almost everyone on social media is guilty. We comment through fictitious personas, we post meticulously curated photos of ourselves engaged in fauxbulous activities—Hot-air ballooning in the Alps! Summiting Everest! Rappelling off the Tower of Pisa!—even if we're actually imploding at home. Even worse, we're confronted with hourly updates of how wonderful everyone else's life is. We can't seem to keep it in our minds that they're pretending just as much as we are. A celebrated 1993 *New Yorker* cartoon prophesied this future: "On the Internet, nobody knows you're a dog."[14]

NOT ONLY ARE we endlessly fascinated by dupers, but we often cut them a lot of slack. We want to hear their repentance, their redemption narratives. Then we reward them for it.

Meanwhile, society generally regards the betrayed—if it considers them at all—with scorn, derision, even blame. *How could those saps have fallen for that scam?* The marginalization is compounded because most victims are so humiliated that they don't want to talk about it.

Our culture is pretty confused about honesty. In theory, we value it enormously. "Throughout recorded human history, treachery and betrayal have been considered amongst the very worst offences people could commit against their kith and kin," said social-evolutionary psychologist Julie Fitness. "Dante, for example, relegated traitors to the lowest and coldest regions of Hell, to be forever frozen up to their necks in a lake of ice with blizzards storming all about them, as punishment for having acted so coldly toward others."[15]

Yet we get—and give—mixed messages about integrity and honesty. Melania Trump delivered a rousing speech at the 2016 Republican National Convention, where she declared that "your word is your bond and you do what you say and keep your promise." It was very inspiring—until speculation arose that as much as 6 percent of her language was lifted from Michelle Obama's speech at the Democratic National Convention eight years earlier.[16] Oops.

Society starts sending us these conflicting messages when we're children, and parents fully participate. Though they say that honesty is the trait they most want in their children, parents are ten times more likely to rebuke a child for snitching than for lying.[17] They lull kids to sleep with parables of George Washington and chopped cherry trees, all the while lying to telemarketers or salespeople or friends. (Don't even get me started on Santa Claus, the Easter Bunny, and the Tooth Fairy.)

This continues into adulthood. After leaving the White House in 2017, former Trump press secretary Sean Spicer went on to teach a class at Harvard's Kennedy School of Government. A few months later, he made a surprise appearance at the Emmy Awards, making light of the flagrant falsehoods he'd told while working for the president. Former New York governor Eliot Spitzer taught an ethics course at Harvard after we all learned that he keeps his socks on when he's with prostitutes.[18] (Hmm. Both at Harvard. Perhaps the school is the one with the problem?)

We're often happy to give those who behave badly the benefit of the doubt: "He was an addict." "She was bipolar." "They were victims of Wall Street culture." We hand over a psychological pass and send them on their way. After all, we all make mistakes! Almost everyone deserves the chance to be forgiven for past "errors in judgment." (Well, most, anyway. We'll see what happens with Harvey Weinstein, Matt Lauer, Charlie Rose, Garrison Keillor, et al. Bill Cosby has already been sentenced and is serving time.)

Duper-cum-doper Lance Armstrong still has his supporters despite his 2013 "apology" on *Oprah*: 173,000 followers on Instagram and 3.75 million on Twitter. There are plenty of people who don't think he did anything so egregious, that he was merely "leveling the playing field," as he put it. *Us Weekly* announced his May 2017 engagement with a fawning headline: "Lance Armstrong Is Engaged to Girlfriend Anna Hansen: See Her Ring!"[19] In April 2018 he settled the government's $100 million "meritless and un-fair" whistle-blower lawsuit against him for a paltry $5 million.[20] Chump change. But who's the chump?

We're entranced by the liars, the perps. We try to figure out how they do it, and why. Are they psychopaths? Sociopaths? Narcissists? We want to know!

Even the Kardashians are not immune to deception. On an episode of their reality show that I found particularly interesting, Kris and Caitlyn (formerly Bruce) Jenner had an intense heart-to-heart.

"You lied," said Kris, dabbing at her eyes. "I thought we were going to grow old."[21]

I realize this was "reality" TV, which is often anything but real. Still, it struck me. Caitlyn was lauded for "living her truth," winning humanitarian awards and gracing the cover of *Vanity Fair*. But what about her wife? Kris allegedly knew all along that her then husband wasn't comfortable in his skin. Still, regardless of what she knew, she based one of the most important decisions of her life on believing he was her man. It's hard to imagine how she hasn't suffered as a result, despite her overflowing bank account.

On some mundane level, of course, we all lead double lives. We might not think of it that way, but most of us live three or four lives concurrently—at work, at home, in love, with friends. We're "social chameleons," with mallea-ble public and private selves.[22] Sometimes these seem discordant. One week we're in sequins and feathers at the Metropolitan Museum of Art Costume

Institute benefit, the next we're in East Texas gorging on barbecue and Wonder Bread. And we're always putting on a public face. As Chris Rock said, "When you meet somebody for the first time, you're not meeting them. You're meeting their representative."[23]

We all inhabit a deceit continuum, but I'm mostly interested in sustained emotional fraud carried out for personal gain. I'm talking about people who lie to their spouses, children, parents, friends, and colleagues, who prolong and expand the lies until they're telling as many untruths as truths, though maybe not to the degree of disgraced New York State attorney general Eric Schneiderman, a staunch anti-Trumpian who prosecuted Harvey Weinstein—and who in May 2018 was accused of choking, slapping, and psychologically demeaning four women while in alcohol-fueled rages. To us this makes no sense. To them, it just might.[24]

I'm not referring to people who live double lives born of necessity, like, say, Rock Hudson, whose career forced him to pretend to be straight rather than embrace his homosexuality. Or computer scientist Alan Turing, who lived in an era when being gay was a crime. Or Deborah Sampson, who disguised herself as a man so she could fight in the Revolutionary War—something a handful of women did.[25]

Nor am I looking at run-of-the-mill dishonesty—white lies of excuse or courtesy, or the occasional business-trip dalliance at the Topeka Marriott. That's a temporary escape from reality, a parenthesis. A wife who drops a fortune at Barneys without telling her husband? Not a double life. But a wife who's been carrying on a fourteen-year affair with her husband's best friend, Barney? Ding!

When I started asking people about their experiences of being duped, two things quickly became clear. First, pretty much everyone has been deceived by someone close to them, or else they know someone who has. If they haven't yet, give them some time.

Over the course of the three years I worked on this book, a good friend learned that her favorite uncle had been cheating on his adored wife for three decades. Another, who swore her husband was a "terrible liar," discovered that he'd been sleeping with their nanny for years. They legally separated, but kept that secret from their extended families. Another friend found out that his father had been HIV-positive since the mid-1980s. A fourth uncovered a half sister from her father's affair with his secretary. Another learned, on his mother's deathbed, that the mother was thirteen years older than his father—which no one knew. She had faked her age on her driver's license and passport.

Second, people's initial reactions to my questions were often guarded. No one wanted to admit they'd been deceived; nothing's more enraging than being lied to. Only when I made it clear that I was a sympathetic audience did they feel comfortable opening up. Then they couldn't stop talking.

The more I listened, the more questions I had. Questions about why this is happening: Why do we keep hearing these types of stories now? Is it because, as a culture, we talk more about deception than we used to? Or are there more pathological liars lurking about now? Is it simply Fear of Missing Out that propels people to do whatever they want, others be damned? Does the Internet, with its alibi networks and untraceable Bitcoin and disposable, prepaid credit cards, make it easier to pretend to be someone else?

With all of this deceit swirling around us, where does our avowed value of honesty come from? And why do we even expect it from others?

And then there are questions about how it's happening: How do people pull it off, psychologically and logistically? How do they split their day-to-day existence into isolated parts, sometimes for decades, participating in seemingly normal, everyday life with spouses, family members, friends, and colleagues, while carrying on an entire existence elsewhere?

Why are smart people sometimes fooled by liars? Are some of us more likely than others to fall for lies? Why do we trust other people at all? Is trust innate and biological, or something we learn to do?

And finally, I had questions about lying's effects. What's the psychological toll of being deceived in major ways over a long period? What's it like to find out you've been living according to someone else's plan? To realize that you've unwittingly been leading a divided life—split between your perceived reality, on the one hand, and the parallel, actual reality that your partner, family member, or colleague has constructed, an elaborate and long-standing deception around your shared experience? Does one recover from that scale of betrayal? Is it ever possible to trust again?

All of these questions feel urgent to me. The word of 2016, according to Oxford Dictionaries, was "post-truth"—an adjective "relating to or denoting circumstances in which objective facts are less influential in shaping public opinion than appeals to emotion and personal belief."[26] Fake news and "alternative facts" are referenced daily. Donald Trump, the Gaslighter in Chief, roams the gilded halls of the White House, tweeting with impunity.

ONE FUNNY THING about researching dishonesty: every answer seems to lead to more questions. First and foremost: given that we all hate being deceived, why do so many of us lie? Why is deception such an inextricable part of human nature? Why do some people take it as far as the Commander did?

And is lying learned or innate? Can you stop doing it, or is it a sign of neurological impairment? What are the biological, psychological, and social factors that predispose individuals to lie or not to lie? If presented with some fantastic opportunity that involved systematic lying, would many of us go for it? I wanted answers. I needed them.

THREE

WHO *ARE* THE PEOPLE IN YOUR NEIGHBORHOOD?

We all have a dazzling lack of authority about the inner
lives of even the people with whom we are most intimate.

—Cheryl Strayed[1]

The infamous double agent Kim Philby's treachery rocked everyone's world, especially his buttoned-up associates at MI6, the British intelligence service. These were some of the greatest minds in the world—trained liars, skilled at spotting deception in others—and they had no idea that their esteemed colleague was doing double duty for the KGB.

A morally, personally, and in all other ways complicated figure, Philby had been recruited by the Russians in 1934 because they believed his father, Harry St. John Bridger Philby, was a British intelligence officer. One of Philby's first duties for the Soviets, in fact, was to spy on his dad. He found nothing.[2]

In 1963, when Kim Philby's betrayal became evident, he defected to the USSR, which welcomed him with vodka and borscht. His fourth wife, the American-born Eleanor Kearns, wrote a memoir chronicling how her husband fled to Moscow while she waited for him at a party—the Cold War equivalent of "going out for a pack of cigarettes."

Eleanor eventually joined her husband in Russia, but by that time the marriage was teetering atop a nuclear reactor. She returned to the States, penned her book, and died not long after, at age fifty-four. Ben Macintyre, author of the Philby biography *A Spy Among Friends*, said, "For all the excitement of spying, the deception at its core wrecks lives. . . . [Eleanor's] bleak conclusion might stand as a motto for the cruel and fascinating trade of espionage: No one can ever really know another human being."[3]

For years, Philby's children had no idea what had happened to their dad. He simply vanished from their lives. Nevertheless, his son Tommy later said that Philby had been a "very good father."[4]

Philby's granddaughter Charlotte Philby noted that he's still so despised in some circles that on a trip to Arizona in 2005, a shopkeeper wouldn't serve her and her mother because of the Philby name on their credit card.[5]

No matter how often Charlotte and her family visited Philby, they never knew his address. Letters were mailed to a post office box; in reply, he signed off under a special code name. On trips to Moscow, they were driven in a deliberately circuitous route so they would have no idea where they were.

Charlotte's father, John, had learned the truth at age nineteen, shortly after Philby's defection. John had just arrived on the Isle of Wight, off the southern coast of England, for a vacation, where he was met by a billboard announcing that his father was "Wanted."

How did John react to his father's betrayal? Charlotte asked him this question before he died. "To betray, you must first belong," he told her. And Philby himself had said he "never belonged."[6]

In Philby's mind, his perfidy was justifiable. Charlotte didn't think her grandfather second-guessed himself about anything. "Every decision he made was done consciously," she said. "Kim sacrificed everything he had: he risked his life and the lives of others, he betrayed his colleagues and duped his family and friends . . . because he genuinely believed—from the point when he joined the movement and set his sights against the seemingly irrepressible rise of Fascism—that Communism was a cause worth holding dear above all else."[7]

I'm not completely convinced that political conviction was Philby's only driver, though he probably told himself it was. In order to live such a huge lie for so long—to endure the prodigious strain of pretending to devote yourself to one thing when in fact you're working to destroy it—you'd have to derive some personal reward from it. What was that for Philby? Was it the thrill of evading detection? Or was it what his son pointed to—his sense of never belonging anywhere? If you feel like a perpetual outsider anyway, maybe choosing to live an exaggerated version of that existence is empowering: you reject your milieu absolutely, so that being rejected by it won't hurt as much. By isolating himself intentionally, completely, irrevocably, and secretly, was Philby establishing control and superiority over a world in which he always felt far from the center of things?

Maybe my armchair diagnoses are wrong; there's really no way of ascertaining Philby's motives for certain. He might not have known himself why he did it. But I can't think of anyone who would choose such a stressful, lonely, dangerous, and morally questionable life over one of privilege and security for solely ethical reasons. His ego must have been in on it.

Most people who commit this level of fraud don't do so in the name of a greater cause, and to my mind, Philby's commitment to a system he believed would save humanity does make his lies to his loved ones a bit less appalling. After all, as his good friend and fellow MI6er Graham Greene put it, "He betrayed his country, but who among us has not committed treason to something or someone more important than a country?"[8]

ONE AFTERNOON IN the fall of 2015, five years after my debacle with the Pentagon Pill Popper, this email surfaced in my in-box, a response to my *Psychology Today* piece on dupers:

Abby,

I was a full-time "deceiver" for eight years when I was on the run from the FBI (for freeing animals from fur farms). Having to lie to everyone 100% of the time for so long gave me a particular interest in this subject. . . . If you want a different angle on the topic ("activist on the run living a double life") I'd be happy to talk.[9]

It was signed "Peter Young," and there was an 818 phone number.

Activist on the run living a double life. Someone who, like Philby, was willing and able to live a long-term lie for his political beliefs. *Perfect*.

I called him. "I'm looking forward to finally unburdening myself," he said eagerly.

I figured we'd probably end up dating.

ANYTIME WE HEAR a story about someone who isn't who he or she seems to be, the first thing we want to know is: Why? Why did he embezzle millions of dollars from clients, or sire a child with the nanny while perfecting the image of the ideal family man, or profess to be a good Christian while secretly pursuing underage boys? Why, why, why?

"Why" is the question people always ask me about the Commander. Why did he make up such insane stories? Was he a psychopath? A madman?

I understand the question: those who break the social contract in such a protracted and consistent manner confound us. What would motivate someone to risk friendship, family, and security like that? How do they sleep at night?

Moreover, if we can understand why people lie, maybe we can protect ourselves from being lied to. So it seems prudent to begin an exploration of serial lying by simply asking, "Why?"

We're all familiar with those stories: a man, maybe powerful, maybe not, lies to his wife, children, employers, colleagues, country about his position, his accomplishments, his romantic entanglements. The deception begins small and then spirals and spirals until it's got everyone running in circles, including the duper. It's Bernie Madoff and Lance Armstrong and Arnold Schwarzenegger and thousands of others.

I know this story especially well. And frankly, by now it feels overly familiar, even expected. Of course, in the huge range of stories about emotional fraud, those about people, particularly men, lying over the long term in order to have more sex/money/power/fame far outnumber other categories.

But I was intrigued by people who led secret lives for different reasons. Philby offered that opportunity. Peter Young, too. They carried out long-term deception not for personal glory (at least on the face of things), but for causes they were passionate about. What made them tick?

HE WAS BORN Peter Daniel Young, though he had a number of aliases over the years, most notably Simon Zimbel. It was an inside joke with himself: Zimbel was the last name of the owner of the biggest mink farm in the United States. Simon he picked out of a hat, because, as he put it, "What kind of criminal would be named Simon?"

In the mid-1990s, Young was an activist with the Animal Liberation Front, or ALF, an extremist group that set fires and vandalized research labs and farms. ALF has no governing body. It's a label that activists can adopt when they carry out illegal actions on behalf of animals, similar to ISIS or Al Qaeda. People for the Ethical Treatment of Animals (PETA) may have splattered fox coats with paint, and served dishes of roadkill to Anna Wintour, but ALF was radical. "The most effective form of activism that I've seen," Young said. "You could wave a sign in front of McDonald's for a hundred years and hope it would close it down, or you could burn it down." ALF opted for the latter.

He wasn't exaggerating about being on the lam. He had run from the law for eight years. He was eventually caught and spent two years in prison.

Young doesn't feel bad about his past. He's proud of it. His Twitter bio is a virtual paean to it: "Stylized felon. Lifestyle optimization. Militant self-employment. Getting away with it. 'A frequent flying hipster'—Forbes; 'An arrogant vigilante'—AP." Talking to me, he was similarly defiant and self-aggrandizing. "This was my purpose in life," he said. "It's no different than feeling like you had just saved a thousand human lives. Like liberating a concentration camp. The animals are not the same as us, but they feel pain. I was alleviating pain."

Young had a privileged upbringing in Los Gatos, California, and then Mercer Island, Washington, and came of age in the flannel-and-indie-rock 1990s. He was influenced by vegan "straight-edge" bands. Unlike traditional punks, straight-edgers don't use alcohol, tobacco, or any other drugs. Neither did he.

Among Young's favorite adolescent reading material was *Scam*, a memoir / music zine / guide to surviving underground. Its author, Erick Lyle, known as "Iggy Scam," published it by sneaking free photocopies at office-supply stores. "I always maintained that *Scam* was not literally about getting free stuff, but was a broader philosophy about how to find ways to own your own time and be free," Lyle said.[10]

Young shared his views. His father, a Seattle disc jockey, had an interesting assortment of friends. One of them was Bill Nye, pre–Science Guy, who advised little Peter never to get a full-time job. Young thought that was sound advice.

Young's activism started around age seventeen, after a visit to a chicken slaughterhouse in Seattle's Chinatown. He was horrified at the way six capons were stuffed into a single small cage. He wanted to stop it.

He leafleted outside McDonald's and disrupted industry functions. Once, at a meat-processing convention in Portland, Oregon, he hid under a table until the event began. Then he jumped out, chained himself to the table, and refused to leave. All this, mind you, while dressed as a cow. The actions invigorated him, sort of, but they were also frustrating. Protests clearly weren't enough. And the bovine costume wasn't his finest moment.

He often thought about Bill Nye. Why tether yourself to an institution working some pointless grind? After graduating high school, he decided he wouldn't get a job. But he was going to do it in style. He had no money, but that wasn't going to stop him.

He found an empty four-bedroom house on Mercer Island overlooking Seattle and the harbor, not very visible from the street. The place had no electricity, but there was a heater and water; it was a perfect place to squat. He took a sleeping bag and backpack and hunkered down in a bedroom. "I was very covert," he said. "I pretty much existed in a single room."

He read, mostly stories and books on '60 counterculture. He skateboarded. He crashed exclusive parties in fancy hotels. He was living his punk-rock fantasy while presenting as a preppy, clean-cut college kid. If he looked like every other sophomore in town, well, no one would think twice about him.

He traveled, hitching rides up and down the coast. He slept in an abandoned boat. Crashed under stairwells on the University of Washington campus, tiptoeing around the library in his socks in the middle of the night. He felt elated, "finally riding the gap between thought and action," as he put it.

He and his activist friends lived hunter-gatherer existences in the lap of luxury: squatting in mansions, shoplifting, dumpster-diving from Trader Joe's. He figured out how to get everything from phone cards to food for free.

His mantra: "Young till I die."

ONE DAY WHILE he was loitering at the university, a scruffy guy in a knit cap approached him and invited him to a meeting of an animal rights group, Students for Animal Liberation.

Young didn't know what the guy was proposing exactly, but he was intrigued. "He said, 'Show up at my house on Friday night at this time and we'll go do something,'" he recalled. "I was so compelled to take action—what I saw happening to animals was so horrific. There was a sense of urgency. I still feel that way. We are looking at every animal that dies as a murder, and we should fight for their lives as if they were our own."

Young teamed up with a fellow organizer. He was ready to break into labs, but his friend envisioned more low-level actions: paint-bombing a taxidermy warehouse, breaking windows at fast-food chains.[11]

The rationale was this: "If we could close down McDonald's for three hours, then that's X number of fewer hamburgers sold, and hopefully the customers won't go somewhere else, and somehow that will translate into one less animal that had to die that day," said Young.

They could never get the press to show up when they waved protest signs. But throw a rock through the window of a butcher shop, or crack the windshield of a meat distributor truck, or spray-paint something, which took all of thirty minutes, and boom! They were the top story on the news that night.

He met Justin Samuel, another activist, around December 1996. The two men would prowl around research labs. Encircled by rats, chickens, pigs, and frogs, they'd look at each other and wonder, now what? Once the animals were freed, where would they go?

But Young soon grew dissatisfied with vandalism-as-protest. He felt that these were the actions of the powerless. "I felt that I found my purpose in life on one level," he said. "We didn't have any ability to influence on the macro level. I wanted to go bigger."

They learned that minks were genetically wild and native to North America, so you could release them directly into the woods. They found targets and instructions in a publication called *The Final Nail*, a kind of how-to manual for militant activism in the fur industry. They sank their money into a red Geo Metro ($1,500), lifted some black clothes from a thrift store, and bought bulk cutters, disposable shoes, wire cutters, and heavy-duty flashlights. In the fall of 1997, Young and Samuel set off for the Midwest with the goal of hitting as many fur farms as they could before pelting season began, usually from mid-November until late December.

During a two-week period in October, they released at least eight thousand mink and a hundred fox from six fur farms in Iowa, South Dakota, and Wisconsin. They'd open a gate, and hundreds of sleek brown or red animals, saved from slaughter, would scurry past. "You're surrounded by thousands of mink and it's the best feeling in the world," said Young.

It felt urgent, too. "Every night we didn't do something, thousands of animals could potentially die," he said. Plus, it was life-affirming. He was living consistently with his beliefs and outside the law. "Being a criminal—if you do it well, it will really serve you," he said.

I WONDERED HOW much of what he told me was real and what wasn't. All his actions were allegedly for the Cause, but Young had been sort of shady even before he got in trouble.

He had chosen to lead a secret life long before he had to elude the feds. Occupying empty houses, passing as a preppy college kid when he wasn't even enrolled at university, committing strategic acts of vandalism and sabotage. His whole life was about undermining "the system" while gaming it and living for free off its excess. He was amenable to living covertly in the name of his cause well before his arrest warrant was issued. He once lived in a broom closet on the UC San Diego campus.

In a 2012 YouTube speech titled "Fugitives Have More Fun: Confessions of a Wanted Eco-Terrorist," he told the audience, "This is the first time I'm unburdening myself. A lot of what I've told you I'm not telling anyone else."[12]

The same words he said to me.

He's the first to admit that he's always been an excellent obfuscator. "I like being clever, or thinking I'm clever," he said. "I liked living in an abandoned house in a rich neighborhood. I like knowing what the loopholes are and how to exploit them. That's how you can be successful as a fugitive. You maintain that discipline."

The performance he made of unburdening himself made me wonder: Did he try on other personas all those years solely for the sake of the animals, or was he also in it for the drama, the glory?

You could look at his actions as a sign of his total and unwavering commitment to animal liberation. Or you could look at it as evidence of his comfort with deception.

JUST AS THERE was a network of activists watching out for each other, there was also a network of fur farmers. Once one got broken into, every other farm went on alert. Sometimes Young and Samuel would run into furriers waiting for them in their trucks.

On October 28, 1997, Samuel and Young tried to sneak into a multimillion-dollar fur farm in Sheboygan, Wisconsin, via a back entrance. But they took a wrong turn and ended up in the main driveway. (Intro to Crime 101: *When you're engaging in illegal activities on someone's property, don't pull up to the front door.*)

The owner's wife saw them, hopped into her car, and chased them, Hollywood-style. Right when they thought they'd lost her, a pack of cop cars screeched up and pulled them over.

They'd also blown the second lesson in Intro to Crime: *Throw away the evidence.* They had bulk cutters, animal rights literature, and fur-farm addresses in the car. The cops impounded all of it and instructed Young and Samuel to return to the police station the following day.

Young and Samuel glanced at each other sideways. *Were they fucking kidding? Did the cops really think they were going to return?*

That night, the two young activists—twenty and twenty-one years old—snuck into a hotel and hid out in the pool area to stay warm. They tried to figure out their next move.

Was Young afraid? Not really. "Fear is what happens when you anticipate something happening," he said. "When you're in it, there's no fear. It was immediately like, 'We gotta fucking get outta town. They're on our tail.'" He likened it to an animal being tracked by a hunter.

They took a two-day Greyhound to Washington, DC, arriving just before Halloween, with no idea if they'd been indicted. In 1997, the Internet was mostly chat rooms and AOL. "Back then either you had to be in the national news or you had to be in the town where the charges are filed to read the local paper," he said.

So whenever he met someone new, he kept details of his life to a minimum, and maintained the pretense. He looked like a mild-mannered frat boy; there was no indication that he was wanted by anyone other than a sorority sister.

"Everywhere I went as a fugitive I had to have a story," he said. He paused. "I still always have a story."

Samuel immediately bolted to Europe. Young became an outlaw in his own country.

I LISTENED TO his saga and I watched his YouTube interviews, and I didn't know how to feel. On the one hand, Young was an entitled rich kid who didn't want to work especially hard and happily took from others. He vandalized. He ruined the livelihoods of many, many people. He lied and misrepresented himself.

But the rebellious side of me was entirely behind him. Like Kim Philby, Young fervidly believed in what he was doing.

I was also a little jealous. Oh, to have such loyalty to a cause greater than myself! I've longed to believe in something—anything—unconditionally, to be so passionate about a person or cause that I'd be willing to risk jail for it. I envied his conviction, the same way I envy people who believe in Jesus or Allah or amethysts. How lucky to be willing to point a pulsing middle finger at convention, repercussions be damned.

I also identified with him. Because here's the thing: I keep secrets. Sometimes, I outright lie.

Not the way Peter Young or Kim Philby did, but I can fib and get away with it. And I get the appeal. Secrets are powerful! Secrets are *fun*! Especially when they are truly that: something totally yours, that no one else knows. In a study, a group of Texas men and women confessed that the relationships they still thought about had been secret.[13] (Oscar Wilde: "The commonest thing is delightful if one only hides it."[14])

Keeping secrets is a way of maintaining mystery. In an age of compulsive oversharing, when we post hourly updates on our irritable bowels or our safaris through the African bush, remaining unknowable is, perhaps, the ultimate power. It's the only way to hang on to yourself.

"In a very deep sense, you don't have a self unless you have a secret, and we all have moments throughout our lives when we feel we're losing ourselves in our social group, or work or marriage, and it feels good to grab for a secret, or some subterfuge, to reassert our identity as somebody apart," said the late Daniel M. Wenger, a psychology professor at Harvard. And, he added, "we are now learning that some people are better at doing this than others."[15]

An old college pal of mine, an observant Mormon, solicited prostitutes whenever he traveled to a new city. You'd never have guessed this about him; he was the quintessential Boy Scout who wouldn't even take a pencil from the office. His hooker habit went against everything he was, which was the allure. He enjoyed doing something so out of character. It filled a perverse need.

Another man I knew, a frustrated college lacrosse player, wrote a pseudonymous sports column in which he regularly criticized his coach, who often benched him. The coach complained about that "bastard reporter," never realizing that the author was one of his own athletes, who nodded sympathetically during his coach's rants: Clark Kent in cleats (minus the saving-the-world part).

I've done plenty of duplicitous things on a grander scale. In graduate school in the early 1990s, I had a boyfriend—and occasional trysts with a woman. Why did I do this? Because I wanted to. Because I could. Because she had a certain stature in my department, and it was thrilling to (secretly) be involved with a mini-celebrity. Because I was twenty-four years old and my boyfriend and I hated each other but we couldn't quite sever the tie. My affair was a big fuck-you to him, even though he didn't know it. I eventually ended both relationships. I felt too guilty.

This situation was my way of trying to have it all. Of course, none of us gets it all, especially not all at once. And in the end, we're all heading to the same place: buried in the ground, spread out over a meadow, or at the bottom of the sea. But one way to seek control is to keep potential alive. If we don't settle down with a partner, there's always the possibility that Prince Charming will come knocking.

THESE DAYS, I prize honesty. In spite of my occasional fantasy life, I'm known among my friends to be honest to a fault. But just for fun, I decided to keep a daily log of every mistruth I told during a six-month period. Some highlights:

Friday, September 9, 2016

Cut a call short. Said phone was dying. It was at 92 percent.

Saturday, September 10

Told my friend's eight-year-old son, John, that I was twenty-three. Well, he guessed that age and I did not correct him. I was forty-eight.

Tuesday, September 13

Told K. my workout ended at 8:30 and that it was too late to get together. Class really finished at 7:30.

Monday, September 26

At the end of my spin class, the teacher asked how many miles we rode.

The goal was fifteen for the hour. I said twelve. Really had ten. Why lie? No idea. Embarrassed.

Sunday, October 23

Sometimes I wear sweatpants in public. If I run into people I know, I tell them I am on my way to or from the gym, even if I'm not.

Saturday, November 19

Told M. I didn't have any more string cheese. I did—three sticks! But I didn't feel like sharing.

Tuesday, December 6

Faked an orgasm. Okay, two.

Friday, January 6

Told a subject that my editor cut him from a story. That would have been true, had I included him in the first place.

Here's what I learned: I lie for convenience, out of laziness, social fatigue, the desire for personal comfort, or a wish not to ruffle feathers. Much of the time I'd rather stay home and cut my toenails than go out. That is: I want to be invited places, I just don't want to show up. Making up an excuse is usually easier than admitting the truth. Lame, perhaps, but easier.

This is what Bella M. DePaulo, an expert on the social psychology of lying, dubbed a "pro-social lie," a kindhearted utterance to make someone else feel good. (Its opposite, an "anti-social" lie, makes *you* look good.)[16]

It's broadly accepted that pro-social lies, also known as white lies, are a daily occurrence. One study suggests that we tell two to three lies every ten minutes.[17] If you doubt this, consider how frequently you feign interest in a tedious story, wave off a compliment you think you deserve, or apologize for a small offense when you don't completely mean it. I'd go so far as to use a word other than "lie" to describe these. They're Social Niceties. Necessary Bullshit. With all the horrors in the world, what's wrong with a little ego stroking?

Life is way too short to hurt other people in the name of "honesty." Honesty can be vicious. If your colleague asks what you think of her new outfit, which makes her look like Yoda, must you tell her? I'm not saying you should bombard her with sucrose, praising her resemblance to Angelina Jolie. If you can figure out how to tactfully suggest she never wear that brown velour jumpsuit again, go for it. But she can't change her clothes now that she's at the office. Why add to her self-consciousness? (For what it's worth, even the Talmud greenlights lies, so long as they're told to foment peace.[18])

Apparently I'm not the only person who thinks this way. A 1999 study by Robert Feldman at the University of Massachusetts noted that the most effective liars were also the most popular kids.[19] They were fun to be around, and they made people feel good about themselves. This is backed up by psychologist Nobuhito Abe, an associate professor at Kyoto University in Japan, who found that people with conditions that compromise the prefrontal cortex in the brain—like Parkinson's, Asperger's, and attention deficit disorder—are bad at telling lies.[20] That's because they can't perceive social cues accurately, and therefore can't assess if conditions are good for lying, and how their lies are received. Introverts also lie less than extroverts. The ability to lie successfully, then, is partly correlated with savvy social skills. Sucking up.

When adults were asked to keep diaries of their own fictions, they admitted to one for every five social interactions, which averages out to about one a day. That number doubles among college kids. (And quintuples for Trump: in his first 298 days in office, he made 1,628 false or misleading claims or flip-flops, according to the *Washington Post*. And those are just his public statements.[21])

"There are very good reasons to lie in your everyday personal life, positive reasons, even in those gray areas where people say it's important to tell the truth," said Edward Reynolds, a communications professor at the University of New Hampshire. "There are some truths that you'll need to tell to keep a relationship strong, some lies that are important to keep a relationship strong."[22]

Comedian Martin Short, whom I once interviewed, told me in his best basso profundo that if you greet a fellow actor backstage after a horrific performance, you do the only acceptable thing and "*lie.*"[23]

Not everyone agrees. Neuroscientist Sam Harris, in his 2013 book *Lying*, argued that when we sugarcoat the truth, "we deny our friends access to reality—and their resulting ignorance often harms them in ways we did not anticipate. Our friends may act on our falsehoods, or fail to solve problems that could have been solved only on the basis of good information."[24]

I'm with him on the big lies. I don't lie to close friends; close friends deserve the truth (though I do have to work on my delivery, which can be a little biting). But I disagree with Harris about white lies when it comes to acquaintances.

I was once set up on a blind date with my parents' friends' son, a one-man Yenta Centa. A lawyer whose wife had recently died, he hadn't been on a date in twenty-three years. I decided to make it painless for him.

We talked about life and children and deception; he had seen my *Psychology Today* article about the Commander. Most people who read it like to prove how upstanding they are, and this guy was no exception.

"You look about twenty years younger than your pictures online," I said sweetly. It was true.

"And you," he said, "look older than yours."

My head jolted back, as if a baseball had whacked into it. He clearly hadn't gotten the memo: *On a first date, don't offend.* It's not like I'd asked if I needed Botox. "Here's a tip," I said. "Next time you meet a woman, try not to insult her right off the bat. It'll work in your favor."

"I'm not saying you look old," he said quickly. "You look great. But you looked like a child in some of your photos. I'm just being honest."

Needless to say, that relationship did not take off. I imagined him telling me every time a sunspot erupted on my cheek or a strand of hair turned white. That kind of honesty is unwanted and unwelcome. I don't need someone else to make me feel bad. I can do that on my own.

SAM HARRIS AND my blind date notwithstanding, most of us accept white lies and understand why people tell them. But the big stuff? We want the truth about that. Usually.

I agree with philosopher David Nyberg, author of *The Varnished Truth: Truth Telling and Deceiving in Ordinary Life*, who said that he "repudiates all harmfully exploitative deceptions such as consumer fraud, insider trading, the misuse of public office and public trust for personal self-interest, kids hiding their dope and alcohol and pregnancies from their parents, husbands and wives cheating on each other, large-scale tax evasion, used car dealers painting over rust and turning back odometers, the false and vicious reasoning of racism and sexism."[25]

Aside from devotion to a cause—the reason Philby and Young lied—or danger to life and livelihood (like those faced by LGBTQ community), other reasons people construct false realities include greed, vanity, entitlement, the desire for power, and the hubris of believing they should "have it all."

Some people lie to gain an advantage. Or to get one over on someone. Or to save face (usually their own). Or because they're used to getting what they want, especially in this Age of Entitlement.

In some cases people lie out of fear—or, if you're feeling less charitable, cowardice. "They do it because it's easy, because they don't want the discomfort of facing confrontation," said Jeanne Safer, a therapist in New York. "It takes a lot to confront people. You have to be willing for somebody to be angry and disappointed in you. You have to be willing to be exposed in some ways. It takes a lot of ego strength."[26]

My friend Nelson, whom I've known forever, has been with his wife for just over seven years. Not long ago he discovered an affinity for transgender women who hadn't had "bottom surgery."

He regaled me with news of a tryst he'd had in San Francisco. It was life-changing. Suddenly, he realized that the one thing that had been missing from his relationships with women was . . . a penis.

Perhaps the genitalia represented some other missing piece in Nelson's life. Whatever the case, he loved his wife and had no plans to leave her. They had a good marriage. But she was much more traditional than he is; there was no way in hell she was going to welcome a third person into the erotic mix.

"I'm really opposed to you leading a double life," I told him. "It's not fair for your wife to be operating one way and assuming you're right there alongside her, and you're not. She deserves to know what's going on so she can make an informed decision about her life."

He agreed. He didn't want to lie to her. But he didn't want to hurt her, either. He also didn't want to leave her and thus hurt *himself.* It was torturous. How to reconcile his very real desires with his very real love for his wife, and his very real need to not blow up his life?

He enlisted the help of a therapist and close friends, all the while continuing to occasionally hook up with trans women. He finally decided to tell his wife that he had a newly acquired interest in this area, without disclosing that he had physically engaged. But these discussions didn't advance things in the way he had hoped. She saw his newfound desire as a benign fantasy that could be explored through online porn. That it might go to something more fundamental—and arguably some kind of shift in sexual orientation—was not something that registered with her. He sadly realized that his double life wasn't resolvable.

They went to a couple's therapist, who pronounced them "sexually incompatible," which they both knew. They're still trying to figure it out. Nelson doesn't know if they'll implement a don't ask / don't tell policy or end the marriage. He hopes the former.

"The options are negotiating some sort of openness, get out, live a secret life, or stay in the marriage the way it is now," he said. "Whatever I conclude, I'm doing this with therapy and in immense good faith. And then if I arrive at a secret life, it's that I've done what I can do. There can be a rational reason for a secret life."

ONE OF THE most basic reasons people lead double lives, and the one that most speaks to me, a compulsive traveler, involves escapism. Specifically, the desire to escape from oneself, or the version of oneself one feels compelled to present. We all probably have a little bit of Walter Mitty inside, but some of us are Mittier than others. We might not imagine ourselves becoming prime minister or scaling buildings like Spiderman, but we fantasize about inhabiting other worlds, if only temporarily. That's the appeal of every movie or play we see, every TV show we binge-watch, every book we read, every trip we take, every Oscar acceptance speech we rehearse in front of the bathroom mirror, every video game we play in which users create digital alter egos. Everyone needs a respite from real life.

The appeal of the concurrent life—the twin who's partying up a storm while you're home in curlers—is the motivation behind many an adulterous liaison. Theoretical physics even has a hypothesis about it, which I learned about courtesy of the TV series *The Affair*: it's about "what would happen if you could travel back in time and make a different choice in your past, how that would affect your life in the future," philandering protagonist Noah Soloway tells his soon-to-be-mistress Alison Lockhart. "So the theory goes that your true life, your first life, continues as it is, unchanged, but at the moment of decision, a new life splits off along a tangent, into a parallel universe. So you could, in a way, live both lives."[27] Or so he wished.

Some people achieve this kind of escape without exploitation. Those who divorce and remarry are often not just angling for another partner, but another self, another chance. A life do-over. How many times do people talk about being a better father/mother/husband/wife the second time around?

It's arguably the same reason we cheat: "Not so much that we want to leave the person we are with as we want to leave the person *we* have become," said marriage counselor Esther Perel, author of *Mating in Captivity*.[28]

This kind of escapism is the premise of the old film *Same Time Next Year*, which has made sense to me ever since I first saw it in the mid-1980s. A couple, George and Doris, played by Alan Alda and Ellen Burstyn, meet every year for twenty-six years at a Mendocino inn for a weekend dalliance. They have spouses at home and six children between them, and neither one is particularly unhappy with their domestic life. But their annual assignation gives them the freedom to talk openly, without risk of judgment by someone to whom they have big responsibilities. They are free to be who they are, and who they aren't.

At various points, each of them considers chucking it all and running off with the other, but, alas, they are never in synch. So they always return to their respective families. It turns out one of their spouses knew about the annual interlude for ten years, and accepted it.

It's an enticing concept, akin to the Celebrity Sex Pass. (I get Ryan Gosling and Keanu Reeves, though not at the same time.) Let's face it: life is in the details, and the details are often big fat bores. The drudgery of life—bill paying, food shopping, housecleaning, carpooling—can be soul-crushing. At times, even the most pleasant of us morphs into an annoying nag. That's why vacations are so alluring. You change not just your location, but also your persona. A vacation is a liminal space. So's a tryst.

I understand the strong pull of escapism: I like the version of myself when I'm on the road much more than when I'm home. I'm easier, funnier, and more relaxed when I'm away from everyday tedium. I am, if I do say so myself, a pleasure to be around when I'm exploring a new environment. It thrills me. I wilt when I'm not in motion.

Some people do manage to pull off a Liminal Life without leaving home. *New Yorker* editor William Shawn had a second family with the writer Lillian Ross. They, along with her adopted son, dined together every night before Shawn returned to his other family.[29] That was public knowledge, at least in certain spheres. François Mitterrand's two families grieved shoulder to shoulder at his funeral. *Vive la France!*

Decidedly less open was the flying hero Charles Lindbergh, who had three families in Germany, a wife in the States, and a gaggle of offspring scattered on the two continents. He was married to Anne Morrow Lindbergh (they had six kids, one of whom, Charles Junior, the "Lindbergh Baby," was snatched from his crib in 1932 and murdered), but he had a seventeen-year relationship with Brigitte Hesshaimer, a thirty-one-year-old German hatmaker whom he met through his private secretary, Valeska, with whom he was *also* involved. Brigitte bore him two sons and a daughter. But why stop there? He also sired two children with Brigitte's sister, Marietta. And, oh! He also had two children with Valeska. No wonder he picked up aviation. How else to make the rounds?

According to Rudolf Schroeck, author of *The Double Life of Charles A. Lindbergh*, Lindbergh would land in Frankfurt, drive to Marietta's home, then see Valeska, and then head to Brigitte in Munich before returning to Frankfurt. He maintained this routine for fourteen years.[30]

Even more astonishing is that Lindbergh was a rabid anti-Semite who believed in eugenics, including the idea that people with disabilities were inferior. Yet neither Brigitte nor Marietta could walk properly, residue from childhood illnesses. But Lindbergh didn't seem to care. He built Brigitte a house and took care of her financially. (It's not known how he behaved toward the other women.)

Lindbergh spent a handful of days with Brigitte and their children each year. They were told he was an American writer named Careu Kent, and no one was supposed to know about him. The kids finally figured out who he really was when his daughter, Astrid Bouteuil, found letters between him and her mother in the late 1990s. Brigitte made her daughter promise not to go public with them until after her death.

Lindbergh's children with Anne Morrow Lindbergh were amazed to learn that they had half siblings in Germany, but a DNA test confirmed it. Lindbergh's youngest child with Anne, Reeve Lindbergh Tripp, now in her seventies, believed her mother "knew something" about her father's philandering, but she isn't sure what. "That strikes me as most believable," she said. "That something didn't seem right but she didn't know what it was."

Her thesis was that her father never recovered from the abduction and murder of her older brother. Despite the fact that her parents had five more children, they led separate lives, and her father, she speculated, propelled himself into the arms of other women because of his inner tumult. (Some speculate that Anne Morrow Lindbergh had her share of lovers, too.)

Lindbergh's Pulitzer Prize–winning biographer, A. Scott Berg, was equally mystified by his subject's double (triple? quadruple?) lives, which came to light in 2003, not long after Anne Morrow Lindbergh died. Charles Lindbergh, who hated people with disabilities, who was a devoted husband and father? None of this made sense.

"He was the most celebrated living person to walk the earth, the first modern media superstar," said Berg. "And yet there wasn't a single clue."[31]

MOST OF US don't lead double lives to that extent, and so we can tell ourselves we're completely different from the Lindberghs of the world. But we all present many different "I's." And the vast majority of us, if only we're willing to admit it, live in a perpetual state of contradictory desires. So many of us are divided, wishing we could have it all by *doing* it all. We might not act on it—hell, we might not acknowledge it—but it's always there, rumbling beneath the surface. We are married, and we want to be out at the bar. We are single, and we long to be snuggled on a couch, binge-watching *Shark Tank* with our sweetheart. We want kids, and then, once we have them, we pawn them off on our in-laws.

Evidently there's a biological explanation for our tendency to want what we don't have. "We're always looking to adapt ourselves to our circumstances in order to survive, and variation lets us do that," said Jordan Grafman, director of Brain Injury at the Shirley Ryan AbilityLab in Chicago..[32]

Matthew Hornsey, a social psychologist at the University of Queensland in Australia, said impostors often have an enormous sense of entitlement but feel they can't reach their potential on their own merits. So they take on someone else's.[33]

Hornsey got into the impostor game after being fooled by a friend from college, Helena Demidenko, who had written a novel "based" on her Ukrainian family, she said. The book won the Miles Franklin Award, Australia's biggest literary prize, and Demidenko became a star.[34]

Except it turned out that Helena Demidenko was really Helen Darville, the Australian daughter of British immigrants. Her book was a work of fiction in a more profound sense than anyone had imagined.

"I certainly didn't feel betrayed or traumatized, but I did feel wildly curious," Hornsey said in an email. "Literally hundreds of people knew her and her parents. Even I—barely an acquaintance—knew that she was called Helen Darville, not Helena Demidenko as she was suddenly calling herself—and that she had British heritage." So when she became a minor celebrity of Ukrainian descent, he figured he'd gotten the facts wrong. When her lie was exposed two years later, he felt a "bit silly" for not following through on his first, confused instinct.[35]

"When I realized that hundreds of people must have done the same thing—just shaken their head and doubted themselves when such a flagrant lie was being mashed in their face—it suddenly became apparent to me how easy it is to live the life of an impostor," he said. "Sometimes the biggest lies are the easiest to get away with."[36]

The story reminded me of Binjamin Wilkomirski, a Latvian Jew whose memoir, *Fragments*, was published in 1995. Wilkomirski wrote in elaborate detail about growing up orphaned in the Riga ghetto and his experiences in the concentration camps.

Wilkomirski *was* an orphan—that part was true. Except he was born in Switzerland and given the name Bruno Doessekker after being adopted. He was not Jewish, and the only time he'd set foot in a concentration camp was as an adult, on a tour.

Here's the intriguing thing: Wilkomirski stayed true to his tale. He wore a yarmulke and tallis, or prayer shawl, in public, and played the clarinet in a Klezmer band. Two books were published on his duplicity, but his position never faltered. That was his story, and he was sticking to it.[37]

Another ethnicity-changer was Rachel Dolezal, president of the NAACP chapter in Spokane, Washington, and an instructor of Africana studies at Eastern Washington University. Dolezal passed herself off as black. She wasn't. She was as white as this page, which her parents admitted on TV.[38]

Dolezal said she'd always identified as black. As a child, she told *Today*, she was "drawing self-portraits with the brown crayon instead of the peach crayon. It was a little more complex than me identifying as black."[39] Still, the public was not very forgiving, comparing her actions to actors performing in blackface.

Hornsey believes we're gripped by impostors because they make us question everything we believe about the world and how it works. While we may fantasize about the other lives we might be leading, or the road not taken, most of us don't have the wherewithal to pull it off. We might dream about becoming someone else, but we don't act on it. Instead, we sigh vigorously and resign ourselves to our humdrum existences.

And that's why we're so captivated by exotic tales of impostors and frauds. We love reading about surgeons who have purchased their medical license on the black market, provided they're not about to operate on us.

Beyond that, Hornsey believes that deep down most of us worry that we're frauds. So we identify with impostors.

"Most of us engage in a low-key impostor-ism every day," said Hornsey. "What if I smile when I'm not feeling happy? What if I pretend to be interested when I'm not? What if I pretend to be confident when I'm really feeling nervous? There's a thin divide that separates impostor-ism from impression management or even social skill."[40]

To compensate, we become social chameleons, adjusting our attitudes and behaviors to fit whatever circumstance we're in, like Woody Allen's character in *Zelig*. This, too, is a form of impostorism.[41]

Donald W. Winnicott, the famous analyst, chalked it up to the "false self," which he said arises in children when they're taught to focus on other people's needs and ignore their own.[42]

"If you have a false self and it's powerful, eventually you get self-destructive," psychologist Joel Weinberger, a professor at Adelphi University, told me. "A false self is normative to a degree. But when the false self takes over to achieve a goal or convince someone of something, then that's when that line gets crossed."[43] That's when the version you present to the world can become exploitative and destructive.

As I look at my own life, I see evidence of impostorism in the little lies I tell about my cell-phone battery, in my fake "diamond," and in my need to escape. But did that make me like the Commander? What if we were the same all along?

FOUR

THE JOY OF LYING

> When you're courting someone, you're always
> willing to pretend you're something you're not.
> For example, when you first start dating some-
> one, you'll agree to go apple picking.
>
> —Seth Meyers[1]

He was dubbed "The Great Impostor" because of his habit of borrow-ing other people's identities.[2] Over the course of his lifetime, he passed himself off as, among other things, a monk, a doctor on a naval ship, a civil engineer, an assistant prison warden, a sheriff's deputy, a professor, a cancer researcher, and a lawyer. And he was all of those, sort of, although he never went by his real name: Ferdinand Waldo Demara Jr.[3]

Demara was born in 1921 in Lawrence, Massachusetts, to a wealthy family who lost everything in the Depression. By all accounts, young Waldo did not enjoy being poor, and at age sixteen he ran away to Rhode Island and joined the Cistercian monks, an order of meditative farmworkers. In 1941, he enlisted in the army; a year later, he took the name of Anthony Ignolia, an army buddy, and went AWOL. Still passing as Ignolia, he joined the navy and trained as a hospital corpsman.

But he didn't reach the position he wanted. So he did what any normal person would do, and faked suicide. Later, posing as a very much alive psychologist named Robert Linton French, he taught psychology at Gannon College in Erie, Pennsylvania.

The FBI soon caught up with him, and he served eighteen months at the United States Disciplinary Barracks. Not for identity fraud, mind you, but for that long ago military desertion. After his release, he went to law school at Northeastern University, in Boston, then joined the Brothers of Christian Instruction, a Catholic education group founded in 1819 to "educate the young and to make Jesus Christ better known and better loved."[4]

But why stop there? He later took on the persona of Joseph Cyr, a doctor he had become friendly with, and during the Korean War "Cyr" landed a gig as a trauma surgeon on the *Cayuga*, a Royal Canadian Navy destroyer. That he had never been to medical school was irrelevant. He was a damn good surgeon—so good that a Canadian newspaper wrote an article about him.

As it happened, the story caught the attention of the mother of the real Joseph Cyr. She knew her remarkable son was not in Korea but practicing medicine in Grand Falls, New Brunswick, in Canada. When she called the *Cayuga*'s captain to inform him of the impersonator in his midst, he initially refused to believe that Demara was not a doctor (or Joseph Cyr). But the Canadian navy didn't charge him, so Demara went back to the United States.

The irony is that Demara was an exceptional employee. He had a high IQ and a photographic memory. As a doctor, he saved many lives. He could have been anything he wanted—when he died in 1982 at age sixty, he was a social worker. So, why would a man who didn't have to pretend, pretend?

In his own words: "Rascality, pure rascality."[5]

"I guess I've always wanted short cuts," he once said. "And being an impostor is a tough habit to break."[6]

He was, quite literally, addicted to lying. "It's almost like an opiate, the high that you get fooling some people," said David Livingstone Smith, a philosophy professor and author of *Why We Lie*. "'Look how smart I am, look how I pulled one over on everybody. I am so great.' That comes through practically every page of his autobiography. It reeks of what we might expect of pathological narcissism."[7]

Smith believed Demara was depressed, lonely, and bored, most probably because he was so bright. The impostorship "represented a defense against his depression," he speculated. "As long as he could maintain it and work at it then he didn't have to think of himself as a depressed and lonely person. A double life is just the way to cover up the turmoil."[8]

It's unclear if Demara had a full-fledged personality disorder. He wasn't without empathy; he understood the psychological ramifications of his actions, and he cared about other people's feelings. "In this little game I was playing, there comes a time when you find yourself getting in too deep," he said in a 1952 interview with *Life* magazine. "You've made good friends who believe in you, and you don't want them to get hurt and disillusioned. You begin to worry about what they'll think if somebody exposes you as a phony."[9]

He even fell in love and planned a future with his "girl." But after his true identity was revealed, he grew deeply depressed, largely because he knew the relationship was over. "All I could think of was the girl," he confessed. "I knew that I would never be able to face her after all this and I imagined what she was thinking about me. It just about killed me."[10]

Today, at the very least, Demara would probably be diagnosed with narcissistic personality disorder. But the extremity and endurance of his deception suggest that he was more than a little off-kilter. His own father said that while he "loved the boy," he really didn't know him. "He's good and he's kind, and he has a really brilliant mind," he said. "But I've never been able to understand him. I don't think anybody else understands him either."[11]

WE LIKE TO think that extreme subterfuge, or the ability to maintain a large-scale deception, is only carried out by those with psychiatric labels— narcissism, Machiavellianism, and psychopathy, part of what Delroy L. Paulhus, a psychology professor at the University of British Columbia, called the "Dark Tetrad." (Sadism was added later.)[12]

Which is to say, people fundamentally different from you and me. We don't want to think *we* are like *them* in any way.

In the early 1800s, psychologists began noticing that some of their patients who appeared normal didn't possess the same ethics as other people. They called this "moral depravity" or "moral insanity."[13]

"Psychopath" was the preferred term until the 1930s, when it became "sociopath" to connote just how dangerous they were to society. Both psychopaths and sociopaths hide their true selves behind a mask, as American psychiatrist Hervey Cleckley wrote in his 1941 book, *The Mask of Sanity*. (The film *Three Faces of Eve*, about a woman with multiple personality disorder, was based on another one of his books.)[14]

Interestingly, "psychopath" has never been listed in any edition of the *Diagnostic and Statistical Manual of Mental Disorders*, the psychiatric bible. Since some psychopathic traits are similar to antisocial personality disorder, which is in the fifth and current edition of the DSM, psychopathy is usually thought of as part of that disorder. About 1 percent of the general population—and 4 percent of CEOs[15]—are thought to be psychopaths. An estimated 9 percent of the population has some kind of personality disorder.[16] Experts disagree on the exact numbers, but they all say that men are more prone to psychopathy than women. Among prison inmates, up to 17 percent of women meet the definition of psychopathy, compared to 25 to 30 percent of men.[17]

(A word on terminology: Laypeople sometimes prefer to use "sociopath" because it sounds somehow gentler than psychopath, which conjures images of Norman Bates and wig-wearing cadavers in rocking chairs. Some experts do use "psychopath" to refer to a genetic disorder and "sociopath" to describe people whose aberrant behavior is shaped by external factors, but the two words are actually synonyms. Today, "psychopath" is the more accepted term, so that's the word I'll use.)

Psychopaths are most commonly diagnosed through Robert Hare's Psychopathy Checklist–Revised (PCL-R), a twenty-item inventory of personality traits and behaviors that include glib and superficial charm, impulsivity, need for stimulation, and pathological lying.[18]

Pathological liars sometimes believe their own fabrications, as I think the Commander did. They usually have a reason to lie, but they don't want anyone to know they're doing it. So they vehemently protest when confronted. Another name for this kind of compulsive lying is pseudologia fantastica, which sounds like a Tchaikovsky ballet.[19]

Liars at this level can't stop making things up. They might not even have a motive; they do it for fun, as Demara did.[20]

We're all capable of lying—the main difference between "us" and "them" is that psychopaths and pathological liars don't sweat their transgressions. Whereas most people feel troubled by their deceitfulness, psychopaths lie and manipulate without feeling any shame, remorse, or guilt. There's often a gamesmanship to it, a grandiosity. They believe there's nothing they can't worm their way out of, and the challenge electrifies them. Psychologist and lying guru Paul Ekman, professor emeritus at the University of California, San Francisco, noted that one can watch people's faces for signs of "duping delight," which can occur after someone has pulled off a major deception.[21]

But although labels can be helpful, they can also be a little too pat. Individuals rarely fit into perfectly tidy categories. And not everyone who leads a double life is a psychopath.

Which brings me down three flights of stairs into the lobby of my apartment building, where I was greeted by a man named Jorge Alvarez nearly every day for four years.[22]

Jorge was my sometime doorman, a Bronx-born Dominican with a shaved head, a gap between his two front teeth, and a roguish spark. He looked eerily like Prabhupada, the Indian Hare Krishna leader with a head as smooth as a cue ball. Jorge probably could have started his own religion if he wanted to. I imagined him getting the kids at school to do his homework for him. He was smart and slick and persuasive—the kind of guy who always knew where the party was, and if there wasn't one, he'd make it himself.

He also knew where to find my ego: smack in the middle of my computer.

"I hear you're a writer," he said a few days into the job. "You wrote a book about fat kids? My daughter has a weight problem. I'd love to show it to her."

So I gave him a signed copy, taking the $25 fee out of his Christmas tip. (Kidding.)

I don't think he or his daughter ever read it, but Jorge knew exactly what he was doing. We became friendly.

"Good morning, Miss Ellin," he'd say with a wink, rushing to hold the door open for me. Or: "How are you today, Miss Ellin?"

He and the night doorman, Dave, were my saviors, zipping up my dresses and scrutinizing my gentleman callers. I don't know why we imbue guards, hairstylists, and bartenders with special insights into human nature; maybe it's because they're constantly dealing with people, so we think they have added wisdom. Jorge and I would swap relationship woes and argue politics. He was active in the political scene in the Dominican Republic, where he owned property. I disagreed with most of his positions, but he was smart. I knew he wasn't long for the job. He wasn't a career doorman. As soon as he saved some money, he was outta there.

THE NEXT ITERATION of our friendship began, as it always seems to, with an email. This one arrived in February 2017. I had been on a winter hiatus in Brazil for a few months, traveling, writing, and avoiding New York until April. I hadn't heard from Jorge since he'd quit working in my building the previous August.

"I have a true story to tell," the email read. "It's ugly, shocking, exciting, and full of your fave, deceit. I know it would make a good movie and if well written or ghostwritten could be a good book. First check out some of my childhood friends and acquaintances."

He threw out names like El Caballon and George "Boy George" Rivera, and I dutifully Googled. They were some of the most notorious drug dealers in 1980s New York.[23]

A few days later another email came in. "Did I ever tell you I was living in Iceland for eight months? I stayed at Litla-Hraun. Look it up."

I did. It was a prison.

IT WAS MAY when we finally got together. He picked me up in his black Toyota Camry, which he was practically living in now that he was a Lyft driver.

I wanted to go to a diner and talk, but he was reluctant to discus his past in public.

"The statute of limitations is up on everything I ever did, but it still makes me a little nervous," he said.

We circled the city, me nursing a Diet Coke and Jorge chain-smoking menthol Newport Lights. I hadn't seen him in seven months, and he seemed different. The accommodating person who "Miss Ellined" me left and right was gone. This guy had a ruthless streak.

He gave me the quick version of his life: big Dominican family, lots of siblings. Jorge was a brilliant kid but bored quickly. Once he figured out a way to make easy money—selling cocaine and heroin in Washington Heights and the Bronx—that's where he focused his energies.

"I'm like the Forrest Gump of the New York City drug underworld. Just not as smart," he said with a laugh. "Know everyone, done everything except real violence, and seen everything. All while pretending to be a regular person to my family and society, of course."

I wondered what constituted "real" violence, especially when he lifted his right pant leg and slid it up to his kneecap. It looked like someone had taken a spoon and scooped a chunk out of his inner calf. "Bullet fragment," he said. "I'm guessing cartilage is growing around it."

We drove around Harlem up to Washington Heights, past the bodegas and churches, past the homeless guys lounging on stoops, past the warehouses where Jorge used to keep his supplies. From what I gathered, he wasn't a kingpin. More like a princepin, earning a paltry $300,000 a month.

According to Jorge, he got busted doing business in Iceland, where he was arrested and charged with "introducing cocaine to the island." He was sentenced to ten months in jail and sent to Litla-Hraun, the largest maximum security prison in the country. The case was all over Scandinavian news, but it wasn't mentioned in the States. He was released after five months, and four days later he was sitting behind the desk in my apartment building.

Jorge was my friend, yes, but he was also a stranger. I wasn't surprised that he had such a colorful past, but it was unsettling. Granted, the power structure had also shifted, and we were now hanging in a completely new context. I imagine it would be like running into your shrink in a pole-dancing class.

Jorge said his mother had no idea about anything; she didn't even know he'd been incarcerated. She thought he'd just been traveling in Europe. He finally came clean to his kids and ex-wife when he returned to the States, but his daughter—the one I'd signed my book to—wouldn't talk to him for two years. His sisters and brothers didn't know the full extent of his antics, and I'm sure I don't, either.

This all took its toll on him, which is why he wanted to talk to me. He knew about my ex-con beau and my fascination with double lives. "I'm tired of hiding who I am," he said. "I'm not proud of everything I did, but it's a big part of the Dominican story and should be told, warts and all."

"How'd you end up in my building?" I asked.

"It was the only job I could get."

"Didn't anyone do a background check?"

"They did," he said, flicking his cigarette out the window. "But I don't have a record in the States."

I DON'T THINK Jorge is a psychopath. He said he took the Hare questionnaire once, just to see where he fell on the spectrum. He had a few psychopathic characteristics, but so what? Who doesn't?

Clinical psychiatrist George K. Simon prefers the term "character disturbance" to describe the array of mental disorders he sees, many of which are fostered by our competitive, materialistic, solipsistic culture. People with character disturbances "love those kinds of atmospheres," he said. "They thrive on them."[24]

Simon suggested that such character disturbances, many of which include serial lying, are currently of "epidemic" proportions, mainly because the concept of shame has gone the way of the pterodactyl.

"We glorify people instead of condemn them," said Simon. "We've lost our sense of outrage and shame, and boy do we need to get it back. I'm talking about the kind of shame that I can't live with myself as the kind of person I am. Some of the worst offenders felt bad every time they did something, but they kept doing it. The only thing that prompted them to change was when they could no longer stand the sight of who they were. Shame saves them, where guilt does not."[25]

Jay Kwawer, director emeritus of the William Alanson White Institute of Psychiatry, Psychoanalysis, & Psychology in Manhattan, believes there's a personality disorder continuum, and we're all on it: *Ich Bin Ein Psychopath*. He has worked with people who have had a "truly secret hidden dimension of their lives—a different professional slant than everyone knows, different friendship patterns, another relationship halfway around the globe or another relationship two floors down in the same apartment building," he said. "They're not psychopaths."[26]

Indeed, the lines are often as fine as dental floss. If you score 15 out of a possible 20 on Hare's PCL-R, what does it make you?

Quite possibly, an *almost* psychopath, a term coined by criminal defense attorney James Silver and Dr. Ronald Schouten, a psychiatrist at Harvard Medical School.[27] "Almosts" carry some psychopathic traits, but not enough to be card-carrying members of the community. While they might be as lacking in empathy as any full-scale psychopath, they're also enchanting, disciplined, and successful, roaming boardrooms and oval offices. They can keep their creepier tendencies under wraps—until they can't.

"It's hard to keep that many balls in the air," said Schouten. "That's where the element of psychopathy comes in, to not be anxious and able to pull this off in a calm fashion."

In a way, the almost-psychopaths scare me more, because they're aware of the kind of harm they're inflicting and they don't care. The half-baked psychos might be *more* dangerous than full-on psychos, because they're everywhere—at the office, on TV, in politics, on the news, and perhaps in your bed.

And then there's this question: If you were an almost-psychopath, would you even know it? I've told lies by accident, unwittingly causing people unnecessary confusion. I regret those things, but they don't exactly torture me. I've knowingly misrepresented or softened my beliefs online or in an occasional conversation. Haven't we all?

I can talk my way into just about anywhere—private parties, fancy award ceremonies I haven't been invited to, concerts when I didn't have a ticket. If you waltz in as if you own the joint, often no one questions you (unless you don't fit into certain demographic categories, in which case you could be suspect just for sitting). This is hardly prison-worthy behavior, but it takes a certain personality to do it.

SOME PEOPLE EXIT the womb with a genius for obfuscation; others develop the ability. For most of us, though, it's probably a mixture of nature and nurture.

Jorge was slick. But he also grew up in an environment where everyone did what he did. His neighborhood was a giant crack den.

Kids usually learn to lie around age two.[28] (Teens tell the most lies; children and seniors tell the fewest.[29])

In an oft-cited experiment in the mid-1980s by developmental psychologist Michael Lewis, children were instructed not to peek at a toy in a room. A researcher then left them alone for a few minutes. Within seconds, every one of the kids looked.[30]

When Lewis returned, he asked each child if he or she had glanced at the toy.

Eighty percent of the kids over age four, about half of the three-year-olds, and a third of the two-year-olds denied peeking. Lewis discovered that the toddlers who lied had verbal IQs about ten points higher than those who told the truth. (The few kids who didn't look at the toy at all were the brightest of everyone, but that's a whole other kettle of wax. Or fish.)

The lying children, Lewis found, were better at remembering instructions, focusing attention, self-regulating, and multitasking. They were also better at putting themselves in other people's shoes, a cognitive development stage known as "theory of mind." The idea is that in order to lie effectively, you have to be able to empathize with others, at least intellectually, if not emotionally (because lying also requires a certain *lack* of empathy; nobody wants to be lied to).

So what did the researchers conclude? That the more intelligent kids were better liars. Also, that kids lie to get attention, to compensate for feeling inadequate, or to cover up a misdeed. Like my friend Mike's son, who filled a wastepaper basket with water and then denied doing it when his father confronted him. Or my eight-year-old buddy, John, who told his father that he had already fed the dog . . . and then proceeded to feed the dog.

When they're young, kids recognize that lying's bad because their parents might punish them. But punishing them can actually backfire, because "it distracts the child from learning how his lies impact others," wrote Po Bronson and Ashley Merryman in *Nurture Shock*.[31] Punishment doesn't make them lie less. They just learn how to do it better.

Around age six, kids begin to get that lying's bad because it hurts other people—except for the fuzzy lies that are permissible, even welcome. And where do they learn that? From us, the grown-ups in the room.

Adults have a knotty relationship to lying—and to truth-telling. We exhort kids to tell the truth but get mad at them when they squeal on their sibling, or when they inform Aunt Thelma that she's fatter than she was last Christmas. Children hear us telling our friends we can't talk on the phone because we're "busy," when in truth we're plucking our eyebrows. We tell them to pretend to love a gift, even when they have no use for Thucydides' *History of the Peloponnesian War*. No wonder they're flummoxed.

THOUGH IT WOULD seem that we're born with the ability or instinct to lie, there's really no knowing how much of a role social influence plays. My friend Melinda is the daughter of a psychiatrist father and a 1960s activist mother. They taught her never, ever to lie, not even a friendly fib to make someone feel good, and that's how she's gone through life. Melinda is a journalist and politically outspoken; she has organized freelance writers in their quest to be treated fairly. To her, justice and truth are interlinked; dishonesty is simply not an option.

She was in her mid-forties when she realized that she hadn't absorbed the same social cues as other people, and so she didn't behave the way they did. "I really had to watch people to learn how to bullshit," she admitted. "I didn't know that you don't tell people no when the answer is no. You tell them you'll 'think about it,' or 'look into it,' or 'consider it.' Life is all office politics. Telling the truth is not always how you get ahead socially. That being said, I know people believe me when I say something."[32]

One thing we can know with more certainty is that the *motivation* to lie is innate. Duping—and being duped—are as ancient as human history, and they've evolved over time.

Let's look at the animal kingdom. "People often turn to animal deception to show how much 'they' are like 'us,'" said Kathryn Bowers, an animal behavior specialist and coauthor of *Zoobiquity: The Astonishing Connection Between Human and Animal Health*. "'Wow—it's so human that blue jays don't steal from one another but only from lower-ranking birds.' I think rather that it shows how deep and ancient these behaviors are—and that they emerged and survived because they enhance survival or fitness."[33]

Animals deceive by camouflage and other physical attributes that make them appear stronger, healthier, or sexier than they really are. Some bugs copy the tastes, odors, sounds, and behaviors of other species in order to deceive—blending in by mimicking, say, a twig, a plant, or tree bark. The phenomenon is called *mimesis*.[34]

"There are insects that look like splattered bird shit," said David Livingstone Smith, author of *Why We Lie*. He was referring, specifically, to the bird dung crab spider. "What kind of bird is going to eat bird shit? It's protective."[35]

Birds are also champion dupers. During courtship, male bowerbirds—the "Picassos of the bird world"—build a sex palace in the trees, decorating it with an array of bright, fancy objects they have found or filched—shells, feathers, flowers—in order to entice a mate.[36] Seduction by (interior) design.

The cowbirds of North America produce up to forty eggs a season.[37] But instead of making their own nests, the females sneak their eggs into other birds' abodes. Although some bird species are on to their shenanigans, the endangered Kirtland warbler is often duped into raising cowbird babies as its own, called "kleptoparasitism."[38] (This is one of the major reasons why the warblers' numbers have declined. They're too busy babysitting someone else's kids.)

In supposedly monogamous bird species, a female may soar over to a neighboring nest and get busy with another bird. The risk of males raising young 'uns who are not theirs is about as high as 75 percent.

So, why would anyone stick around, knowing that his mate's tramping it up a few nests down the block?

Inertia. Rather than seek another partner, which is laborious no matter what species you are, the male birds weigh the odds and decide they're better off minding eggs that might not be theirs. No one wants to raise someone else's offspring, but at least this way they ensure that their own eggs are also part of the family.[39]

Animals higher up the food chain also deceive. Jane Goodall noted in the 1970s how a male chimp lured his peers away from a heap of bananas . . . then crept back in to snack on them alone.[40]

Chantek, the male orangutan raised in captivity in Georgia and Tennessee, once pilfered food from a researcher's pocket while pulling her hand in the opposite direction. Another time he signed the word "dirty" in American Sign Language to get into the bathroom. But he was sparkling clean. He just had to pee.[41]

If a male topi antelope senses that his darling is getting a little restless, he'll snort loudly, as if danger's lurking around the corner, thus catapulting her back into his arms. "This is the clearest example of tactical deception between mates in animals other than humans," said H. Kern Reeve, an expert at Cornell University specializing in the evolution of cooperation and conflict in animal societies.[42]

A sneaker male cuttlefish will dress in drag to avoid being attacked by an even bigger male. To get even trippier: a cuttlefish can appear to change colors and genders on demand. Say the cuttlefish sneaker is swimming across the ocean with a male on his left side and a female on his right. He can make himself look female to the male and male to the female. So the male fish would think he's surrounded by two women, and not a budding romance. (Or two lesbians, I suppose.)

A whole new definition of "transitioning."

IN ADDITION TO these evolutionary roots of deception, evidence suggests that the human ability to lie comes from deep in our brains.

A study published in *Nature Neuroscience* found that the brain adapts to dishonesty, making it easier to continue to fabricate over time.[43] When you first tell a lie, the amygdala and insula, areas associated with emotion, light up. By the twelfth time you do it, the brain has acclimated and so the response is less potent. "After a while, the negative value of lying—the negative feeling—is just not there, so much," said coauthor Tali Sharot, a cognitive neuroscientist at University College London.[44]

Children's brains, psyches, and values are greatly shaped by external forces, but what about adults'? For a quick answer, we need only turn to social media. Facebook, Instagram, and the like not only allow but *encourage* us to emphasize—maybe even exaggerate—the lucky, fun, and enviable aspects of our lives, and to downplay or conceal our struggles.[45]

We're creating our own doubles in our Facebook profiles, said Alissa Wilkinson, an assistant professor of English and humanities at The King's College in New York.[46] "I call it our 'better double'—that is, a sexier, smarter version of yourself who steals your girlfriend and your friends like more than they like you."

Let's go back to Walter White, of *Breaking Bad* fame, and Don Draper, *Mad Men*'s incandescent Lothario. "Those characters root in Jekyll and Hyde, and that's a pretty modern story of someone provoking a split personality," Wilkinson said. (Robert Louis Stevenson, who invented Jekyll and Hyde for his 1886 novel, grappled with his own conflicting states of consciousness: he saw that he had "myself," who was laid back and chill, but then there was that "other fellow," who was creative and brooding.[47])

Does the ability to construct new "realities" online merely satisfy our escapist desires, or does it embolden us? Is our culture forcing all of us to move from our stable identities to more mutable ones? Are more people fabricating and committing emotional fraud because of Facebook?

It's probably much too early in the social media era to know the answer (although researchers did find a link between high narcissism scores and tweeting about oneself).[48] But it's definitely changed our relationship to presenting and obscuring the messy, multiple truths of our lives.

Massachusetts Institute of Technology psychologist Sherry Turkle labels social media an "identity technology" because it gives us the chance to indulge our fantasies and become anyone or anything. "You can have these friends," she said.[49] "You can have these connections. You can have this love and appreciation, followers, people who want to be with you." Online, anyway.

People have long mucked around with their identities, albeit not in as public a forum as Instagram. You probably tried on different "you's" in high school or college. Maybe one week you were a hippie, wearing flowing skirts and Birkenstocks, and the next you were a prepster in a crocodile T-shirt.

Was it active deception? No. It was trying to figure out who you were and carve out a Self. But it was an image you projected, and it often changed with the wind (or at least with your clique).

Now you can do this without ever leaving your air mattress. Turkle researched games where people create virtual communities and families, as in Sims Online. In interviews with nearly two hundred semiregular players, she discovered that many used the game to explore alternate versions of themselves and the lives they wished they led.[50]

"I think what people are doing on the Internet now . . . has deep psychological meaning in terms of how they're using identities to express problems and potentially solve them in what is a relatively consequence-free zone," Turkle told the *New York Times*.[51]

Maybe Facebook, Instagram, Twitter, and Snapchat aren't merely a means of showing off to others. Maybe social media also allows us to *create* the life we long for—the one in which we have time to craft beautiful breakfasts with artisanal butter and heirloom tomatoes; engage in fun, enriching activities with our Ralph Lauren–perfect families and friends; and harbor only generosity and righteousness in our hearts. On Facebook, we don't have to think about the percentage of our lives taken up by obligation, ennui, and frustration. Maybe we gravitate to social media because it lets us fool *ourselves* into believing our lives are bigger and better.

Whomever we're trying to impress, Instagram and the like certainly assist us in our lands of make-believe. Just how different is the real world from the world on social media? In the real world, "*The National En-quirer*, a weekly, sells nearly three times as many copies as *The Atlantic*, a monthly, every year," noted economist Seth Stephens-Davidowitz. "On Facebook, *The Atlantic* is 45 times more popular. Americans spend about six times as much of their time cleaning dishes as they do golfing. But there are roughly twice as many tweets reporting golfing as there are tweets reporting doing the dishes."[52]

THE DESIRE FOR another life, another self, is a longtime staple of literature and film, and it's easy to see why. A double life generally consists of two opposing forces, one good and one bad. Most of us feel these forces competing inside us, Jekyll and Hyde high-fiving each other as they skateboard around our neocortex. This internal conflict makes for good storytelling.

This kind of duality has often been represented in literature by the doppelgänger, German for "double walker," which represents our dark side or the potential Other.

Besides Dr. Jekyll and Mr. Hyde, there's Charles Dickens's *A Tale of Two Cities*, a pair of biblical stories (Cain and Abel, Jacob and Esau), even Dostoevsky's *The Double*, in which a government clerk meets his opposite. The ancient Egyptians had the concept of the spirit double, or *ka*, and the Greeks had the demigod Dionysus, who was both raucous and serene.[53]

Carl Jung called it "the Shadow" inside all of us. Wholeness, he believed, required a *coniunctio oppositorum*—a coincidence of opposites, an amalgamation of ego and the unconscious. The ideal human integrates these opposing tendencies. Good and Evil need each other for their own existence, and they know it.

Jung defines the double as neither good nor bad, but a "replica of one's own unknown face," as philosophy professor Milica Živković put it. "It acquires a demonic aspect only because one side of the personality is repressed and subordinated to a faultless and absolute good. . . . Jung defines the double as a manifestation of desire"—the desire, specifically, for a life other than the one we are leading.[54]

There it is again: escape.

Jung had his own shadow perfectly worked out. He had two separate selves, which he called Personality No. 1 and Personality No. 2. Number 1 was a gregarious, extroverted Master of the Universe. No. 2 was an insecure, anxious, tormented introvert.[55] Both were him.

Many of us embrace and acknowledge these paradoxes and integrate them into our lives. The destruction comes when we can't.

So what's the difference between the sort of pretense in which we all engage, on the one hand, and the type perpetrated by the Commander, on the other? Where do we draw the line between acceptable boasting and predatory behavior?

It's partly a matter of the size of the lies and partly a matter of whom you're trying to fool. Posting flattering, smiling pictures of ourselves on Instagram that may tell only half the story, and exaggerating a tale at a party, are both fairly benign. Doctors dissemble every time they give a placebo or spin a diagnosis. Social psychologists lie every time they tell study participants that they're measuring their ability to smell when they're really examining memory.

The Commander's deceptions were gargantuan, encompassing, and nonsensical ("The Secret Service is following us!"). He lied elaborately to people who loved him. That's exploitation, and it causes real damage.

But those examples come from opposite ends of the lying spectrum. There's a lot of leeway in the middle, and ultimately, we have to judge liars and lies—including our own—on a case-by-case basis.

All of this brings me back to the seemingly unavoidable question of why the Commander fabricated so much of his existence. I really don't know the answer, but I would bet he tilts mightily toward one end of the psychopath continuum. He may even be legitimately delusional, truly buying into his own lies, at least in the moments he utters them.

I also believe his early failure to become a brain surgeon weighed so heavily on him that he spent much of his life trying to seem not merely successful, but extraordinary. He wanted desperately to be a hero. This would explain the faux meetings with Hillary Clinton and President Obama, his fake SEAL rescues, and his heroic endeavors in Kabul and at DC Metro stops. But who knows? Maybe he would have been a compulsive liar even if he had become a brain surgeon. Maybe it's just in his chemistry. Or maybe there were external circumstances I'm unaware of—maybe his childhood was more traumatic than anyone knew. But Kate told me that he came from good people on Long Island with no noticeable oddities.

I contacted his first wife, Robin—his *ex*-ex-wife—to whom he'd been married for five years. After verifying that we were talking about the same man, she wanted to make sure I wasn't taping the call. I wasn't and I gave her my word, but, of course, what good is that? "You don't have to believe me," I said. "But I'll send you an email and put it in writing that I'm not taping the call." (She gave me permission to use this exchange.)

I wanted to know what his behavior was like back then. Was there any crossover? Some. He had screaming nightmares. He had stomach problems from a pole-vaulting accident. He couldn't eat much during the day. But that was it. No secret missions. No Mossad. No capture in China. No gunshot wounds. He was a sweet guy. They were happy.

Well, she was, anyway. One night he came home and announced that he wanted out of the marriage. Just like that.

She was thunderstruck. She'd supported him through medical school! They were trying for a baby! Divorce? What had she done wrong?

"My initial shame was at not being 'good enough' to keep this wonderful person," she wrote me in an email. "Over the years I changed my internal narrative about him—'he must have been crazy,' but I did not get confirmation about this until I read about the indictment."

There it is again—the desire to label someone as "different" in order to comprehend. But it's only a partial explanation—it accounts for the why part of the equation, which is what people always asked me about first when I explained what I was researching. What it leaves out is the second question people always ask: *How?* How is it possible for some people to split their day-to-day existence into isolated parts, conceal various aspects from the people central to their lives, and carry on as if everything were normal? Are they that different from you and me? And if most of us can't pull it off, how exactly *do* successful liars do it?

As for Jorge, he's not quite a model citizen, but he's careful. "I won't be getting into any more trouble," he told me. "I can't afford it." Besides, he said, "spending time in a maximum security prison thousands of miles from home with white supremacists, a biker gang I owed a lot of money to, and antisocials gave me the incentive and time to rethink some things."

So then why did he engage in such risky behavior?

Because it was exciting. Fun. Every day was different. The money was excellent, and he liked being *el jefe*. Plus, he got to meet some interesting people.

I asked him who were the worst people he'd ever encountered.

"Liars," he answered speedily. Even criminals hate people they can't trust.

FIVE

A LIFE DIVIDED

He who permits himself to tell a lie once,
finds it much easier to do it a second and third
time, till at length it becomes habitual.

—Thomas Jefferson[1]

As soon as the cops pulled him over, Peter Young ceased to exist. Somehow—he's still not sure how—his synapses instinctively clicked into place and he knew exactly what he needed to do.

He severed contact with his parents and friends. He bought books on identity theft and forging signatures. He got a post office box under his fake name and staked it daily to make sure no one else was monitoring it. He regularly went to the library to log online and see if he'd been indicted. Eleven months later, he still hadn't been, so he figured it was safe to return to Washington State.

One afternoon as he was leaving a record store in Bellingham he bumped into an old pal. The friend had learned that Young and Justin Samuel faced eighty-two years in federal prison for domestic terrorism, and showed him some information from the FBI to prove it. "Run!" the friend said, stuffing a fistful of cash in Young's pockets.

So he did, floating from state to state. He'd settle in somewhere, usually for a few months at a time. He made sure never to get his picture taken. He didn't have a bank account. He never talked about family or friends (although, through an extremely circuitous channel, he sent word to his parents that he was okay). "I was not dead but not alive," he said. "It was a game of dodgeball. I had to lie all the time." His mug shot stared back from post office walls, right next to bank robber Nova Guthrie, who was half of a modern-day Bonnie and Clyde.

The best liars stick as close to the facts as possible, something impressed upon me by "Luke Jackson," the nom de whore of an international male escort. Luke works at a nonprofit humanitarian organization by day and earns thousands of dollars by night servicing women and couples. He keeps his evening job hidden from his friends and family—as far as they know, he's just a do-gooder (and not a good-doer).

Most people massage the truth rather than pound it out of existence. The majority of online daters, for example, are fairly accurate in their profiles.[2] Which is to say, they reside in the neighborhood of truth, even if they don't quite wind up in its exact location.

Eighty percent of male online daters upped their height about nine-tenths of an inch. Women rounded their weight down. And everyone lied about their age. They wanted to turn themselves into a reasonably better specimen, but not make it seem like they were, um, *lying*. What if they claimed to be six feet tall but were a mere five foot three in real life? People would notice that kind of discrepancy. But if they said they were five four and were really five three? That was a little more plausible. What's an inch among lovers?[3]

Behavioral economist Dan Ariely, author of *The (Honest) Truth About Dishonesty*, said we all cheat by a "fudge factor" of roughly 15 percent.[4] But some of us advance to such big lies that we're practically drowning in the gooey concoction.

The Commander certainly used fragments of the truth, combined them with *un*truths, and shot it all out of a cannon. He really was a doctor in private practice in Beverly Hills, and had a PhD and an MD. He did have an ex-wife and two kids, and his mother really had been a radio actress in the 1930s. He was a navy doc, working on a task force at the Pentagon, and trying to open a hospital for kids with cancer in Iraq and Afghanistan. All those things were real, but he riffed on them, improvising the facts as if he were Charlie Parker mixing melody and discord.

Peter Young also stuck close to the facts. He said he grew up in Silicon Valley, where he really did live until he was ten, though in Los Gatos and not Cupertino, as he claimed. His typical line was a variation of "I'm twenty-one and running around the world." Also true. Never mind that he was running *away* and not simply running *around*.

He stayed for a few months in a rooming house in Gainesville, Florida, a college town where it was easy to blend in. He had an early-morning job cleaning a bar, earning minimum wage. It was humiliating. This was a guy who prided himself on never having a real job, and he was making $7.56 an hour.

He was lonely. Not in the same way most people feel lonely, with a longing to connect with others. But more like, *I am one of two people on this planet who knows who I really am. I could die, and no one would know my real name.*

"If you tell people who you are—that will be your demise. She tells one person, and they tell one person, and pretty soon you're in handcuffs," he said. "No matter how much I trusted someone, the potential consequences of sharing it outweighed the benefits."

Samuel was in England, and Young decided to join him. A friend picked up his birth certificate at his parents' house and smuggled it to him, an Underground Railroad of activists. Since he hadn't yet been indicted, he was able to use his real information to buy plane tickets. At the airport, he was scared—were the feds going to pounce? But he sailed right through.

Samuel was working and living at an animal sanctuary near Liverpool. Young was miserable as soon as he joined him. "I remember thinking— *prison can't be worse than this*," he said. "I was cut off from everything I knew and in a foreign country and had no friends except him. I was just killing time."

Within seven months, he was back in the States. After researching the easiest place to get a fake ID, he moved to South Dakota. He walked into the DMV with $12, a forged power bill, and a fake birth certificate and walked out with a new ID, no questions asked.

But he missed his friends, and he started getting in touch with people he felt he could trust, though he never told them where he was living. He would just show up for an unexpected visit, and when he left he didn't say where he was going. He hitchhiked to Boulder, slept on the roof of a Toys "R" Us, loitered in a Whole Foods Market, and enjoyed the fact that he wasn't doing menial labor.

Where to go next? He pulled Tucson out of a hat. He lived there for six months, working at Goodwill and speaking to no one, before moving on to the next place. He was on the run for a total of eight and a half years. In all that time, he only came clean to two people, both of them activists who understood the need for secrecy.

"If I was wanted for bank robbery I would feel differently," he said. "But they shared my feelings about the cause. You don't have to like anyone to keep that secret."

He's right. You don't. Unless your ethics don't jibe with his.

Once, he dipped a baby toe into full disclosure. He ran into someone wearing a "vegan" T-shirt. "Did you ever hear about those kids that got indicted?" he asked. "I'm one of them."

"I didn't get anything out of it other than the immediate satisfaction of getting it off my chest," he told me later. "I think I wanted some validation for what I was going through. I wanted to unburden myself."

It's a phrase he used often. And that was what he was doing in talking to me. Unburdening himself. He was still processing his past, still trying to understand it and make it right.

Santa Cruz was his longest stop—two years, from 2003 to 2005. That's where he met Maggie Barber, a jewelry maker from Greenville, South Carolina, who became his girlfriend. The two of them moved to San Diego, where the weather was divine.

They stayed a few months, camping out in dorm lounges and broom closets at universities in town, attending lectures, and pretending to be regular students. Then Justin Samuel got arrested at an antinuclear protest in Belgium.

When Young got word, he told Barber that he wanted to focus on his writing and go somewhere quieter than San Diego. This wasn't a lie, exactly: their life in San Diego *wasn't* conducive to writing. They were basically homeless. He never told her the truth about who he really was.

How was Peter Young able to maintain the facade? The anxiety and stress, the logistical difficulties, the isolation. It was wearying and lonely. Yet he managed.

For starters, he didn't think he did anything wrong—the minks *shouldn't* have been caged. What good would his arrest have done? "The animals didn't get put back in cages if I got arrested," he reasons. As for lying, well, duplicity is part of the activist culture. It's required to survive. He was facing eighty-two years behind bars, so he had no other option. It was self-preservation, an instinct all animals share.

He still doesn't think of himself as a "liar." Not in the traditional sense.

"It's not a lie you're telling on a daily basis," he said of his hidden identity. "It's a lie of omission 100 percent of the time, but when it comes to telling overt lies, that only happens every few months. Like, my girlfriend would go—'Why do you never talk to your parents?' And I'd have to come up with something."

This is all part of so-called security culture, a set of practices maintained by people the government has targeted.[5] The way Young sees it, the people he deceived should thank him for *protecting* them.

His one regret was lying to Barber in order to leave San Diego. "I've always felt indebted to her after that," he said.

"Would you do it again?" I asked. "Lie like that?"

He paused. "I won't," he said. "But I *could*."

Most of us have the capacity to manipulate. To some extent that's a social skill. Still, there's a difference between stage-managing a situation and being calculating and unscrupulous.

I'd like to think that I couldn't maintain an extended fabrication like

Philby or Young, that the stress of it—the "work" or cognitive load—would cause crow's feet, migraines, and ulcers. I'm pretty sure I'd have difficulty keeping my stories straight. Did I tell him I was anti-KGB, or pro-? Did I grow up in Omaha or Detroit? And what do I do for a living again? In extreme circumstances, like if I lived in Nazi Germany and my survival was at stake, I suspect I could do it. But hiding my true identity every second of every hour of every day, just for the hell of it? Exhausting.

A double life requires wagonloads of inner reserve, dedication, and impeccable organizational skills. It takes great dexterity and commitment to oversee two households and the demands of two partners and multiple offspring, or a secret cocaine habit, or three women chained in your basement.

So how do some people split their day-to-day existence into isolated parts, conceal various aspects of their lives from the people central to their existence, and carry on as if everything were normal?

From a purely practical and logistical standpoint, how do they sustain extended lies? From a psychological one, how do they live with the stress, and the guilt? We know how psychopaths do it: Since they don't experience guilt or empathy, they don't care about other people's feelings. And since they don't care what people think of them, they don't feel stress. But the non-psychopaths who lie long-term: What exactly is happening in their minds that enables them to pull off an elaborate con for years?

A big part of the answer is compartmentalization.

We all compartmentalize. We draw lines between different aspects of our lives; we present ourselves differently depending on the situation. Especially now, with social media, we have endless opportunities to appear better/sexier/happier than we actually are (I call it The Facetwitgram Effect). We often paint different faces for the world—sometimes literally, with makeup—to create multiple versions of ourselves, especially in the early stages of love.

The word "person," in fact, stems from the Latin word "persona," Etruscan for "mask." We put our best self—the self that is not scratchy and needy and jealous and insecure—forward when we're getting to know new people. In the beginning, our masks are locked tightly in place, even among those of us who are not Etruscan. Once we become close, our real selves unfold.

That's one of the main reasons I believe we tend to like each other less the more we get to know each other.

Long-term partners know exactly who you are, or at least it feels that way. You can't hide from them. Or yourself, when you're in their presence. As my friend Benita said, "It seems like the main point of marriage is to find out how annoying you are."

The difference between seasoned dissemblers—undercover agents, people who fake their own deaths—and the rest of us is that they have a virtuoso's knack for putting unwanted intrusions on a shelf, inside a Tupperware container, wrapped in tinfoil, under a dishtowel, and never think about them again until they have to.

At their core, skillful deceivers give Oscar-worthy performances, according to Dutch researcher Aldert Vrij, who compiled a list of eighteen characteristics common to good liars.[6] Good liars are *manipulative, confident, eloquent, quick-witted, able to balance guilt and fear,* and, yes—*attractive.* The hotter you are, the more you can get away with. What a shallow species we are.

Successful liars also rehearse their stories before telling them, avoid follow-up questions as much as possible, and tell the truth more than they lie. Last, they go on the offense when challenged, which good liars do with gusto. To wit: Richard Nixon, Donald Trump, Bill Clinton, Bill O'Reilly, and Harvey Weinstein, all of whom, when faced with clear evidence that they were misbehaving, went after their accusers, just as the Commander did to me.

When I confronted him about the email to his ex-wife, the one where he told her he'd try to get back together with her if he managed to survive Afghanistan, he flew into a self-righteous rage. "You violated my privacy!" he screamed into the phone. "I never know who I'm going to get. Sometimes you're so sweet and loving, and then you're Mr. Hyde. We are DONE!"

Then he'd calm down, and the contrition would begin: "I'm sorry. I didn't mean to, I'll make it up to you, I'll do better next time. I love you more than you know." It's the sort of thing abused women repeatedly hear from their tormenters.

Another time he told me that his friend's son-in-law—a music teacher at an elementary school—had been arrested for possession of child pornography. I asked what the friend's daughter was going to do.

"Probably leave her husband," he sneered. "If she truly loved him she'd stick by him."

That took me aback. "He's a pedophile!" I said. "He had a separate world she knew nothing about! Why should she stay?"

"Doesn't matter," he said. "She should stick by him. That's what you do with someone you love." Really? Were my values that out of whack? Did I really have no understanding of love?

It reminded me a bit of Waldo Demara's edict: "The burden of proof is on the accuser," and, "When in danger, attack."[7]

Or, in Philby parlance: "Deny everything."[8]

Lance Armstrong must have studied Philby religiously: for years he assailed anyone who dared challenge him. When he finally came clean, he said this about Betsy Kramar Andreu, the wife of his former teammate Frankie Andreu, who'd heard him admit to doping and refused to cave to his bullying: "I said, 'Listen, I called you crazy. I called you a bitch, I called you all these things, but I never called you fat,'" Armstrong told Oprah. "Because she thought I said, 'You were a fat crazy bitch.' And I said, 'Betsy, I never said you were fat.'"[9] A real gem, that one.

I actually met Armstrong in the mid-1990s when I worked in the press room of a bike race called the Tour DuPont, formerly Tour de Trump. Lance was the angriest son of a bitch I'd ever encountered, which I informed him of at the closing night party. "But that's what motivates you, isn't it?" I said. He nodded.

I later tried pitching stories about him to *GQ* and *Esquire*, but nobody cared. He was known in cycling circles, but he hadn't reached mainstream superstar status. It wasn't until he got sick and came roaring back that editors began paying attention.

Like so many others, I was surprised when he finally confessed to doping—I'd assumed that his ego wouldn't have allowed him to cheat, that he'd have wanted to win on merit alone. Apparently not.

The best liars know how to cause chaos. "It's called *maskirovka*—little masquerade—where you create so much confusion and uncertainty and mystery that no one knows what the truth is," said Philby biographer Ben Macintyre.[10]

Interestingly, most of Vrij's eighteen traits are related to personality, which is mostly fixed, psychiatrists say.[11] Which means that some people are naturally better prevaricators than others.

"Some people make better kreplach, some are fabulous at amassing great wealth, some are architects of note and renown," said psychologist Jay Kwawer. "More typically, successful lies are so well practiced and well rehearsed that people can pull them off with their eyes closed, like a grand-scale master actor or actress who can recite lines in their sleep and make them sound convincing."[12]

Elizabeth Greenwood is the author of *Playing Dead*, a book about people who pretended to be deceased but were very much alive. This is called pseudocide (Waldo Demara tried it), and it's more pervasive than you might think. "What I saw again and again was a combination of hubris and the ability to compartmentalize and rationalize in the most extreme sense," Greenwood said of the subjects she interviewed. "The hubris is reflected in the idea that you could pull off a complex ruse like faking your death, and getting family members, law enforcement, and the state to believe it. Most of us fantasize but don't go through with it because we have morals, and also are perhaps daunted by the logistics."[13]

One of the more notorious death fakers was John Darwin, a British ex–prison officer who, after mountains of debt, "disappeared" in a kayak accident on March 21, 2002. His two sons thought their father had been swept out to sea, but his wife, Anne, knew the truth.[14] She collected hundreds of thousands of dollars from insurance and pension funds and helped him hide.[15] After four years of living in a tiny flat in Seaton Carew, County Durham, England, John stole the identity of a dead baby named John Jones, and the couple moved to South America. In 2006, Anne told their sons she wanted to move to Panama to start over as a widow, but she really went there to meet up with her "deceased" husband. A year later, after trying to get a visa to remain in Panama, John turned himself in to a police station in London. Anne initially denied any knowledge of the scam, but the *Daily Mirror* discovered a photo of the smiling duo in a Panamanian realtor's office.[16]

In July 2008, they were each sentenced to six years in the slammer. Anne went to jail for three and a half years, and later claimed that her husband had victimized her. He was a narcissistic, controlling, and manipulative man, she wrote in her 2016 memoir, *Out of My Depth*. But what was his excuse?

"The second bit of compartmentalizing and rationalizing is, I think, what sustains somebody like death faker John Darwin, whose initial motivations were indeed financial, but kept it up for seven years," said Greenwood. "He told himself the story that his family would be better off without him, and that while his children did think he was dead, they were adults living their own lives, so it's not as if he abandoned them as babies."[17]

At a secret trial held at MI5 headquarters in Mayfair, London, in November 1952, eleven years before the truth finally came out, Kim Philby convinced his interrogator that he wasn't a Soviet agent partly by stuttering whenever he was asked a question. Such skills bought him time to come up with another lie. He added that he was basically immune to detection, because he was born to the "governing class" and knew many people of great influence. "They'd never try to beat me up or knock me around, because if they had been proved wrong afterwards, I could have made a tremendous scandal," he said.[18]

PHILBY WAS A natural deceiver. So is Bob Hamer.[19]

Hamer spent twenty-six years with the FBI, many of them as an undercover agent, successfully persuading bad people into believing he was one of them. He was a Sanctioned Duper.

Hamer, who is now retired, thinks he was born with the ability to lie. He's a devout Christian, and he believes that God granted him a "screwed-up brain" that allowed him to "compartmentalize and be the contract killer and then turn around and coach Little League games," he told me in a phone call. He could play the role of a drug dealer by day and still make it to his daughter's school plays.

Why didn't he just go to Hollywood? "I'm too stupid to memorize lines," he said.

Originally, he wanted to join the CIA, but he flunked the agency's personality test. They were looking for independent thinkers who could go to parties, schmooze government officials from other countries, and coerce them into cooperating. That wasn't his strong suit. "I said, 'I don't really like people. I can be alone,'" he recalled.

But he wasn't interested in sitting in a car in a T-shirt and shorts, staking out the bad guys. He wanted to go head-to-head with them.

His family knew when he was undercover—it was obvious by his appearance or by the hours he kept—but they never knew the specifics of each case. Had they known exactly what he was doing, they wouldn't have been overjoyed. He posed as a pedophile and infiltrated the North American Man/Boy Love Association, or NAMBLA. He penetrated the Los Angeles Mafia family. He worked gangs in South LA, buying drugs from members of the Bloods and the Crips, all of which he wrote about in *The Last Undercover*.

During Hamer's early career, the four members of his family lived in a nine-hundred-square-foot home in Southern California. More than half of his pay went to house payments. During the day, on assignment, he'd zip through town in a Porsche 911, eating at the finest restaurants. On their monthly date night, he and his wife, Debbie, would hop into his beat-up Buick and head to McDonald's, the only place they could afford. Could you blame him if he went to the other side for good? It's not uncommon.

A survey of Hawaiian officers found that 21 percent felt their true self was "unreal" while they were undercover. The more clandestine operations they did, the more drug- and alcohol-related problems they developed.[20]

The same researchers investigated forty-eight federal police officers who had spent three weeks training to go undercover. Sixty-six percent of them said their false work identities unwittingly seeped into their real lives.[21]

Another report argued that living with the secrecy necessary for a covert job caused an inflated sense of power. Secret agents become addicted to the excitement and perks of doing something illegal. And because they so often work alone, without being able to confess to anyone, they become isolated and begin to question their own sense of self.[22]

Hamer understands this risk, but he managed to avoid falling into the trap. Why? An undercover agent or deceiver often has "the ability to compartmentalize," he said. "I knew who was Bob Hamer the undercover contract killer and arms dealer and who was Bob Hamer the father, the Sunday school teacher, the youth league coach. When I'm in each role, I'm thinking like that role, and I'm responding in that role."

HAD PETER YOUNG not stopped for a latte, he might still be on the run. One day in 2005, he went into a Starbucks in San Jose. He picked up several Ray Charles CDs, walked across the room with them, and sat down. A cop asked to search his bag. Young coughed up his fake ID and refused to talk. They ran his prints, and that was that. He was no longer Wanted. He was Found.

To many people, he was a hero, a martyr who took one for the cause. When the FBI finally arrested him, his vegan activist friends and acquaintances rallied around him. Donations covered his lawyer fees. He didn't believe any of his friends were pissed at him for pretending to be someone else. "No one ever said they felt deceived," he said. "Even my meat-eating grandma could get behind what I'd done."

After about six months being shuffled around county jails, he accepted a plea deal: 360 hours of community service, $254,000 in restitution, and two years in federal prison in Victorville, California. When he arrived, the other inmates stared at him.

"What'd the motherfucker do?" he heard one ask loudly. "Cheat on the SATs?"

Prison didn't suck. He wasn't harassed or threatened, because he was seen as standing up for what he believed in, which held enormous cachet. But he was bored as all hell. He got out in February 2007.

What was Young's lesson from all of it? He thought about it for a few seconds. "I think life serves the risk taker," he said. "It could have gone a lot worse had I not taken all the chances I did. I was on the track to live a very boring life and I think I lived a full life. And I think that's much better than a life in the middle."

IF YOUNG THINKS he might've wound up being boring, Mr. Spock disagrees.

Leonard Nimoy was not only everyone's favorite Vulcan, but also a gifted photographer. One of his projects, *Secret Selves*, focused on how people compartmentalize parts of their personalities. It was inspired by Aristophanes' speech in Plato's *Symposium*, in which he alleged that at one time humans were double, with four arms, four legs, and one head with two faces. When the humans got a little too cocksure, the gods sent Zeus—himself no slouch in the duplicity department—to deal with it.

"Zeus took a big sword and split everybody in two and sent them on their separate paths," said Nimoy. "According to Aristophanes, ever since then people have been searching for the other part of themselves in the hopes of becoming whole again."[23] In the meantime, we fill that void with friends, hobbies, lovers, work, family, travel, food, or opioids.

Nimoy wanted to photograph people as their "secret," "lost," or "hidden" selves, and the results were staggering: people dressed as milkmaids and Vikings and dancers and children. "It seems to strike a chord in a lot of people," he said. "We put on a mask and we grow our face to fit it. I find that a very provocative idea. We make a decision about what we want the world to see of us and what we want it to think of us. But it's not the whole story, is it?"[24]

Interestingly, when asked if he had a secret self, Nimoy said no. "I have acted out so many aspects of myself over the last 60 years—I've been bad guys, I've been good guys, I've been crazy people, I've been intelligent people, I've been aliens, I've been foreigners of all kinds with dialects and makeup," he said. "I can't imagine any kind of character that I haven't played. . . . I don't have any more hidden, lost selves. I'm integrated. I'm very happy with the way I am."[25] (I believe him: Vulcans never, ever lie.)

Therapists define being integrated as feeling and behaving like the same person in all situations, because the various parts of the psyche communicate. Since Nimoy was also an actor, he got to try on other identities and get paid for it. Most of us probably fall somewhere between Kierkegaard's view—that we never present our true selves to the world—and Nimoy's personal experience. That is, most of us aren't wholly integrated into a single, authentic self but instead float between various versions of ourselves, ideally in a fairly fluid and organic way.

Of course, compartmentalizing our lives is only workable and healthy if it doesn't exploit anyone else, and self-awareness is crucial. Just because you're smart and capable of deceit doesn't mean you have to do it; you can use your superpowers for good and not evil. Some people find ways to address their various desires without betraying other people. Others consciously forge feasible parallel lives by making an active decision to play a part—for instance, people who do S&M role-play, or Civil War reenactments. Many do it through travel, hobbies, or work—such as fiction writers, who create fake worlds on paper.

Most of us unthinkingly incorporate distinct, even contradictory versions of ourselves—city mouse / country mouse; angel/devil, Madonna/whore, and so on. We show different sides in different situations; we play one role when we're in a business meeting, another when we're chilling with our family, and another when we're out with friends and mates.

I have multiple interests and, in a sense, multiple selves. I have my cello friends and my cycling friends and my writing friends and my hippie friends and my snooty Upper East Side friends and my hipster Brooklyn friends and my suburban married-with-kids friends and my single friends and the people with whom I can hike for days on end without showering. They all appeal to distinct parts of my personality, and I behave somewhat differently with each group. But at my core, I am who I am—inquisitive, curious, irreverent, prone to existential dread. I almost always crack myself up, perhaps to a fault.

I've always admired the kind of relationship my friends Jill and Neo have managed to establish. They've been together for thirteen years and married for five. He's Brazilian, she's American, and for eight years they split their time between Manhattan and the mountains outside of Rio, but not always together. They'd spend two months together, and the next two months apart. She got to maintain her autonomy as a "single" woman in New York and then experience married life in Brazil. They were not unfaithful, but they got to enjoy seemingly opposing aspects of their personalities that might otherwise lie buried amid the minutiae of everyday life.

"I liked missing him," Jill told me. "And I liked having alone time. I got to explore both sides of myself."

WITH THE POSSIBLE exception of Leonard Nimoy, we all occasionally do things that seemingly contradict who we are and what we believe, whether it's being an ardent vegan in public and enjoying veal piccata in private, or being vocally anti-drug and then smoking pot on the sly.

"Consistently inconsistent" is how evolutionary psychologist Robert Kurzban puts it.[26] In simpler terms: we're all fucking hypocrites.

Almost everyone despises a hypocrite. It's one of the worst things a person can be—8 out of a possible 9 in Dante's *Inferno*. As Tennessee Williams once said, "The only thing worse than a liar is a liar that's also a hypocrite."[27]

But while we're quick to condemn *others* for hypocrisy, we're almost all guilty of morally opposing something and then actively engaging in it. But we're no good at acknowledging our own contradictions.

According to Kurzban, the mind is punctuated with independent areas of cognition.[28] (Philosopher Jerry Fodor's 1983 monograph, *The Modularity of Mind*, had a similar argument, though Fodor only believed part of the brain was modular, whereas Kurzban argues that the whole brain is this way.) This modularity allows for gulfs to occur between thoughts and behavior, so that different parts of the brain can oppose each other.[29]

So if we're all hypocrites, why do we find hypocrisy so distasteful?[30]

For starters, we're not all hypocrites to the extent of someone like Harvey Weinstein, who supported Hillary Clinton and donated money to pro-female causes and was later accused of sexual harassment, assault, and rape. Or former Pennsylvania congressperson Tim Murphy, who sought to reduce reproductive rights and then urged his mistress—*his mistress!*—to get an abortion. Or Bible thumper Roy Moore, former chief justice of the Supreme Court of Alabama, who was accused of preying on underage girls.[31]

Kurzban believes that the brain is like a giant computer system. Each wire and tube has a different function. A command might travel down one wire without being visible to the rest of the machine.

Or you could look at it as a Fortune 500 company, where each department operates in isolation. Accounting doesn't know what HR is up to, HR
doesn't know what goes on in the boardroom, and the boardroom has no
clue what marketing does.[32] According to Kurzban, hypocrisy is nothing
more than competition among departments (or modules), but most of us
aren't consciously aware of what's going on.

"Most of the brain's activities influence our motives, emotions, thoughts,
and behavior without us being conscious of them at all," said Mark Leary, a
professor of psychology and neuroscience at Duke University. "As a result,
we do many things without really knowing why (although we can usually
generate a plausible story) and even while adamantly claiming that we are
not being driven by motives that are obvious to everyone else. We simply
do not have conscious access to the workings of most of our processing
modules."[33]

The bigger question is whether or not people like Tim Murphy believe
their lies. Many of them might. But—work with me here—they might not
be conscious that they're lying because their modules are hiding their actions from one another.

Or, back to the company analogy, HR keeps its employees' behaviors
hidden from other employees, and this causes self-deception. They literally
don't see what's going on a short walk down the hall. Or they don't care.
"The hypocrisy arises when the PR department says 'cheating is wrong' and
the accounting department cheats," Kurzban told me.

For another analogy, say the sex drive part of someone's brain doesn't
know what's going on in the ethical part. The truth might be floating
around in the ocean of the person's mind, but it's as if there were a dam in
the brain blocking it from consciousness. For most of us, the truth comes
flooding into our psyche, making us feel bad. But for the hypocrites, those
who have the dams installed, the truth stays tucked away, allowing them to
live the lie—until the dam breaks.

It's easier to get away with lying if we actually believe our own bullshit,
because it "eliminates the costly cognitive load that is typically associated
with deceiving," said evolutionary biologist and sociobiologist Robert Trivers, whose 2012 book, *Folly of Fools*, is all about self-deception.[34]

Trivers, who was counted among *Time* magazine's one hundred greatest thinkers and scientists of the twentieth century, believes that we must deceive ourselves in order to deceive *others* more easily. "The key to defining self-deception is that true information is preferentially excluded from consciousness," he told an interviewer. "In short, self-deception makes deceit more effective. And since we are all in the business of inflating ourselves to look and even be better than we actually are, this contributes enormously to an individual's greater reproductive, or rather genetic success."[35]

In plain English: people who lie to themselves make good liars. And good liars usually have more sex.

So, HOW CAN the Self be both duped and dupee in the same instance?

"Kurzban hypothesizes that what appears to be self-deception occurs because some modules conceal their activities from other modules," said Leary. "If we assume that a module of which a person is consciously aware is itself not in contact with another module of which the person is not aware, two parts of one brain could both know and not-know something at the same time without any deception at play."[36]

Basically, Kurzban is contending, as Buddhism does, that there's no True Self, that we're an aggregate of multiple selves. This is not a popular argument, because it implies that no one's in charge.

To my maybe-modular mind, this is equal parts frightening and liberating.

DURING HIS YEARS in hiding, Peter Young wasn't lying to himself. Not fully, anyway. He was conscious of, and intentional about, the lies he told all day, every day. And even though he believed absolutely in his cause, the nonstop mendacity did take a psychic toll. He might have benefited during those years, actually, from a little more modularity in his brain, to protect him from the knowledge of his own deceit. For most people, it's stressful to live like that.

"I was good at it for two reasons: discipline and because I had to be," he said. "It's that force where, when you have a strong enough 'why,' the 'how' takes care of itself. Looking for loopholes to problems has been my core passion as long as I can remember."

Most people would, like Young, experience psychological stress if they perpetuated a major lie for many years. In Caroline Knapp's best-selling memoir of grief and addiction, *Drinking: A Love Story*, she shares a conversation she had with her father, who was dying of brain cancer. The tumor, a glioblastoma—the same type of tumor the Commander wanted to cure, and the one that killed my grandmother—was smack in the center of his skull. Her father, Peter Knapp, believed it was a psychosomatic manifestation of his own conflict. A renowned psychiatrist, he'd been having a long-term affair while married to Knapp's mother. After the mother discovered it, he called off the extramarital relationship, or so he said. On his deathbed, he confessed that he'd been lying all along; the affair had never ended. His paramour had even visited him at the hospital just weeks earlier.

"Although she took care of him until the day he died, my mother never quite forgave my father for his betrayal, and he never really forgave himself," wrote Knapp. "He died believing in his soul that he'd somehow brought the brain tumor on himself."[37]

Kim Philby didn't appear to suffer any psychological damage from his more than thirty years of living a lie, but there is evidence that he struggled with the mental calisthenics.[38] Again, it might have helped him manage all the chess pieces if he'd been able to compartmentalize fully, and sometimes keep bits of information hidden from his conscious mind. Luckily for Western democracy, the modular brain is not an on-demand kind of operation.

THERE'S NO KNOWING exactly what goes on in the brains of people who lie for decades without any seeming anxiety. But research beyond Kurzban's and Trivers's theories may help explain it.

In the early 1960s, psychologists divided people into two categories, "repressors" and "sensitizers."[39] Repressors always had a smile on their faces; they skipped through life joyfully. But though they always claimed to be healthy and adjusted, "if you measure their physiological and behavioral responses to things—particularly negative emotions—they react very strongly," said organizational psychologist Adrian Furnham. "They seem to be either deceiving themselves or trying to manage the impression of being tough, resilient and calm when they are far from it."[40]

If they were about to undergo a life-threatening operation, repressors pushed their thoughts aside, usually by keeping busy. Think of women who've given birth. Immediately postlabor, they're reeling in pain. But check in with them a few months after they've got their little bundle of joy, and they minimize the level of pain they experienced, or have maybe even forgotten all about it (it's called "motivated forgetting").

Sensitizers, on the other hand, ruminate. They're fearful. In one study, nurses who were sensitizers were more worried about contracting AIDS than those who were repressors.[41] How do repressors repress? Researchers suspect they're able to block distressing thoughts by focusing on happy things. They're immaculate deniers. Over time—with practice, in effect—this becomes habit.[42]

"This talent is likely to serve them well in the daily struggle to avoid unwanted thoughts of all kinds, including unwanted thoughts that arise from attempts to suppress secrets in the presence of others," Daniel M. Wegner, of Harvard University, told the *New York Times*.[43]

Aldrich Ames, the former CIA agent who, like Philby, was a secret KGB mole, was most probably a repressor. "I adapted a little more in the sense of being able to deny things, to avoid thinking about consequences," he said. "I never spent a lot of time thinking about my relationship with the K.G.B."[44]

As a full-on sensitizer, I wish I could distract myself like that. It seems like a good tactic for feeling less anxious.

Could any one of us learn the way of the successful repressor?

"Some types of lying are, by definition, learned," psychologist Nobuhito Abe, an associate professor at Kyoto University, told me in an email. "So-called skillful lying by a con artist would be based on learning."

In a sense, the capacity to lie is developmentally linked to, or at least broadly coincides with, our ability to put ourselves in someone else's shoes (called, once again, "theory of mind").

"We learn pretty early on that you and I aren't the same person, that we see the world differently," said Timothy Levine, a communications professor at the University of Alabama. "In order to deceive, you have to know that the other person doesn't necessarily know what you know. Anyone with basic human cognitive skills can do that. But some people can do that much better than others. Those people can be very successful as undercover agents or police or great at closing arguments in the courtroom. They're great politicians and great salespeople and great at picking up people in bars."[45]

ONCE PETER YOUNG left jail, he felt like a bandit all over again. He didn't know what to do with himself; his purpose was gone. So he started a software-related business. That's as specific as he'd get, because he operated his company under a pseudonym. He had to. "I don't enjoy having to conceal my identity, but my real name has a huge Google footprint," he said.

"Oh, really?" I asked.

He heard the catch in my voice. "I get how you could be going, 'This is a pattern of deceit,'" he said. "But consider for a second—if I were to do business under my name it would be totally problematic."

His company, whatever it was called, seemed to be doing really well, and he was pleased. He referred again to the times when he'd slept in broom closets at universities. Every night, he and his girlfriend would sneak into the hot tub at the Hyatt hotel up the street. "Tomorrow I have a room at that hotel," he said. "My life's changed a lot."

YOUNG AND I finally met in person in December 2016, at a vegan restaurant in Philadelphia, where he was living for a spell. He had moved every six months or so, from San Francisco to Boulder to Atlanta to Savannah. A nomadic existence made sense to him. He was used to it.

I'm not sure what I expected, but he was cute. Canvas shoes, jeans, a mint green sweater over an untucked paisley shirt, and an undershirt. John Lennon glasses. Dark hair. A chin dimple.

At the moment, he had girl problems. A woman he'd dated a few years ago was being a little too elusive for his tastes. "She's just like me," he said. "Hard to read." The irony didn't escape him.

He knew that his own compartmentalization hurt him in his personal relationships. When he was on the run, he'd had to pull away whenever anyone got too close. That was his survival mechanism; it made it easier to bail when he needed to. But then he met this woman he couldn't shake. Not long ago, he dreamed they attended a Christmas pageant together, and so maybe the dream was a portent, and they could be together now.

"For the first time in my life, I proposed to someone that we pick things up where I torpedoed them two years ago," he said. She wasn't fully on board, but he was taking her to the kitschy but quaint New Hope, Pennsylvania, on some kind of Yuletide outing with dinner and caroling. He didn't expect a happy outcome.

"Well, you never know . . . ," I said, trying to be encouraging. "Let me know how it goes." I wondered if his choice of a town called New Hope was unconscious or not.

He nodded. There was a sadness to him, a melancholia, that I suspected was real. I felt bad for him. But not as bad as I would have felt if I'd been involved with him and later discovered he was lying.

I heard from him a little while later when he told me his Christmas date went exactly as he'd imagined. They ate some nice (vegan) food, took in the decorations, talked for six hours, and said goodbye. "I don't expect I'll ever see her again," he said. "The fugitive part of my brain has its latest and most tragic casualty."

It sounded a little dramatic to me, but he seemed to mean it. He'd reached a new level of awareness.

"I don't think I fully acknowledged how much my past has affected me," he admitted. "I'm constantly accused of holding back, and it's totally subconscious at this point. I have a hard time getting close to people."

He knew why this was, and he knew that it had to be this way. "I was a fugitive or in prison for all but eight months of my twenties!" he said. "Prior to that, there was a short but consistent history of normal relationship patterns. This is the first time I closed a door, caught myself, went to reopen, and found no one waiting for me on the other side."

HIS NEW AWARENESS was well and good for Young, but what about Maggie Barber, his girlfriend during some of his fugitive years? For the duration of their relationship, Barber didn't know who her boyfriend really was, much less that he was wanted by the government. They broke up before he got caught, and parted ways amicably enough. But he actively lied to her for two years.

But here's the thing: when he got arrested and she learned the truth about him, she didn't experience it as betrayal. Nor had she been emotionally damaged by his lies. Once she knew the truth, she was sympathetic. "It's really hard for someone who's on the run to never be honest with anyone," she said.

The fact that she was so young, and the relationship relatively brief, meant it didn't derail her life. She was eighteen when they met; he was twenty-four and "dreamy." "That might be a part of why I wasn't upset," she admitted. "Maybe I was too young or naive to have a response."

But he didn't really lie about who he was. He said he was a social justice activist; that's who he really was. "I never felt ill will or issues with trust because we were interested in that scene, animal activism," she said. "There was an awareness that people have to go underground."

And she condoned—and still does—the criminal activity that had gotten him into trouble. "I so wholeheartedly stand behind what he was accused of," she said. "My support for people doing this important—and illegal—work is at the forefront of any grace I'd extend to someone who was deceiving me. It would have been different if his crime had been harmful to another person, or hiding some very terrible part of himself. But he was hiding a part of himself that was really heroic, sexy. I still support it. Everybody should release some mink from a farm!"

They finally had an eye-to-eye, knee-to-knee conversation after he got out of jail.

"It was great to be open," she said. "I never doubted his emotion, and I still don't. I never doubted his mental faculties; I never felt that he was crazy or a bad guy. He was a good guy who was responding to a set of circumstances as best he could. I feel fondness for him as a friend."

She was actually grateful to him. "There are some secrets you don't want to know, especially when there's illegal activity involved," she said. "Now I'm thankful that he never told me. He protected me legally."

Having a personal stake in the emotional fallout for the duped, I was riveted by Barber's perspective. Bob Hamer's wife similarly reported no sense of betrayal. It seems to matter what the liar's intentions and motives are. If he is perceived to have lied out of altruism, or in order to protect himself and his loved ones, the deceived parties don't feel harmed, and don't struggle with trust issues.

For Barber's sake, I'm glad she was able to make peace with her boyfriend's betrayal. But let's not kid ourselves. Most liars leave behind a massive trail of psychological and emotional wreckage.

SIX

POST-DECEPTION STRESS DISORDER

> When we discover that someone we trusted can be
> trusted no longer, it forces us to reexamine the universe,
> to question the whole instinct and concept of trust.
> For a while, we are thrust back onto some bleak, jut-
> ting ledge, in a dark pierced by sheets of fire, swept by
> sheets of rain, in a world before kinship, or naming, or
> tenderness exist; we are brought close to formlessness.
>
> —Adrienne Rich[1]

It was a spectacularly romantic essay, published in a "How We're Celebrating Valentine's Day" section of a small New England newspaper. A little purply, perhaps, and too cloying for my tastes. But it was the kind of tribute most girls dream about: "The pure harmonic in which she moved through life somehow ambushed me," the Commander wrote. He had truly outdone himself.

Only it wasn't about me. It was an homage from the Commander to his college girlfriend, Emma, with whom he was madly in love. Apparently they had never not been in love, and now, praise God, they could finally be together.

I stumbled across it in February 2012, fourteen months after I'd left him, one month before I got the call from NCIS, during a late-night Googlefest. I indulged in these self-destructive activities every so often before I knew the real truth about him, usually when I was lonely and bored and feeling particularly masochistic.

My obsessing usually went something like this:

Did I give up too soon?
I gave up too soon.
Did I make a huge mistake?
I made a huge mistake.
Have I ruined the best thing that ever happened to me?
I ruined the best thing that ever happened to me.
I was horrible.
I was untrusting.
No wonder I'm alone.
I deserve to be alone.
No one will ever love me.

Then I'd surf the web to see what kind of intel I could gather on him, just to make myself feel even worse.

As I read his article, my pulse sprinted up and down my body. He wrote, in part, that not long after he and Emma had connected, life had pulled them in different directions.

I ended up in the military, qualifying as a Special Forces operator, then finally, after nearly dying at the hands of the enemy, I made it to medical school and fatherhood. . . . We both made the decision to establish meaningful life with marriage and children, and while each set of kids were jewels, our marriages were eerily similar and difficult.

In a twist of fate, we located and reached out to each other recently. We were both free of relationships. . . . We revealed that at various key points in our life trajectories, victory over all odds was attributed to dreaming of the other. Our reconnection was seamless.

My head felt like it was about to explode. It hurt more than I expected. He had said similar words to me—written them on scraps of paper. Had he been pining for this Emma person the whole time?

And how did he move so swiftly from our relationship to another? Why did he get to reconnect with a long-lost love, while I, the loser, spent five hours a week schlepping to DC on the Megabus?

I remembered seeing Emma's name on his Facebook page when we were living at the Watergate. "Who's that?" I'd asked.

"Someone I knew from college," he said, clicking off the computer. "A photographer. She keeps reaching out to me."

"Maybe she can shoot our wedding!" I said.

He quickly squashed that idea, hinting that she was somewhat of an amateur and rather annoying.

Not long after that, I tried to research Emma but I couldn't find her profile again. She had disappeared, and I didn't think about her again until I saw the story.

RIGHT AROUND THIS time, another woman was scanning the same article. Her name was Eileen Morrison, and she was an emergency room doctor in Jacksonville, Florida. She was the Commander's other fiancée. They'd been living together for a year when he proposed in December 2009. Right when he reached out to me.[2]

I'd heard Eileen's name a year earlier; his five-year-old daughter had mentioned her the previous Christmas. He'd told me they'd briefly dated in Florida. He felt slightly guilty for the way it ended—abruptly, with no real closure.

"Why don't you call and apologize?" I'd asked.

He shook his head. "No need to look backward."

A couple of years later, when I began working on this book, I found Eileen, courtesy of Whitepages.com, and emailed her. I wanted to hear her side of the story.

"Holy shit!" she wrote. "I know exactly who you are! You're the reporter. You quoted him in that story! I was so excited to see your name in my mailbox."

I sat on a bench in Union Square with the phone pressed to my ear while she uncorked a bottle of wine at her home.

They had been set up in October 2008 by a mutual friend who had worked with him at the naval hospital. He was new to the area and eager to meet women.

Eileen was a shiksa goddess from Toledo, golden of hair and creamy of skin, with an unflustered midwestern affect. When her marriage had fallen apart, she'd put herself through med school while raising three kids. She didn't think twice about it. She did what she had to in order to survive.

She had liked the Commander. He was older, but a "young old," as she put it. "Fit." Plus, she had heard that Jewish men made the best husbands.

"I accepted that this was the man who would change my life and my kids' lives and take care of me," she said. She met all of his friends and family, including his mother, who had died before I came into the picture. Eileen especially loved his three-year-old daughter. Finally, after three boys, she was getting a girl! It didn't hurt that they always flew first class, stayed at the Ritz, and dined in all the best restaurants—just as we had. "I fell for the package, not the man," she admitted. The Commander wrote her middle son a letter of recommendation for law school. When his acceptance arrived in the mail, the son called the Commander before his mother—that's how close he felt to him.

In April 2009, the Commander was sent to Guantánamo as the medical director, but she "wasn't allowed" to visit. She had no reason not to believe the things he told her, even the bit about capturing bin Laden.

He returned to Jacksonville six months later, armed with a memory card full of photos of Gitmo life. Eileen was an amateur photographer and took great pride in her skills, but his talent was sublime. His pictures were artistically superb. She kept commenting on the composition and subject matter—they looked as though a professional had taken them. The Commander told her not to show them to anyone—although the prisoners were photographed in such a way that they couldn't be identified, they were top secret.

"I starting doubting my own abilities," she said. "I thought, 'I suck as a photographer!'"

(He also showed her the same shot he sent me, a long-distance picture of "him" rappelling from a helicopter into the ocean. The email subject line was the same, too: "BDawg Taking on AQ Pirates." BDawg!)

He proposed in late October at a friend's home in the Hollywood Hills. The friends offered to hold the wedding there, and plans unfolded.

And then one morning in February 2010, the Commander packed up his valise and kissed Eileen on the cheek. He was off on a secret mission and would be "out of pocket" for about a month.

These little excursions bothered her, but she understood they were part of the deal. She wasn't from a military family, but everyone she worked with in Jacksonville was. "They all kept telling me that it happens, that's the way it goes, I might not hear from him," she said.

But this time felt different. Something seemed off. Usually when he went away she received a call from his mother, his aunt Millie, or his college friend Howard. But she heard nothing.

After a month with no word, a knot growing in her stomach, she wondered if he was comatose or dead. But wouldn't someone have been in touch with her if that were the case? She called everyone they knew in common, including his brother, but no one returned her calls.

Eventually, around month two, while shopping at Target, she received a brief call from him telling her he had just been "to visit the kids in LA" and couldn't talk long. He told her he "might have a position at the Pentagon."

"I'm thinking, 'What? You were in LA and you didn't call me?'" she said. "It was very rushed and he wouldn't answer any of my questions."

After that, she summoned her inner stalker.

His phone was on her AT&T plan, so she inspected the bills and called the unfamiliar numbers. She noticed that after the strange Target call, he had called his old friend Howard and spoken to him for forty-five minutes. She also saw calls to restaurants in DC and his family, including his son. At that point, she understood that he—her fiancé—was never coming back.

"I took off the ring, got rid of his shit, and processed things in my way," she said. At the end of May, she called AT&T to cancel his phone; they told her he had reported it "lost or stolen" about a month earlier.

One night she logged on to her computer and came across the Gitmo photos that had been uploaded into her iPhotos. Months earlier, she had showed them to her best friend, who had wanted copies. But Eileen demurred; he had asked her not to even show anyone.

"Even after all that shithead did, I told her I wasn't supposed to give them or even show them to anyone," Eileen recalled. "Still protecting him."

She finally decided to email her friend the pictures, but first she had to reduce them in size. That's when she saw the time and date stamps, and realized he hadn't taken a single one. He couldn't have.

"I'm not sure how he got them, but they were all taken at different times and none of them while he was there," she said. She was relieved that he hadn't shown any artistic advantage after all, but she was also freaked out with the lies.

Before leaving for Gitmo, he'd left twenty-six garbage bags of "important stuff" in her garage. Six months after realizing he was gone for good, she rummaged through the highly sensitive material.

She found handwritten notes from his parents, a crayon drawing by his young son, some family photos, and Hermès cufflinks. She wrapped two boxes of family heirlooms and shipped them to his friend Howard in Delaware. She sent his shoes to a humanitarian organization in Haiti and a homeless shelter in Jacksonville. "He hated the homeless, so that felt good," she said. She brought his books to the Chamblin Bookmine, the largest bookstore in the United States. The clerk said he'd donate them to a local prison.

"Maybe he'll come across one of his books while he's in jail," I said.

She never heard from the Commander again. "He never said goodbye, or fuck you, or thank you for forwarding my mother's handwritten note," said Eileen.

He was off on his next secret mission: Operation Abby.

EILEEN LEARNED OF his arrest when the friend who had introduced them sent an article about it from a Washington newspaper.

"I wanted to blow his fucking brains out," she said. "He conned my parents and he conned my kids. I'm a physician! I have a license to practice medicine! He could have taken me down just by association."

She never saw him use drugs, but she had wondered if he might be an alcoholic. Once she heard about his pharma fraud, she came to suspect that he'd been crushing up pills and snorting them through his nasal spray, which was practically cemented to him. "We always had to stop for that fucking inhaler," she said.

And then she said the saddest, truest thing ever: "Isn't it amazing how one small little guy can make us feel so bad about ourselves, despite the thoughts and adjustments that have gotten us to the places we are in our lives?"

I hung up the phone unable to contain my fury. What kind of person walks away from the woman he's engaged to, from her children, and never even sends a flare? And then takes up with someone else, and proposes to *her*?

After the Commander fiasco, I spent the next year feeling like a deflated balloon. Suddenly, anyone had the potential to hurt me. Everyone was suspect. I was a target, raw and exposed.

But unlike so many dupees, who refuse to talk about their ordeal because they feel so ashamed, I shared my story with taxi drivers. And my cello teacher. And my doormen. And my personal trainer, who'd spent ten years in jail himself.

Initially, my way of coping was to think of what had happened to me as a made-for-TV movie, a yarn that happened to someone else. I also felt that if I told people about it in my own words, I could reclaim the narrative. Like a fat person who announces they're fat before anyone else can—"You can't get anything over on me!"

But I could feel people judging me. Not *him*, but me, as if I were tainted. After I told the story to two potential clients who were considering hiring me to ghostwrite their memoirs, I realized that I should be less cavalier about it.

"Did you tell them that you had a fiancé who went to jail?" asked the literary agent who introduced me to them.

"I did," I said. "They wanted to know what I was working on, so I told them I was writing a story about my ex-fiancé in jail. What's the problem?"

"They thought it didn't reflect well on you," she said. "Maybe you should hold back on that in the future."

It hadn't occurred to me until then that my experience was something to be ashamed of. It was real. It happened. It *happens*. Plus, everyone was fixated on the Commander. They were curious about him and his psyche. I was another matter. What did it say about me and my judgment to have been cavorting with this sort of a creep?

I didn't get the gigs.

I tried to keep it in perspective. I wasn't Maria Shriver, whose hubby the governator, Arnold Schwarzenegger, had knocked up the family's maid. And I wasn't Elin Nordegren, whose husband, Tiger Woods, had had affairs with everyone but, it seems, the maid. And I wasn't Ruth Madoff, or Silda Spitzer, or Jenny Sanford, or a passel of wives of other prominent figures who were dragged onto the front pages of tabloids but stood by their men again and again when they clearly should have shoved them off a cliff. (To be fair, Jenny Sanford and Silda Spitzer did finally give their men the heave-ho. Ruth Madoff's husband, of course, went to jail for life.)

Still, I'd been taken. All I'd wanted was to find a partner and get on with my life. People do this on a regular basis: they meet, fall in love, build lives, create worlds. Sometimes it doesn't last, but at least they get the chance. Apparently not me. (Cue violins.)

WHAT HAPPENS TO your psyche when you find out that someone you trust has lied to you so extensively? When you discover that the life you've been living has a giant hole at its center? That the person you thought you knew is evil or sick? What does it do to your sense of self, of reality?

It depends on whom you ask, the duper or the dupee. A 1990 study found that 26 percent of betrayers claimed their transgressions had made the relationship *better*. More than 41 percent said the relationship hadn't changed at all. Only 29 percent admitted that their betrayal had ruined it.[3]

But guess what? That's not how the victims saw it. Eighty-six percent of them said the betrayal had destroyed their relationship.[4]

"A double life hurts all the people you supposedly love," said Sonia Desai, a thirty-nine-year-old engineer whose husband had another family nearby. "It changes the orbits of everyone else, except they have no idea. The people who lead them are slave masters. Someone leading a double life is playing God, toying with the emotions of the people around them and getting away with it."[5]

She discovered her husband's long-term affair after giving birth to their second child. She'd had a hunch something was off, so she hired a private investigator to follow him around. Seek and ye shall find. When her husband found out what she had done, *he* felt betrayed. "He was furious that I didn't trust him!" she said.

The discovery that you've been exploited in this way is often so deeply bewildering, unsettling, and hurtful that it constitutes real trauma, with the resulting post-traumatic stress disorder, or PTSD. (A woman I know calls it PDSD, for post-deception stress disorder.) Moreover, researchers believe that the changes in the brain caused by PTSD can increase the likelihood of a person developing other psychotic and mood disorders. The word "trauma" comes from the Greek for "wound," a precise description of most victims' emotional fallout.

In a widely heralded *New York Times* op-ed, Anna Fels, a psychiatrist, wrote about patients who discover that the life they've been leading is a sham.

These people—the duped—"struggle to integrate the new version of reality," Fels wrote. "For many people, this discrediting of their experience is hard to accept. It's as if they are constantly reviewing their past lives on a dual screen: the life they experienced on one side and the new 'true' version on the other. But putting a story together about this kind of disjunctive past can be arduous."[6]

Amber Ault, a clinical sociologist and psychotherapist, has spent the better part of the past decade working with partners, adult children, siblings, and parents of people with narcissistic, antisocial, and borderline personality patterns. She believes that when a trauma is caused by someone we know—someone with whom we have a relationship—and it feels targeted and personal, it's much harder to recover from than if a trauma is accidental and impersonal.[7]

Research backs this up. A 2000 study found that PTSD is less toxic when it's caused by a natural disaster, like an earthquake, a tornado, or a tsunami, than when it's caused by humans.[8] Still, the betrayal doesn't have to be perpetrated by a loved one to cause real distress. Eight to ten months after Bernie Madoff's Ponzi scheme came to light, social worker Audrey Freshman conducted an online survey of 172 Madoff victims using the list of 17 symptoms of PTSD as listed in the DSM-5. Almost 56 percent of the victims met criteria for a presumptive diagnosis of PTSD. Nearly 61 percent had high levels of anxiety, 58 percent had depression, and 34 percent struggled with other health issues.[9]

Many of the respondents were Jewish, like Madoff, and either knew him personally or had him recommended to them by their own financial advisers, all of which exacerbated their distress. He had played to their shared religion and community. Many victims were also distressed that regulatory agencies like the SEC had failed to protect them, despite warnings about Madoff that went as far back as 1999.

"HUMAN REALITY IS mostly built on agreements that we have with other people about what's happening and what's real and what's true," said Ault, who coaches clients worldwide. "Reality is in some ways interpersonal. So when we have conceived an interpersonal reality and taken it to be true, it's very traumatizing to discover we've been operating out of a false set of assumptions, that without our consent, we've been living a lie through someone else's manipulations."

Imagine you're involved with someone who tells you he owns his house. He invites you to move in, and you do. As far as you know, that's really his home.

But what happens if you discover six months later that the house really belongs to his ex-spouse? And that he broke in and won't budge? "Then your basic sense of reality has been violated and manipulated," said Ault. "And that's crazy-making."

That was certainly true for me: I didn't merely lose confidence in my judgment after the Commander; I became paranoid about my ability to *perceive* reality. One of the biggest casualties of this kind of deception is one's trust in oneself, which opens the door for all manner of self-doubt and self-loathing.

For a long while, Eileen also blamed herself. I understood. Almost every duped person feels similarly. With the added weight of society's judgment of us "suckers," it's all but impossible not to feel like it's at least partly our fault, though mental health professionals emphasize that self-blame is harmful, and usually misguided.

"It's an assault to the ego to recognize that we were sucked in," Ault said. "People stigmatize themselves because they feel it reflects badly on their judgment, and that others will say, 'What's wrong with you that you went out with someone like that?' Or put up with someone like that? Or gave your money to someone like that? There's a stigma attached to being in a toxic relationship. Our social belief is that if the person has been the victim of deception then somehow that's indicative of a failing on *their* part, rather than simply, 'They've been conned.'"

WHAT ABOUT THE brain itself? What happens to us neurologically when we learn that a vital relationship was fake? Scientists are still learning about the physical changes that happen in the brain in response to pain and trauma, but there appears to be a direct effect.

Severe emotional trauma causes the ventromedial prefrontal cortex region in the frontal lobe to decrease in size.[10] Trauma also increases activity in the amygdala, an area of the brain that helps us process emotions and is also linked to fear responses.[11] Trauma can cause such hyperactivity that PTSD patients freak out when they're shown pictures of other people experiencing some kind of tragedy—even if it has nothing to do with their own triggers.[12]

Neuropsychologist Rhonda Freeman puts it a bit more plainly:

"Emotional abuse absolutely affects the brain. 'Oh, but he didn't hit her,' means nothing to the brain!" said Freeman, who was in an emotionally abusive relationship herself and founded Neuroinstincts.com to help others. "The amygdala is built so that it remembers what happens bad in our life. So if I get bitten by a dog at age nine, every time I see a dog I'll still remember. The amygdala puts me in this guarded mode. That's why certain aspects of the stress system do not return to baseline or go back to normal. This type of 'learning,' initiated automatically by the limbic system, often serves as a form of protection from future harm."[13]

This is a good thing from an evolutionary standpoint—we'll be safer if we constantly keep our guard up. But in most other ways, the enduring impact of traumatic betrayal is a real bitch.

Eileen hasn't been in another romantic relationship since the Commander. "He truly changed my life when he left," she said. "I have very little desire to search for love or any capacity to enjoy it if I find it. I am having consistent trouble with trust in romantic relationships, and I have built a wall around my heart that even Trump would envy."

That's an accurate description for me, too. I've dated a few people since the Commander, and one semi-seriously (in my mind, anyway—but more on that later).

Life, love, friendship, work, and society depend on trust. When it's broken, the consequences can be long lasting.

I ASKED ONE of the duped how she defined trust—in this case, Lisa Lawler, a vivacious sixty-year-old with shoulder-length dark hair, hazel eyes, and dimples. Her ex-husband was convicted of pocketing $2.6 million from a Massachusetts hospital in 2009.

Lawler was living at a friend's house in Montclair, New Jersey, when we met in October 2017, a plate of sushi and a vodka and cranberry waiting for me. She'd been renting a cottage a block from the ocean on Cape Cod for two years, working as the development director for the Cape Cod Center for Women, when her landlord announced that he needed his house back. So

Lawler put everything in storage and headed for New Jersey to cohabitate with an old friend, also a divorcée, like a twenty-first century *Kate and Allie*.

This move was just one of many since the arrest. Up to that point, she had been a "professional corporate wife and mother," she said wryly.

She insisted that she'd had no idea what her husband was up to, and that most other wives of white-collar criminals don't either. Lawler believed Ruth Madoff was another "innocent spouse," which is actually a legal term the government grants wives of white-collar criminals who are eligible for tax relief from their husband's illegal financial gains.

"The term also describes the majority of white-collar wives who are stigmatized by the general public," said Lawler, who in 2014 founded the White-Collar Wives Project, an online support group to bring awareness of the social stigma and financial ruin suffered by women, like herself, and their children.

The nightmare continued when she had to fight the feds. She applied twice for "innocent spouse" relief and finally received it, but not before being threatened with having her driver's license revoked and even jail time.

That's because innocent spouses are often held accountable for their partner's crimes, and can end up paying thousands of dollars in legal fees to clear themselves of any criminal implications and to fight for innocent spouse status.

"Families are tangled and maimed in the wreckage left behind by their white-collar criminal head of household as much as any victim of a financial crime can be," she said. "Guilt by association places spouses and children in the position of being either accomplices or collateral damage with little recourse to remedy their own losses."

Based on my own experience, I have no trouble believing that Ruth Madoff and Lisa Lawler were blindsided by the men in their lives. I can barely do arithmetic; if my husband were manipulating numbers or moving money from one account to another or forging complicated bank documents, I'd have no idea what he was up to. But people weren't just angry about Ruth not knowing how badly her husband had screwed over his clients. They were furious that she seemed to side with her scheming husband rather than their two sons, both of whom died. (One committed suicide; the other died of cancer.)

"I think people were disgusted that she chose Bernie over her kids," I said.

Lawler shook her head. "People were disgusted that she *initially* chose Bernie over her kids," she said. "I understand he was her life partner, but when it became clear that that was not the choice she wanted to make, she dropped him. She went with the kids. I think she was in shock initially. It takes a long time for the denial to wear off." (Self-deception!)

Lawler knows all about self-deception, and she agreed that lots of women keep their head in the sand like an ostrich. ("Ostrich syndrome" is actually in the Urban Dictionary.) But she doesn't let the guys off the hook.

"They're master manipulators, so you basically believe whatever they tell you, even when it doesn't make any sense," she said. "It's so hard for people to understand."

She would have had no way of knowing what her husband was up to—he had a secret checking account where he placed his extra money, and his paychecks stayed the same.

"For a lot of white-collar wives, when you're living a modest lifestyle and the paycheck gets larger and larger, you don't question it," she said. "A lot of wives sign things or the husbands have things forged, and most of the wives don't want to question anything that could do the family harm. You shut down the logical part of your brain that says, 'This is impossible.' You don't want it to be true."

Lawler believes that her own husband, like most white-collar criminals, suffered from what she calls "More Disease." "He was generous, bright, and self-confident, but nothing was ever enough for him. Nothing could fill that hole of a monster childhood," she said. "He wanted more and more." He eventually went over the rails, and took his family down with him. The whole process from investigation to sentencing took three years, which is about average.

"During and beyond this time, you suffer guilt by association, and go through hiding, physically and emotionally," she said. "Being married to someone who has done something so abysmal to society and the family—it's embarrassing. It's shaming. When you deal with shame, it makes you want to shut down. It causes such instability." She spent those years after this horrific event making sure her son got back on his feet. Her focus was getting her son and herself through the mess. The hardest part for her was watching her son struggle through his new identity as a child of a criminal.

Lawler knew she and her husband were doomed the day his black convertible Porsche arrived. "Midlife crisis time!" she thought. Soon after, she said, she discovered his affair with a "friend" of hers. She confronted him, and he swore it was over, but there were inklings that it was still going on. "I was gaslighted," she said.

Still, she stuck around. She knows she sounded like a fool. "It's like what people say about domestic violence—'Why didn't she just leave?' But it's not that easy, psychologically, emotionally, and financially. It's easy to judge from the sidelines. But when you're in it, there's nothing you can do. It wasn't me being naive, it was—*This is my life partner.* You just don't want it to be true."

She wanted to wait it out, but eventually she formally separated from her husband, and shortly thereafter discovered the embezzlement. It was validating.

After he got out of jail, her husband took an apartment near their home, and his first night back from prison she invited him over for pot roast. She was, she admitted, "leaving the door open just a smidge." "It's the psychology of loving someone. I didn't want him in my life, but I still cared about him." But he hadn't changed, not at all, she said. "He walked into the house as if the last two years never happened. He was like, 'That was all in the past. You need to get over it.'" She ended up escorting him to the door between the first and second courses.

Lawler had about seventy women in her White-Collar Wives group, and they came from places as far flung as Melbourne, Australia, and Burlington, Vermont. She acted as kind of a sounding board and advised them on how to navigate their new roles as women whose husbands lied to them. She almost always suggested they divorce to protect their assets, but not all of them wanted to.

"The women want to live back in the safety of the bubble," she said.

Many of them defend their husbands: *He's a good father, a good husband, a great member of the community.*

"I'm like—'No, a good man protects his family and knows his place and role in society!'" she said. "Good guys don't toss themselves and their families over a fucking cliff. Love and trust go hand in hand.

"Time and again there are women in my group who turn a blind eye and see their husbands as victims. It's mind-blowing how many wives and girlfriends will put up with affairs and abuse: 'But I love him.' Ugh. It's an epidemic."

EMOTIONAL BETRAYAL IS so traumatic that many women have likened it to domestic violence.

Joyce Short, a former bond trader on Wall Street, runs ConsentAwareness.net. Her slogan: "Sex is a privilege, not an entitlement!"[14]

Short wants a universal law stating that "nonconsensual sex is sexual assault," and that "consent is freely given, knowledgeable, and informed agreement."

This is personal for her. Short was in her twenties and a Wall Street bond trader when she met Brian, a thirty-two-year-old divorced Jewish man with an accounting degree from New York University (NYU). A Vietnam vet, he had been born in South America and had two sons, both of whom lived with their mother, Roxanne, in Brazil, who was dying of cancer.

Short fell in love and they soon became inseparable. A year and a half into their relationship they began talking marriage and she became pregnant. Although she was elated, he wanted her to have an abortion, so as not to put his children through the pain of discovering the existence of a "love child" while their mother was so ill. Reluctantly, Short acquiesced.

The night she had the abortion, he brought her home from the hospital, left to put his kids, who were back from Brazil, to sleep, and called her.

"Honey, I have something to tell you," he said. "I'm married."

Short threw up, dropped the phone, rushed to the medicine cabinet, and downed an entire bottle of sleeping pills. The housekeeper found her the next morning and called Brian at work. He sped over, plied Short with coffee, and called the doctor.

She survived and struggled through the turmoil of separating from him. But once he and his wife split, she took him back. Why?

"Betrayal, which is a type of abandonment, can augment the intensity of attachment, causing us to long for and cling to a toxic partner," she said. This type of "addiction," which psychologically binds the duped to the duper, is commonly called the "Betrayal Bond."

"When we hear stories of abused victims remaining with brutally aggressive predators, and ultimately being gruesomely attacked or killed, it's not unusual to learn that they were concerned or scared, but failed to protect themselves," she continued. "A betrayal response, along with a moral code of commitment to a loved one, can confuse and deter the victim from simply walking away."

The truth finally unfolded courtesy of Roxanne. Brian was a Catholic, draft-dodging high school dropout, eight years younger than what he'd told Short. There had been no degree from NYU. There was no Jewish family. He hadn't been to Vietnam.

It was like someone took a sledgehammer to Short's head. "I couldn't wrap my head around the concept that he was a total stranger to me and the man I loved really didn't exist," she said. "He had been an actor. I was not his audience; he was his own audience. I was simply a dehumanized prop in a play he crafted to satisfy his need for power, sex, and anything else he could take."

As part of her healing, she wrote *Carnal Abuse by Deceit: Why Lying to Get Laid Is a Crime*, which was published in November 2013. Through her research, she concluded that she'd been "raped," but she hadn't understood that earlier "because nobody talked about the form of rape I'd experienced," she said. "There were no words out there in common language to help people reconcile their experience and express their agony. Once I could put a name to what happened to me, I could deal with it and begin to heal. And I knew I was far from alone."

To comprehend sexual assault by fraud, she said, you first have to understand the difference between *assent* and *consent*. The American Law Institute, a group of some four hundred lawyers who review the law of the land, created the Model Penal Code back in 1962 to help standardize laws across the United States. Many states adopted parts of its language, including its provision about "consent." According to Model Penal Code for sexual conduct, consent doesn't count if it's induced by force, duress, or deception.[15]

"Most people think all types of agreement are consent," said Short. "They're not. Consent means 'freely given, knowledgeable, and informed agreement.' Assent means 'agreement on the face of it.' So, when someone tells you a lie, you can be agreeing on the *face of it* but you're not knowledgeable or informed. You can assent and agree, but that doesn't mean you're *consenting.* The person who told you that lie, they know they tricked you into thinking you're consenting, even though you don't know until you finally learn the truth.

"No one should be tricked, deceived, coerced, violently overwhelmed, drugged, or intoxicated into sexual conduct," she said. "Everyone has the right to determine who they engage with sexually based on both knowledge of the action and clear and informed knowledge of the actor. People say, 'Isn't it a slippery slope?' 'People take off their wedding ring. That's not rape.' Yeah, it is, if by 'rape' you mean sexually defiled."

Short defined fraud in basic terms: someone lies, they know they're lying, they intend for you to believe their lie, and you believe it. The difference between fraud and a lie in this context? Fraud harms.

"There's no crime committed by attracting a person with a lie," said Short. "But there's a significant crime committed by *having sex* with a person based on a lie. Until you harm them in a criminal way, a lie is just a lie. At the point at which you sexually defile them by lying, you've committed a *fraud.* Before you go to bed with that person you have a responsibility to straighten out the lies you told. Because they're counting on those lies to be truth."

WHETHER ALL OF this can be prosecuted or not depends on where you live. Under Missouri law, for example, "consent or lack of consent may be expressed or implied. Assent does not constitute consent if it is induced by force, duress or deception."[16] Rape by deception is a felony in Tennessee.[17] In September 2013, California governor Jerry Brown signed two bills into law making certain types of rape by deception a crime in the state.[18]

In Alabama, it's a crime for a man—the law specifies a man—to have sex with a female where her "consent was obtained by the use of any fraud or artifice," said Jed Rubenfeld, a professor of law at Yale.[19] But it's classified as "sexual misconduct," which is a misdemeanor and a much lesser offense than rape.[20]

In Short's opinion, it's criminal, but shouldn't be punished as severely as violent rape. "Think of it this way," she said. "If someone beat you up to take your wallet, that would be robbery. If you left your wallet sitting on the front seat of your car and they broke in to take your wallet, that would be burglary. Your wallet would be stolen either way, right? But the crime has a different name in the penal code and is punished at a different level of severity because violence was used in the robbery. Whether the crime is called larceny, robbery, theft, or stealing, someone makes off with the victim's property. Whether you call sexual defilement rape, sexual misconduct, sexual battery, or any other name used in criminal codes across the country, a crime against the person—*a sexual assault*—was committed."

Some American laws also criminalize two kinds of situations: if you impersonate someone's partner (e.g., you climb into their boudoir at 2:00 a.m. and fornicate with them as if you were their mate), and if you abuse medical privilege, like Larry Nassar, the doctor for the US Olympic women's gymnastics team. Nassar was accused of molesting more than 160 girls and in 2018 was sentenced to 40 to 175 years in prison. He had told them that touching their genitals was medically necessary.[21]

Failure to disclose being HIV positive is also a criminal offense nationwide, although states vary about not revealing other STDs, such as herpes.[22]

Short was quite clear that we should all do our due diligence before hopping in the sack. If someone said to you, "I'm Brad Pitt's cousin," and you say, "Oh, great," and go home with him hoping he's a gateway to Pitt, you won't have a prosecutable case. She also maintains that the term "sexual assault" needs to be standardized, albeit with varying degrees of punishment.

A cybercrime case that Short thinks should have been rape fraud took place in Missouri in September 2017.[23] A thirty-four-year-old man named Mario Ambrose Antoine posed as a woman called "Nikki." Nikki reached out to women on Facebook to see if they wanted to model. He eventually steered the conversations to adult modeling, telling them they could earn thousands of dollars by making porn videos. He promised that no one in the United States would see the videos; they would only be available on private websites overseas.[24]

The women would show up at the home of a videographer named Chris or Mario, which was really Antoine's place. Antoine would show them an array of fake tax forms and checks to other models—to seem legit. The women were instructed to sign contracts and release forms. He would then film their sexual activity in the guise of auditions—while he played their partner. When they left, they were told that the check was in the mail. Nothing ever came. He was sentenced to ten years in federal prison—but with a charge of cybercrime, not with rape by fraud.[25]

Short maintained this was another example of how "loath prosecutors are to raise the issue of crime in defilement by deception cases." (Her second book on the subject, *Combating Romance Scams: Why Lying to Get Laid Is a Crime!*, came out in 2017.)

"Gender fraud"—when people misrepresent their birth gender to potential sexual mates—is another type of sexual assault by fraud. Sean O'Neill was convicted of this in Colorado in 1996; five people have been convicted in the United Kingdom since 2012.[26] One of them was Gayle Newland, a twenty-five-year-old British woman who was sentenced to eight years in prison for pretending to be a man while having sex with her female friend about ten different times. Newland apparently disguised her voice, bound her chest, and wore a knit hat and a bathing suit because she had just had brain surgery and was "self-conscious" about the way she looked. Newland's victim had always worn a blindfold when they were together. One night, she removed it and discovered the prosthetic penis. She was shaken to discover that her "boyfriend" was really a girl.[27]

In a controversial case in Israel, Sabbar Kashur posed as a Jewish bachelor in search of a serious girlfriend. When his girlfriend found out he wasn't a Jew, but a Muslim—with a wife and two children—she filed a police complaint that led to charges of rape and indecent assault. He was convicted and sentenced to eighteen months in prison.[28]

The head of the Noga Center for Victims of Crime, in Kiryat Ono, Israel, Dana Pugach, supported the verdict. "We all have different characteristics, and it is a person's right to have sexual relations with a person knowing the facts about those characteristics," she told *Haaretz*. "I see no difference between impersonating a Jew if you are an Arab and a wealthy pilot when you are penniless, if those are relevant characteristics to the decision to have sex."[29]

But what about in the United States? Is Short's dream of national sexual-assault-by-deception laws a possibility?

"I think it would be difficult to enforce," said Carrie Goldberg, a lawyer who focuses on online harassment, blackmail, and sexual attacks. "I could see it being more of a civil sort of action, the infliction of emotional distress."[30]

"Stealthing"—the clandestine removal of condoms during sex—gets into rape territory, she said. And there are laws to protect against "catfishing," or impersonation. "But factual information—one's identity or their background—unless it was used for some kind of financial gain, or coercion, I think it would be difficult to find an applicable law," she said. "A lot of times it's going to fall on the target to do their due diligence and to take precautions against being gullible to an offender. Not everything horrible needs to be legislated."

Rubenfeld is also against the expansion of rape-by-deception laws. "Think about the results that would follow if we really had a law that said it's rape whenever one person agrees to have sexual intercourse with another person on the basis of a misrepresentation," he said. "If a seventeen-year-old lied about her age and a thirty-year-old man slept with her who wouldn't have, had he known her real age, he'd be guilty of rape. If two people deceived each other about their marital status, they'd be guilty of raping each other. I don't think these are acceptable results."

And those are examples where the facts would be straightforward to prove. But what about misrepresentation of feelings? Or religious beliefs?

"The instinct to criminalize some sexual lies makes good sense," said Rubenfeld. For example, some lies, like lying about an STD, can cause physical harm. He thinks those should be subject to criminal liability. "But I can't accept a general rape-by-deception statute," he said.

After I shared my Commander story with Short, she told me that I, too, was a victim of sexual assault by deception. "Women don't like to call it what it is," she added.

I thought about that, and I still think about it. She had a point. If we expand the definition of sexual assault to include deception, then technically, I was a victim of it. But I classified my experience as emotional abuse rather than sexual.

Because where do you draw the line? Is it deception if I'm seeing two guys at once and they don't know about each other? Or what if I color my hair to look younger, or inject Botox into my crow's-feet, or pretend to like golf even though I despise it? This happened on an episode of the new-and-updated *Will & Grace*. Grace played golf just to please her ex-husband, Leo, but she really hated it. The twist was that Leo had done the same thing to make *her* happy.[31] Ah, sweet sitcom love.

THERE'S NO DOUBT that I see myself and my experiences in many of these stories about the emotional damage of betrayal. But the question that keeps nipping at me has to do with the self-blame that nearly all of the duped experience.

I agree that it's critical not to judge ourselves for getting drawn in by these predators. But I do wonder—often—if there was something in my personality or behavior that made me vulnerable to this sort of betrayal. It seems not only possible but necessary to move past self-judgment, but it's also necessary to ask the question: In some way, are we too gullible? *Are* those of us who've been duped unwittingly complicit in our own betrayal?

SEVEN

"I KNEW BUT I DIDN'T KNOW"

> Like everyone else, I feel betrayed and confused.
> The man who committed this horrible fraud is not
> the man whom I have known for all these years.
>
> —Ruth Madoff[1]

This is the part of the story where I crawl under the bed with enough sushi and Diet Coke to last six months. It's a mortifying tale, and arguably more embarrassing than the Commander. But there's a larger point to it, so, pathetic though it may be, I'll take one for the team.

Here's the thing about trust. You will be vigilant and you will be strong and you will steer clear of bad actors and then one day you will go to an art opening for a friend and you will meet someone who will, quite literally, charm the pants off you, and all your caution and hesitation and reticence will fly out the window and then you will be in really big trouble.

In March 2015, my friend Ethan, a sculptor, had an art show downtown. The evening was cold and gray, and I would have preferred to stay home. But it was a big deal for Ethan so I forced myself to go. And wouldn't you know, I met a very funny abstract painter, slightly rumpled with a full head of silver hair, who was separated from his wife of twenty-five years, which he shared in an email the following day.

On our first date at a Greenwich Village café, I must have asked eighty-two different ways the specifics of his situation. What exactly did "separated" mean? Had he and his wife had an open marriage? Had they taken an annual Marital Rumspringa, where they used electricity and drove real cars before returning to the dry Amish homestead?

All I wanted was information, so I could make an educated decision about my life—what Immanuel Kant, who was against lying in all circumstances, called a "moral" decision. Kant believed that every choice we make should be made freely, of our own volition, and not through coercion or deception.[2]

I was pretty certain the painter was legit. We had friends in common and I knew lots of people who were friendly with his soon-to-be-ex, so I didn't think he would lie to me. It wouldn't be prudent. Plus, he was the father of a daughter. *A daughter!* Men with daughters don't jerk women around, do they? *Do not do unto others what you wouldn't have them do unto your offspring.*

And I wasn't some random hookup. I was different. *Special.* But I'd learned my lesson, damn it! I needed to know what I was dealing with. I don't date married men. My ego is too big, and too small.

The next time I saw him I asked him point-blank: "Are you legally separated?"

Well, no, he admitted. Not yet. "I guess that's the next step."

"Does your wife know you're separated?"

"My wife doesn't give a shit what I do," he said. He actually may have chortled.

It wasn't that he was so unhappy, he explained. But he could be *happier*. He wanted to laugh more, poor guy.

"I'd like to be Amal Clooney," I said.

He swore that he and his wife led parallel lives, and, more importantly, slept in separate quarters. "We haven't had sex in six years!" he said triumphantly, Atticus Finch resting his case. He'd wanted to leave for a long time, but he couldn't for the sake of his kid. "How old is she?" I asked, taking a sip of wine.

"Twenty-four," he said. "She lives with her boyfriend in Vancouver."

I nearly aspirated on my Merlot. *Twenty-four?* It sounded insane, especially to the wiser, smarter, learn-from-her-mistakes gal that I now was. Except. Well. I'd heard about grown-up kids devastated by their parents' later-life divorce. He was trying to extricate himself from a long marriage. These things take time.

I didn't want to let the experience with the Commander ruin a potentially great thing. Isn't that what we say after a terrorist attack? *We won't let hate win.*

Rather than retreat, I went Reagan. I would trust, but verify. Not only would I listen to what he said, I'd watch what he did. Most importantly, I'd listen to how I felt.

There were lots of signs supporting his claim of separation. In an early email, he made mention of *A Fish in the Dark*, the Larry David play on Broadway that cost $400 for two tickets and was a "massive disappointment." "My date almost got thrown out of the theater for audibly groaning at the jokes," he wrote.

Eureka! said Nancy Drew. *A "date"! He said "date"! A "date" is not a wife.* A good sign.

He always referred to his life in first-person singular. As in, "I'm going to dinner," or "I'm heading upstate." Most people in long-term relationships default to third-person plural. Again, a good sign.

He was often free at night, even Fridays and Saturdays. He invited me to join him and a few friends for a four-day weekend in London.

And what I believed to be irrefutable evidence that he was playing it straight: he knew the Commander story. What kind of cad would mess with me after hearing that?

These all amounted to a shimmering green light, and I felt secure enough to move forward.

LET ME STOP right here to express what you're all thinking: What the fuck is the matter with this girl?

I'm with you; it's galling. But I was trying to strike a balance between healthy skepticism and not losing out on what might have been the love of my life. Yes, some things gave me pause, but they weren't deal breakers. He had an excuse for everything, and bizarre though they were, they were also plausible—and didn't involve secret missions (a must-have quality for any future mate of mine).

So I did what any *Cosmo* reader would do. I made a list of PROS and CONS.

CONS

Con: Sometimes he'd bolt from my apartment at midnight, as if his penis might turn into a pumpkin.

Con: He was addicted to Happy Endings at Asian massage parlors.

Con: I once found a white envelope full of little blue pills before he set off on a trip to Europe. His?

"A guy I know gave them to me," he said quickly. "I use them when I go to Chinese massage parlors. I can only get an erection if I have an emotional connection with the person. Why pay for something if I can't enjoy it fully? I don't want to waste my money." (Isn't it nice that Viagra is always "from a friend" or "for a friend"? I find it heartening, if not hardening, that these guys are so invested in each other's sex lives.)

It was the most preposterous explanation—I don't even think the Commander could have come up with anything so asinine. But I decided not to push the issue. Clearly, he was insecure about his Manhood. No need to rub it in.

Con: I was never invited to his place. Why?

"It's complicated," he said, sighing heavily.

The terms of his spousal disunion were indeed peculiar. His niece, his wife's sister's daughter, was living with him while his wife was staying across town with her sister, who was recuperating from ovarian cancer.

Okay, plausible might be overstating it a bit. But people are weird.

And the Pros significantly outweighed the Cons.

PROS
Pro: I liked him.
Pro: I reaaaaally liked him.
Pro: Oh boy, did I like him.

He was as charming as the Commander but funnier, sexier, and successful in a real New York way. When we were together I felt witty and sexy and alluring and sharp. We had a visceral, animal chemistry. I delighted in delighting him. He was exactly, and unexpectedly, what I wanted.

He said he was in love with me, too, and it certainly felt like it. I was one of "four people" he'd ever felt emotionally close to. In order of appearance: his first wife, his second wife (whom he took up with while still married to the first), another woman who was "batshit crazy," but they shared a "connection in suffering," and me.

So you can imagine my surprise when I received an email the night he was scheduled to return home from Berlin, where he was on a "working vacation." The email, clearly errant, mentioned a nerve-wracking experience at the airport when a Teutonic security guard yanked him out of line, frisked him, and practically slapped a yellow star on his left bicep. "My wife called out, 'What are you doing to my husband?'" he wrote.

Ah. Time to clear some more space in the Con column.

I'd been in Prague this same week and had hoped to meet up with him somewhere on the Danube. He had squashed that idea—he was sharing a suite with his colleague, and there was no time for fun. Now I understood the real reason. "I don't think you meant to send this to me," I shot back. "I didn't know you were traveling with your wife."

His reply practically flew into my in-box. "She was with her sister in Amsterdam visiting my nephew, and they decided to stop over in Germany at the last minute. We had breakfast and went to the airport. But we didn't sit together!" he said proudly, as if he had discovered the cure for lupus. "The plane was empty, and we didn't sit together!"

I knew he was lying.

I hoped he wasn't.

But I knew he was.

I SHOULD CUT this little episode right here; it clearly does not portray me in the coruscating light in which I'd like to shine.

Slowly, over time, the truth eked out. He and his wife were separated. Sorta. That is: they were separated the way you're separated from your neighbor at a movie theater—by an armrest. The sister-in-law really did have ovarian cancer—two years earlier. As for the Audible Groaner at the Larry David play? That was his wife.

His mother died when he was a toddler; his father married three more times and had multiple affairs. He felt the world owed him for his peripatetic upbringing, so he followed in Dad's Casanova footsteps. He had once overheard his wife say she didn't mind if he got an occasional extracurricular blow job. As long as it didn't threaten their emotional connection or break up the family, who cared? He took that ball and ran with it so hard he practically won a Heisman.

Three months in, I discovered texts not only from his soon-to-be-ex-wife but from *another* woman, a professor whom he had met at an art opening months before me. ("She cornered me and propositioned me!" he said.) He denied that it was anything serious—"It's just sex, I'm in love with you"—but there it was in Times New Roman.

In his head, he had it all worked out: there was his wife, there was the woman he was "just fucking," and there was the woman he allegedly loved: me, Compartment Number Three.

Maybe the world owed him something, but I didn't. "What are you *doing*?" I asked. I wanted to tell him to use his Viagra to go fuck himself.

"I don't know," he said. "I'm weak!" And then he blurted, as if by accident: "I'm not going to blow up my life!"

"*You don't cheat on the mistress,*" was all I could think to say.

I asked him if he wanted his daughter to be with someone like him, and he said no, he was too flawed. "So why should I?" I asked.

His behavior was worse than mean. It was clichéd.

I GHOSTED HIM. No emails, no phone calls, no texts. It's not like I hadn't learned anything from the Commander.

But I don't think the Cliché, as I christened him, is a psychopath. Whereas I'm pretty sure the Commander truly believed his lies, this guy knew he was obfuscating. He had deliberately, intentionally misled me—not outright lies, but "doublespeak," George Orwell's term for language that purposely conceals or twists its true meaning.

How could this have happened again? All I'd asked for—begged for, really—was to be told the truth. But he couldn't do that, because that would have gone against his own interests. Anyone with a shred of decency in his situation would have extricated himself from a relationship with me—or better yet, never even started one.

But he articulated his position quite bluntly: "If I told you the truth you would never have gone out with me."

I believe the clinical diagnosis is "asshole."

I CAN HEAR the screeching as I type. "Again? She *was duped AGAIN*?"

I read this and want to stab myself in the head with a fork. I also expect to be crucified for being "bitter," which is what every woman is called who voices anything unsavory about a failed romance. Or better yet: a "scorned woman with a vendetta," à la Anita Hill.

But it's not bitterness that's fueling me. It's rage. Not so much at him, though that's certainly there, but at myself. It sickens me that it happened again. Yes, the experience took place in a shorter time span—five months, max—and with fewer consequences than the Commander. And I fled when his deception came to light. Still, someone I trusted—someone I loved—had lied to me for his own benefit. *Again.*

But this happens more than you might realize. Maria Konnikova, author of *The Confidence Game*, told me that "the best sucker is one who has already been suckered. There are so many repeat victims. You think, 'This could never happen to me again.' The more confident you are in your invulnerability, the more vulnerable you become."[3]

MAYBE THE SIMPLEST and most powerful reason I trusted both the Commander and the Cliché is that I *wanted* to.

This is natural. Trustworthiness is the number one characteristic we seek in people.[4] Because of this very real need, we see what we want to. To some degree, we all have a "truth bias"—that is, a desire to believe in others so strong that it's impossible to do otherwise. Trust is embedded in us.[5]

Most of us think that trust grows over time. You meet someone, you get to know him or her, you watch his or her actions, you like what you see, and you begin to trust. But the opposite is sometimes true. "Average initial trust tends to start at somewhere around 5 on a 1-to-7 scale and then either grows or decreases, depending on experience with the other person," said D. Harrison McKnight, a professor of business at Michigan State University.[6]

Most of us can't—or don't—live our lives anticipating exploitation. Even when there's actual evidence to the contrary, we give the other person the benefit of the doubt. *He's really a good guy. She's going through a tough time.*

We trust every minute of every day, sometimes without good reason. We trust that the car behind us won't bash into us. We trust that the pilot won't deliberately nosedive into the sea. We trust that our bosses will pay our salaries on time, that the company won't abscond with our pension plans, that our "populist" governor is not shuttering the bridges we use every day just to prove a point. We trust that the surgeon really has a medical license. We trust that the nutritional content on the label is accurate. We even trust strangers. Or, at the very least, we behave as if we do.

But why? *Why* trust anyone? On what grounds do we believe that most people are generally worthy?

Because it's usually fruitful. "Most people, most of the time, are honest," said Jeff Hancock, a communications professor at Stanford. "If you trust people, 99 percent of the time things go really great. Equity is built into the way humans interact with each other."[7]

Even if we're not looking for goodness in other people, trust is useful. "Think about how much of what we know has to be accepted on faith rather than through independent observation," said Vikram Jaswal, an associate professor of psychology at the University of Virginia. "This is particularly clear in science: How many of us can actually demonstrate that the earth is round or that the structure of DNA is a double helix? So our receptiveness to information other people provide, even some things that on the face of it seem outlandish, can serve us well."[8]

Taking this pragmatic line of thinking further, there are evolutionary explanations for why we trust. We're wired to believe that people are inherently good, primarily because society couldn't function without that default. If we all operated in isolation, we would achieve very little, as individuals and as a species.

We've evolved to trust and cooperate, even with non-kin. "It's a big leap forward in evolution to trust others and take a chance on that," said Roy Baumeister, a professor of psychology at Florida State University. "Is it adaptive to be a trusting soul or skeptical and fearful of being duped? Back with hunter-gatherer bands it was probably adaptive to trust. Out of purely self-interest you have to be trustworthy if cooperation is how your species survive. Once we started relying on that, trusting became important."[9]

Trust is *de rigueur* in society. Likewise in intimate relationships.[10] And this, too, is adaptive: If we don't trust, we might not have sex. If we don't have sex, the species doesn't continue. And then where will we be?

Our biology shuffles this along. When you're in love with a person (or institution or political candidate), you're not great at detecting the beloved's less-than-awesome behavior.[11]

In one study, male and female participants were given a whiff of oxytocin, the so-called cuddle hormone that has been tied to mother-newborn bonding. Others were given a placebo. Higher levels are associated with empathy, generosity, reciprocity, and trust. The men and women who'd inhaled the oxytocin had a diminished ability to accurately classify statements made by members of the opposite sex as truths or lies compared to those who'd taken a placebo. "This effect was based on a lower ability to detect lies and not a stronger bias to regard truth statements as false," the authors wrote.[12] Not only that, oxytocin is thought to increase the release of dopamine, which causes even further attachment between partners.[13]

"When you fall madly in love with somebody, activity in the prefrontal cortex, which is linked with decision-making, begins to deactivate, so you can overlook all kinds of important details," said anthropologist Helen Fisher, who's built her career studying love. "You begin to have positive illusions, the ability to overlook what you don't like and focus on what you do."[14]

Another reason we trust people is to not hurt their feelings. In experiments, David Dunning, a retired Cornell psychology professor, found that 62 percent of 645 students would hand over $5 to another person if the only two choices were that the original recipient could keep the whole thing or they both would get back a bigger amount if the second person chose to return it. But no one gave the money away just because they were pillars of generosity; it was because they didn't want to seem rude—even if they were going to be screwed. They didn't want to hurt the other person's feelings by implying that he or she was untrustworthy.[15]

"That tells us that people are responding to issues in the other person's character," Dunning told an interviewer for *Time*. "The signal they are sending is that 'I respect your character.' As soon as you take out that issue, people gamble at the rate that would be consistent with greed."[16]

The study was done in a lab, of course—as many studies are—so the stakes weren't very high. Still, the findings were interesting: it's not that people selflessly want to help their fellow humans, it's that they don't want to *appear* cynical and distrustful. "The situation causes internal conflict," said Dunning. "We get 30% to 40% of people saying something like, the odds are that I am going to get screwed, or not get the money back, but they still give up the $5 to the other person."[17]

NOT ALL OF us trust in the same way, or to the same extent. Some of us trust more easily than others; some are better able than others to sniff a scoundrel from thirty-two thousand feet in the air.

Our past experiences affect whether we trust or not. A child who has reliable authority figures who make her feel safe and secure will view the world in a very different way from someone whose parent was absent or abusive.[18]

"The kid who reached for his mother who said, 'Stop that silly whining and go to your room!' grows up knowing it's dangerous to need people," psychologist Sue Johnson told me. "He takes it into his romantic relationships."[19]

More recent experiences can also have an impact on our ability to trust. Since the Cliché knew all about the Commander experience, I trusted him. I believed he was my prize after suffering through a horrible relationship, and that I needed to have that terrible experience to get something good. I was wrong.

OKAY, SO THE reasons we trust so readily are numerous and layered, and possibly include our biology. But surely there must be some kind of allowance for new information that contradicts previously held beliefs and undermines the trust. That's the question that still nags me about the Commander. How did I miss this?

One answer is the psychological construct of cognitive dissonance, which posits discomfort when someone is faced with inconsistent evidence and driven to resolve the discrepancy.

Like when my cousin told her eight-year-old son that she got pregnant with him because of sperm that swam fast to the finish line, and in the next breath told him the stork dropped him off in her lap. How could both be true? They could not. Still, somehow he managed to accept both ideas. That's cognitive dissonance.

The theory of cognitive dissonance was developed in the 1950s by Leon Festinger, a social psychologist who believed that humans needed internal consistency.[20] He argued that we become psychologically uncomfortable with any kind of irregularity, and so we do everything in our power to diminish this dissonance. Consequently, we avoid situations and information that might increase it.[21]

Festinger and his colleagues penetrated a cult run by Dorothy Martin, a self-proclaimed prophet who believed that a flood was imminent and that aliens called Guardians were on their way to scoop everyone up in their flying saucers. No little green men or heavy rains appeared. But Martin didn't back down. *Tomorrow*, she promised. *They'll come tomorrow.* Her followers stuck by her.

In their 1956 book about the cult, *When Prophecy Fails*, Festinger and his coauthors concluded that "a man with a conviction is a hard man to change." This applies to women, too, by the way.[22]

Cognitive dissonance is actually quite valuable, because it causes us to believe we have made intelligent, reasonable decisions.[23] Our response is also called "motivated reasoning," or motivated bias.[24] It's what we do when we seek out information that jibes with our previously held convictions. We discount anything that challenges our views.

This response is particularly pronounced in politics. If our candidate utters a falsehood, we're lenient. But if the other guy does it? He's the most conniving person under the sun.

"Once you hold a belief centrally related to your core worldview—religion, politics, and who you see yourself as—thoughts that are contradictory to that are spin-doctored out," said Michael Shermer, publisher of *Skeptic* magazine and author of *The Believing Brain*.[25]

Take Richard Nixon. Even after his crimes were irrefutable, some supporters still rationalized his behavior. This enabled them to hold two opposing views: "I believe in Nixon" and "Nixon broke the law." For example, someone might say, "Nixon broke the law, but he did it to protect America," said Jim Taylor, a psychologist in San Francisco and the author of *Your Children Are Under Attack: How Popular Culture Is Destroying Your Kids' Values, and How You Can Protect Them*.[26]

"People defend Lance Armstrong by saying, 'Everybody did it,'" said Taylor. "Because he was such a hero to so many, and it's hard to admit that your hero lied to you. If you have an emotional investment, then you do what you can to rationalize it. Or it's a 'right-wing conspiracy,' because that's consistent with my ideology and my beliefs. Plus, it makes me uncomfortable that someone I love would lie."[27]

To some degree we're all Charlie Brown, running toward the football and expecting that bitch Lucy not to snatch it away at the last second. And then we're stunned when we land flat on our asses, gazing up at the heavens and wondering how we ended up here yet again.

CHARLIE BROWN MAY be guileless, but he's definitely not stupid. He's actually a pretty smart kid. So why does he keep falling for Lucy's tricks? What makes him think *this time* will be different? Why does he trust a mean girl?

Charlie Brown is all of us. Lots of smart people are deceived. The fact that I'm a journalist, ostensibly well versed in bullshit detection, could have actually worked *against* me with both the Commander and the Cliché.

"We immunize ourselves because we think we're above it: 'Of course I can't be duped, I'm the smartest guy in the room,'" said Kurt T. Dirks, a professor of managerial leadership at Washington University in St. Louis.[28]

Also, when our self-control is diminished in any way—when we're "ego-depleted," in the psych biz—"We tend to ignore warning signals and just quickly try to ease the pressure," said David Modic, a senior member of King's College, Cambridge. "If you come across an opportunity to fulfill a desire, you are likely to not check it out thoroughly."[29]

Nothing will deplete an ego quite like falling in love.

Some psychologists contend that being familiar with a con can actually *contribute* to being deceived, because it makes us overconfident. In a 2009 study, researchers at the University of Exeter found that people with excessive knowledge in a specific area were often duped more than those less well versed.[30]

This is because people who know things may hold delusions of superiority. They know enough to assume they know more than they do, and can jump to conclusions that are false. "There's a sense of, 'Nobody can take me for a fool; I know so much about it,'" said Modic. "They feel no need to fact-check."[31]

Jack Levin, a professor of sociology and criminology at Northeastern University, interviewed one of John Wayne Gacy's neighbors. In the 1970s, Gacy had raped, tortured, and murdered at least thirty-three young boys outside Chicago. He'd buried most of the bodies in the crawl space beneath his home.

Gacy's neighbor used to visit him on death row. "I said, 'How can you visit this man? Don't you know he killed thirty-three people?'" Levin recalled. "She said, 'That's what they tell me, but I only knew him as a great neighbor.' He had been a clown at children's parties and fundraisers, and had held themed events for the neighbors. They had loved him.

"It's not only the killer who compartmentalizes," Levin continued. "It's also those around him that help him get away with murder."[32]

It's been some consolation to learn that I'm far from alone in having believed my fiction-spouting fiancé. We see what we want to. Loneliness and the promise of its eradication can cause people to do all sorts of unwise things.

Remember *M. Butterfly*, the Broadway play about a French soldier who fell in love with a female opera star, had a child with her, dated her for eighteen years, and didn't know she was a man? That was based on a true story.[33]

Or Billy Tipton, the revered jazz pianist, who had four wives. Due to an "accident" in his youth, he had to keep his chest bandaged, he had told people. This was also his way of cloaking decidedly female breasts. No one—not even his wives—knew his gender until his death: female.[34]

One thing that has made me feel better is that some of my fellow journalists, people a lot smarter than I am, have also been duped. Editors at the *New York Times* and the *New Republic* were deceived by Jayson Blair and Stephen Glass, respectively. Walter Kirn was blindsided by "Clark Rockefeller," which he chronicled in his book *Blood Will Out*. Benita Alexander, an Emmy Award–winning TV producer who worked for Meredith Vieira, was deceived by her fiancé, renowned surgeon Paolo Macchiarini. Among many other lies, he told her the pope was going to officiate at their wedding. Not only was that impossible, but Macchiarini had been married to someone else for thirty years. (Alexander made a terrific documentary about the ordeal, *He Lied About Everything*.)

When writer Jonathan Van Meter discovered that Anthony Weiner had lied to him in an interview for the *New York Times Magazine*, he was so distraught that he stayed in bed for two days.[35]

But not only scoop-hungry journalists are susceptible to deception. MI6 was bamboozled by Philby and the Cambridge Five, a ring of British spies who were really working for the KGB during World War II and beyond. (They were recruited while they were students at the University of

Cambridge, which is where the name came from.) The FBI was deceived by Robert Hanssen, an FBI agent who was also in cahoots with the Russians, as was the CIA by Aldrich Ames, who was selling secrets to the KGB for millions of dollars in cash.

The Agency was not happy. As former CIA agent Jack Devine told me, "We do that to *others*, not internally."[36]

ANOTHER VERY INTELLIGENT person who was nonetheless swindled is Stephen Greenspan, an emeritus professor of educational psychology at the University of Connecticut. Two days before he held an early copy of his book, the aptly titled *Annals of Gullibility: Why We Get Duped and How to Avoid It*, he discovered that Bernie Madoff had made off with a large chunk of his nest egg.

Oof.

Greenspan never met Madoff in person—that was literally above his pay grade. Like most Madoff victims, he went through a feeder fund; he had no need to see the Big Man in person. Nor did he have any reason to be suspicious. "I was dealing with a supposedly reputable firm," he told me.

It's not surprising that Greenspan trusted the firm. The closer we are to people who've seemed to prove themselves, the more we trust them (truly trust them, that is, and not in the way we "trust" strangers in Dunning's experiment). Many Jews and Jewish organizations believed Madoff wouldn't cheat them precisely because he was a tribe member. Similarly, Kim Philby said his colleagues trusted him because he was an upper-crust Brit, like they were.

"Establishing trust foremost comes with your in-group—friends, people of like color, religious beliefs, like gender, things that seem to make us similar to other people and that engages our trust," said Jordan Grafman of Northwestern University.[37]

That's why it's so excruciating when those in our perceived in-group deceive us, known in the financial world as "affinity fraud." Affinity fraud includes investment scams perpetrated by a member of an identifiable group—say, a religious or ethnic community or a professional group— against others in the same group. Bernie Madoff is a perfect example: a

Jew himself, he defrauded other Jews. The victims were ideal marks—they never imagined that one of their own would hurt them. They trusted him fully.

The state of Utah provides similar examples. Utah is about 60 percent Mormon, which makes the state a major target for religious-based affinity fraud.[38]

In 2010, the FBI ranked Salt Lake City fifth in the country among Ponzi scheme hot spots, after New York, Minnesota, Texas, and Florida. In 2011, Utah was listed as number five for a "Ponzi propensity ratio."[39] In an effort to combat the problem, in 2016 Utah became the first state in the union to have an online registry for white-collar crime offenders.[40]

AN IMPORTANT CAVEAT: some liars are just really good. "A kid who is duped by a parent into believing in Santa Claus may not be duped by a peer who claims to have seen a ghost," said Vikram Jaswal, the University of Virginia psychologist, in an email. "Belief in what other people say is likely to be influenced by characteristics of the speaker (e.g., age, past accuracy, confidence, apparent expertise), the information (is it totally implausible, or just somewhat?), and the context in which the information is given (e.g., was it provided in school, when talking about science, etc.)."[41]

But while some people are such brilliant manipulators that almost anyone could be duped by them, personality type also factors in. "An extremely trusting person can be duped; sometimes a very non-trusting person can, too," Jaswal said.[42]

Greenspan wanted to make money, which he gamely admitted. That could have affected his decision to invest with Madoff, because "when emotions, such as greed, kick in, we tend to put our skepticism on the shelf," he said. "While as a rule I tend to be a skeptic about claims that seem too good to be true, the chance to invest in a Madoff-run fund was one case where a host of factors—situational, cognitive, personality, and emotional—came together to cause me to put my critical faculties on the shelf."[43]

He doesn't think he was at fault for investing in the hedge fund. "Gullibility is a form of induced social risk," he said. "There is one or more people who are trying to suck you into doing something not in your interest."[44]

But trust and gullibility are disparate concepts. Trust "typically means you have sought some basis for that willingness to depend on others," said McKnight, the business professor at Michigan State University, in *New York* magazine. "You're making a conscious decision to trust them." But gullible people "buy into a relationship swiftly with less evidence than most trusters."[45]

JUST ABOUT EVERYONE I talk to who's been deceived said that they, too, knew something was amiss with their spouse/colleague/friend/parent/sibling/neighbor, yet they proceeded to trust anyway, self-doubt clouding their suspicions.

Self-deception on the part of the victim is a big component of long-term betrayal, especially when the heart's involved. Not because we're stupid, but because the line between delusions and dreams is flimsy.

"We want to believe that love exists," my friend Nell said. "We want to believe that we can fall in love. Even when we know that someone's kind of messing with us, we want to believe that they're not, and so we keep going down that road."

Nell was married to a man she didn't know at all.

She knew he was from Colombia, and that his ex-wife was hateful.

She knew that his parents had shipped him off to the States as a teenager so he could attend a military school. She did not know that was because of an "incident" involving a gun and cocaine.

She knew that he inherited $800,000 after his mother died. And she knew that it disappeared, but she didn't know where it went.

She knew he had four kids, which was a large part of his appeal. She did not know he had another child back in Colombia whom he never discussed.

She did not know that the reason he kept accusing her of cheating on him was because he was cheating on her.

She didn't know he was a crack addict, though she knew something was off.

"There were a million times in the middle of the day he was out of it," she said. "But I didn't smell alcohol. When we were moving I had a few bottles of Klonopin and Valium in my dresser drawer. They were all gone."

She asked him where they were. "He said, 'I don't know what you're talking about,'" she told me. "But who else took it? I didn't want to admit just how bad it was."

Here is the most interesting part. Despite the fact that there's "collateral damage," as she put it, she thinks trust is a positive—in general, but specifically, too, because it got her something she desperately wanted: those kids.

"I knew I was crazy to marry him and I went ahead and did it anyway," she said. "I sacrificed a lot to get what I wanted at the time, and if I had to do it again I'd probably do it because I wanted those kids. I have to sleep in the bed I made, but I'm now getting out of bed."

By deceiving ourselves, we protect ourselves from information that's too painful to digest, especially when we have a lot invested in it being true. We want the truth, but we want the truth to be what we want it to be.

"Liars are so successful not because they're expert fabricators, but because the target of the lie wants to believe them," said lying expert Paul Ekman. "Do you really want to find out whether your lover is betraying you? Of course you do. But of course you don't. It's a terrible thing to discover that someone has been taking advantage of you. That's why liars succeed. Because we want to believe them."[46]

To be sure, certain personalities are more susceptible to being duped than others. George K. Simon, a clinical psychologist and author of *In Sheep's Clothing: Understanding and Dealing with Manipulative People*, said that victims of emotional fraud are usually the "conscientious, neurotic types who always want to see the good in people, hate to be the bad guy, hate to be perceived as overly judgmental. They're the perfect dupes."[47]

Still, I believe that anyone can be deceived under the right circumstances, especially when they're intimately involved with the deceiver. It's to our benefit to believe them, and all the more so if we've built a life together.[48] The same general rule also applies to a boss, a colleague, a sibling—anyone we rely on and, well, trust. A kind of willful blindness sets in, all the more so if they're telling us what we want to hear: that we're smart and talented and gorgeous and excellent kissers. Because we want to preserve a relationship or job, or maintain harmony, the betrayal simply doesn't register.[49]

We are so beautifully delusional. We know something's off, and we know we know it, but we don't want to know it, so we ignore it. We don't want to know that not only is the emperor prancing around in the buff, but he also has psoriasis, cold sores, and a back full of bristly black hair.

When I told people my Commander story, they all agreed that self-deception—my own—had interfered with my judgment. His own mental health notwithstanding, the Commander must have met some pretty strong needs of mine.

Initially, I resisted that idea. Of *course* he met strong needs of mine, like the need for companionship and intimacy and love! Like the promise of a family! *Duh.* I felt like people were blaming me for his craziness. I understand this tendency to blame the victim; I sometimes catch myself partly condemning the duped when I hear a story in the news, and I should know better.

I've gradually come to accept my own complicity. I believe it's possible to see our own participation in a situation where we were deceived. I don't blame myself for it, but I definitely played a role.

"Complicity and collusion are very much part of the process of being duped," said psychologist Jay Kwawer, director emeritus at the William Alanson White Institute in New York. "It raises the age-old question of, 'Is there such a thing as seduction?' The successful seduction requires the thorough complicity on the part of the seduced, to close the eyes and not notice everything that is there to be seen."[50]

Kwawer believes that willful blindness exists in every such interaction. Most of his patients who were deceived, he said, "acknowledge that they did have some questions in that first six months or the first year, but it was so enticing and intoxicating to be in this relationship that they told themselves, 'Stop being your usual suspicious self, give people a break, be nice.' I've never worked successfully with someone who self-identified as a victim who didn't acknowledge that they sensed or knew something from the start. That's the paradox—'I knew but I didn't know.'"

We overlook gaps in someone's story because we have an incentive to do so. We get something out of it.

"If you're enmeshed in some kind of repetitive pattern of being with others—even after it is called to their attention and they're aware of it and they continue to do it—there's got to be a payoff," said Kwawer. "Something that rewards them emotionally or psychically for continuing to do what they've been doing all along."

It doesn't have to be acrobatic sex or millions of dollars or a home-cooked meal every night. It could be something as simple as, "Oh, he was so good to my mother and father. Finally, I brought someone home they could approve of." (For more on that, see: "Commander, the," and "Doctors, Nice Jewish.")

Also, I like men with big personalities who have a facility with words and score high on the Narcissus-o-meter. These people usually have their own best interests at heart, and not mine.

NEARLY EVERYONE I'VE spoken with who's been betrayed has said they'd realized, upon learning of the deceit, that they'd had a gut instinct, consciously or unconsciously, that things were not hunky-dory. But they dismissed it—just as I had the very first night I was out with the Commander at the Four Seasons.

Donna Andersen, the author of *Love Fraud: How Marriage to a Sociopath Fulfilled My Spiritual Plan*, developed a Love Fraud Romantic Partner Survey and posted it online. Of the 1,300 respondents, 90 percent said that a third party had warned them to be wary, but they carried on with the relationship anyway. So painful and scary is the idea of being betrayed by the person with whom you share your life that many of us would prefer to believe ourselves wrong.[51] This response is known as "betrayal blindness," and it's the idea that we overlook clues to deception because it's to our benefit not to see them.[52]

So how can the self be both duper and dupee at the same time? Because not all our beliefs are conscious. In a 1979 study by Ruben Gur and Harold Sackeim, people were matched for age and sex and asked to read the same paragraph out loud. The passage was from Thomas Kuhn's *Structure of Scientific Revolutions*.[53] (Kuhn was the physicist, philosopher, and historian who introduced the term "paradigm shift" to mass audiences.)

The researchers recorded the participants and then sliced the recordings into segments of two, four, six, twelve, and twenty-four seconds. The participants then listened to a master tape that played back a mixture of everyone's voices.

Each person was also hooked up to a machine that measured his or her galvanic skin response (GSR), which doubles in intensity when you hear your own voice instead of someone else's. The participants were told to press a button when they thought their own voice had popped up, and another button to indicate how certain they were of it.[54]

Some people didn't recognize their own voices—but their skin did. Time after time, the machine showed the same increase in GSR when participants heard their own voice. Even when people thought they were hearing themselves (when in fact it was someone else), their skin got it right, and "knew" they hadn't actually heard their own voice.

What this showed was that unconscious self-recognition worked better than conscious recognition.

Then the researchers asked participants uncomfortable questions, the sorts of things no one really wants to answer truthfully: Have you ever doubted your sexual adequacy? Have you ever thought of committing suicide in order to get back at someone? Have you ever felt hatred toward either one of your parents?[55]

Here's the kicker: those who responded no to most of the questions were the same people who weren't able to identify their own voice. They were also happier, in general, than those who could identify their voices.

The upshot? "The people who were the happiest were the ones who were lying to themselves more," Sackeim told an interviewer. The realists, according to his colleague Joanna Starek, a clinical psychologist, "tend to be slightly more depressed than others." Sackeim said, "They see . . . how horrible people are . . . what their weaknesses are . . . and the problem is they're right."[56]

I like to think I see things pretty accurately. But one glorious Manhattan afternoon I strolled along Lexington Avenue and caught my reflection in a store window. I checked out my calves, my ass, my thigh muscles rippling below my skirt. They looked especially taut, and I was pleased with myself. All that spinning had paid off.

And then I realized they weren't my legs. I was looking not at my own reflection, but at the image of the person walking next to me. Self-deception in action.

THIS SEEMS LIKE as good a place as any to bring up Henrik Ibsen.

In his 1884 play *The Wild Duck*, Ibsen wrote about Hjalmar, a Loser with a capital L. Hjalmar's father had some underhanded business dealings that ruined him. He and his family earn a paltry living from a photography business.

Despite his bleak circumstances, Hjalmar was a happy fella. Every day he goes to work on a fabulous machine that's going to change the world. He's convinced that money will rain down on him and his family. Every afternoon he returns home in a great mood, believing he's an inch away from finishing his masterpiece. It's self-deception on steroids. A Life Lie.

Life Lies are the sound bites we feed ourselves to inspire us to get out of bed in the morning.[57] They're the hope that we might still win an Olympic Gold, or find the love of our life, or "neutralize bad guys" with the CIA.

This sort of self-deception can actually help people succeed. In 1991, Starek gave Gur and Sackeim's questionnaire to members of the University of Colorado, Boulder, swim team at the start of the season. Those who said no to all the questions tended to be the fastest, most successful swimmers on the team.[58]

"Look at how athletes talk to themselves—they visualize, 'I can catch that person. I am the best, etc.,'" said Starek. "Denying facts about the real world produces people who are better at business and working at teams."[59]

Starek, I should add, made a clarification after NPR's Radiolab aired a story about her work. "The purpose of the research was to understand if self-deception aided performance in athletes, not whether their psychological profile was something to aspire to," she wrote on NPR's website. "I agree, the research is disturbing! It insinuates that the qualities many of us aspire to in western society to succeed actually draw us away from our true selves."[60]

THERE'S ONE MORE element at play, and it is this: we assume that other people share our language and define things the same way we do. But the older I get, the more I realize that people have their own frameworks and lenses for almost everything. That we manage to communicate at all astounds me.

Words and concepts mean different things to different people, especially abstract terms like Love, Trust, Fidelity, Hate, Friendship, Lies. Each one of us defines things in our own unique way, and our definitions are often at odds with other people's.

(My friend Bobby and I once got into an enormous fight over when, precisely, "New Year's Eve" takes place. I defined it as sundown—the "eve" in evening!—on December 31. To him, it was the entire day of the 31st. He thinks it's because I'm Jewish, and Jewish holidays start at sundown. I just think he's wrong. But I digress.)

Just as we assume everyone defines words and emotions the same way we do, most of us believe that people share the same "psychological contract," that we all operate under similar rules. Because he knew my history, I figured the Cliché would treat me with kindness. But that didn't seem to matter to him. Betrayal shatters the illusion that we're in synch.

The Cliché and I thought about things differently. I had created a fiction about our relationship. It meant one thing to me, something else to him—the same way we may craft strong romantic narratives around the people we fancy, while they may view us as mere interludes.

Predictability on the part of the trustee also matters.[61] Close friends tend to share unspoken rules about one another's behaviors, based on their shared understanding of the rules of friendship.[62] These rules often include things like keeping secrets, respecting each other's privacy, and not criticizing one another in public.[63]

To me, trustworthy people do what they say they will, mean what they say, and won't lie to my face or malign me behind my back. When I trust people, I expect them to be who they say they are. I presume they're not falsifying their academic records or stealing my identity.

But that's not always the way it is. And that's not always the way others see it.

One of the guys who helped me move out of my apartment told me he had two children who were both three years old. "Twins?" I asked.

He shook his head. "Two different moms."

"You were seeing them both at the same time?" I said.

He nodded.

"Did they know about each other?"

He shook his head.

"Did they think you were monogamous?"

"Yes," he said.

"So, you lied!"

"I did not lie," he said huffily. "I just didn't tell them about each other."

"That's a lie," I said. "They trusted that you were being faithful to them and you weren't."

"That's not a lie," he said.

"You deceived them."

Around and around we went. "People want to know what they're dealing with!" I said. "They need to have all the facts so they can make informed choices. They want to know how much of an emotional investment they should make in another person or situation." But I failed to convince him to see it my way.

Here was more evidence that different people see trust, and lying, differently. Whether he knew it or not, he was distinguishing between lies of commission (speaking blatant untruths) and lies of omission (leaving out important details).

I wondered why that is. Certainly, broad social factors—our cultural background, the time period in which we live, our country of residence—influence our beliefs, fears, and actions. And so do specific personal experiences, like our parents' behaviors, the pop culture we consume, the friends, romantic partners, colleagues, and acquaintances we've chosen or fallen in with. Then there's individual character, molded by biology and upbringing. What determines how much and whom we trust? What about other men and women—do different genders have different ideas about truth-telling, lying, and trust?

IN A FINAL attempt to persuade the mover to see things my way, I told him about a woman I know who learned that her beloved boyfriend was married with a child. She was heartbroken. "If you're not serious about me, why should I be serious about you?" she asked him. "I want to know how deep I can let myself go. I think that's only fair."

It is only fair. Alas, there are no Geneva Conventions for love. Only war.

EIGHT

LITTLE PINK LIES

The one charm of marriage is that it makes a life of deception absolutely necessary for both parties.

—Oscar Wilde, *The Picture of Dorian Gray*[1]

People tend to think that men have a lock on duplicitous, malicious, erratic behavior, but that's a myth; women are just as capable of all sorts of seriously bad conduct. And we do it well, too (yet another reason to bridge the wage gap). While it's tempting to place blame on the XY chromosome set, men aren't the only ones who keep major secrets.

I've always wondered why Prince Charming wasn't furious that Cinderella pretended to be someone she wasn't. I guess the party line is that the pouffed-up gal at the ball was her true self, not that ash-covered waif by the fireplace. Still, there's a lot she left out of her story.

KARL ROBINSON MET Ashley McNichol at work, the breeding ground for deception. He was creative director at a New Orleans content marketing firm, and she was the finance manager. Both were married, but not to each other.[2]

The relationship wasn't supposed to happen. He was a good Southern Baptist, wed to his high school sweetheart, with two young kids and a golden retriever. He even coached his son's Little League team. In high school, he was the sort of guy who befriended everyone, from band geeks to jocks. He always tried to do the right thing.

Okay, so he wasn't thrilled in his personal life, but how could he be? Who's happy in the sameness of a twenty-year relationship?

Here's where I could quote him uttering the typical clichés about his wife, to whom he'd been married about nine years when Ashley first crossed his path: that they'd "hooked up when they were too young," that they'd "drifted apart," that they "hadn't been intimate in years," that they were "never truly in synch." "I thought she was sweet," said Karl, now forty-two. "But even on my wedding day, if an angel tapped me on the shoulder and said, 'Is this who you really want to marry?' I think my answer would have been no. She was cute and nice. She fit the bill."

Ashley was everything his wife wasn't: magnetic, "borderline brilliant," with a zest for life. Six years younger than Karl, she had a smile as wide as the Grand Canyon. She even taught Bible class! A hottie with a God thing—how could any man resist?

She was a little too concerned with outward appearances, but that was okay. We all have our issues, right? It was the South. People cared about keeping up with the Joneses, whoever they might be. "She would love it when other women would say things like, 'Oh, my god, you're a size 2!'" Karl recalled. He was thrilled to have her on his arm when they went out in public.

Beyond all that, she elicited hope in him. She made him feel like Batman, Ironman, and Aquaman rolled into one.

Every morning, Karl zipped over to Ashley's house in his black Infinity and waited around the corner for her husband, Darren, to leave. They'd scuttle up to her bedroom for half an hour or so and then head into the office together. Their colleagues knew what was going on. "We were open," said Karl. "Plus, you could see how close we were. We walked at the same speed. Our body type was the same. We laughed at the same time. It was obvious."

Ashley had a newborn baby girl, and Karl helped change her diapers. "Her daughter saw me as a father figure," he said. On weekends, Ashley and

Karl would convene in a parking lot at the mall. She'd pull up next to him, leave her car idling, and hop in the backseat with him. The two would have sex right there, straining their necks every so often to make sure her daughter wasn't crying in the neighboring car, like a reverse Peeping Tom.

Three months in, Karl told his wife he had "feelings" for someone at work. He didn't tell her he had acted on said feelings—why upset her further? "I didn't feel guilty about the affair, but I felt bad that she was sad," he said. They went to counseling, and Karl did his damnedest to avoid Ashley. But that lasted only so long. She was his crack cocaine.

They began plotting their life together. They would leave their spouses and raise their kids in one happily blended home. It would be hard, they knew that. Darren was a corporate lawyer whom Ashley had married at twenty-four, and she liked their lifestyle: the $1.3 million ranch home, the European jaunts, the Mercedes. She wanted custody of their daughter, and so she had to plot very, very carefully. Karl was willing to be patient.

But a funny thing happened on the way to the picket fence: Ashley got pregnant, and not from Karl. At least, she didn't think it was his, she wasn't sure. This came as a twenty-five-megavolt shock to Karl, since, according to Ashley, she and her husband hadn't had sex in two years.

Ashley explained that Darren had "forced" himself on her one night. She had no choice but to comply.

It bothered Karl, sure it did. He wondered if Ashley had been trying to get pregnant all along, if she was regularly sleeping with her husband. But he tossed that thought aside; he understood the pressure she was under. Darren was humorless and domineering. Ashley had to play her cards right or she'd lose everything. (Just to be certain, Karl and Ashley plunked down $1,000 for a DNA test. The baby wasn't his.)

When Darren went away on business, she'd often tell Karl: "There are two ways for my problems to be solved: either his plane will crash on the way there, or on the way home." Ashley often made comments like this. Sometimes, Darren would go on hunting trips and Ashley would sigh. "Why can't I get that phone call—'Sorry, Mrs. McNichol, but there was an accident. Your husband was killed.'" Karl didn't think she was joking.

It was Karl who took her to her sonogram appointments, who painted the baby's room, who assembled the IKEA furniture. He even came up with the name: Hunter. "The doctors thought I was her husband," he said. "I was called 'Mr. McNichol' a bunch of times."

He and Ashley carried on this way for two more years, during which time Karl's wife finally filed for divorce. Karl gave her credit: "She wanted love and intimacy and friendship, and all that had disappeared, if it was ever there." He swore she knew of Ashley's existence, though maybe not the specifics. Like, she had no idea that he and Ashley vacationed together in Cabo and New York when he was on those ubiquitous business trips. Nor did she know that little Hunter, who was now two years old, considered Karl a surrogate father.

Still, some things bugged him. Despite their closeness and the risks Ashley was willing to take on his behalf, she didn't seem to be making any major effort to leave her husband. Every so often Karl would erupt. What was she doing? He never made a move without considering the impact it might have on their future. His life was Ashley-centric, but it didn't feel like she reciprocated.

And yet he understood her psychological makeup. Her parents had divorced when she was seven years old and had remarried each other three years later. Her mother, not her father, had been unfaithful. "It's in Ashley's DNA to be a manipulator," said Karl. "I think she was damaged by her mom's actions. She felt a tremendous amount of abandonment, so she decided not to give herself over to somebody. She would make big decisions for herself and her family and never lean on her husband."

In the summer of 2013, Ashley told Karl that she and her husband had separated. They still lived in the same home, but they were never together. Either she would spend the night at her brother's house, or Darren would. A few months later, Ashley removed her wedding ring. A few months after that, she announced, gaily, "I'm getting divorced!"

He howled with joy. Finally! He'd taken a four-bedroom, two-bathroom home in an affluent suburb, a place big enough for them and their brood. But he only had his kids every other weekend; he was lonely when they weren't there. Now, he wouldn't be.

Things were looking up for their relationship. For the first time, Ashley didn't celebrate Thanksgiving with her husband. Instead, she took her kids to her parents' home and spent the weekend there. She was going to tell them all about Karl. "They'll love you," she assured him.

He was even more ecstatic when she asked him to take the photograph for her Christmas card, a sweet rendering of Ashley and her two kids, *sans* husband. "I thought, 'Whoa, that's a massive public sign,'" said Karl.

And then.

KARL BLAMED TECHNOLOGY for the unraveling. If it hadn't been for Facebook, he would never have seen the photo of the three-carat emerald-cut diamond glittering on her fourth finger—her wedding ring from Darren.

"I just put it on when Darren and I went to a party," Ashley explained. "I didn't want people to gossip."

Right around Valentine's Day, 2015, Karl snagged her digital camera.

That's when he saw the photographs of Ashley, Darren, and their kids grinning cozily over turkey and cranberry sauce. The four of them. Together. Rather than spending Thanksgiving with her family, as she had claimed, she had been with her husband and his parents in Alabama. "She said he begged her to go," Karl recalled. "The kids were crying and she felt trapped, so she went."

As a father, he understood the sacrifices people made for their kids. He was willing to give her a pass. But then he saw photos from Christmas: same place, same scenario. He flipped.

For two weeks, Karl cut off all contact with Ashley. No texts, no emails. When he ran into her at work, he ignored her. She begged him to come back. "She was on her knees," he said.

"You have to get a divorce," he said. "I'm not messing around anymore."

"I will," said Ashley. "I promise. By June, I'll be divorced."

He believed her. She even showed him a divorce decree, which he'd held in his hands like the Shroud of Turin. After that, they were more solid than ever. They spent time with all of their kids, so they could get to know each other. In May, the six of them went to California. In June, they visited New York City. In July, she took a solo trip to Colorado, then back to Manhattan with Karl, then to the Texas coast with her kids and parents, and then to Jamaica with Karl.

But in August, she canceled a vacation to Disney World with Karl and his kids. Her divorce still wasn't final. Frustrated, one afternoon a week, after they were supposed to be in Florida, Karl did something he'd never imagined doing before. He paid a visit to her parents. He thought of it as a charm offensive. Karl was going to seduce them into giving their approval for him to marry their daughter. They'd think so highly of him that they'd practically thrust Ashley into his arms.

"Ashley had been using her parents as an excuse, saying they weren't supportive of her," he said. "That they were pushing her to stay with her husband, even though she told them she wasn't in love with him."

Karl drove up the gravel driveway to their sprawling home in the garden district. He had it all mapped out. He would knock on the door, and when her father answered, he would say: "You don't know who I am—we only met once in passing—but I come from a good background. I'm a Christian. Yes, I was carrying on an affair with your daughter behind my wife's back, but I told her about it. I love your daughter and pledge my faith to her forever." Or something like that.

Her father was an intimidating man, six foot three with slate gray eyes and a strong jaw. He was a former newspaper columnist; people feared his snark. When he came to the door, Karl stuck out his hand as planned. "I'm Karl," he said.

Her father nodded politely, but with no trace of recognition. For all he knew, Karl could have been a Jehovah's Witness hawking magazines.

Karl paused a beat. "I'm Karl?" he said again, less assuredly. "Ashley's Karl. You know . . . Ashley and Darren are divorcing. She's told you about me, hasn't she?"

Her father shook his head. "I recognize your face, but I don't know who you are," he said. He held the door open and invited Karl in. Poured them both an iced tea.

They sat across from each other, sipping silently and sizing each other up.

Slowly, the truth drizzled out: As far as her father knew, Ashley had no marital problems. She'd never mentioned Karl. He had not taken a beach vacation with his daughter over the summer; she had gone away with Darren and the kids. When she was supposedly in Colorado by herself? She was with her husband and family. She had phoned Karl from rest-stop bathrooms, drugstores, anytime she could sneak away from her husband. Sometimes the call would drop because of a bad signal. Except Karl now realized the "signal" was named Darren.

Karl's eyes pinged toward the row of family pictures lining the shelves. Among them: a Christmas card Karl had taken of Ashley's kids during their photo shoot, and another one of Ashley, Darren, and the children. That, Karl discovered, was the real Christmas card that she had sent out. The one he had snapped of just her and the kids was a fake, done exclusively for his benefit. She was never planning to end her marriage.

The divorce decree was fraudulent, he later learned; she'd downloaded it from the web. Her friends knew nothing about Karl. Neither did Darren.

"I love my daughter, but she's not perfect," Karl recalled her father saying. "She has an idea of how her life is supposed to be lived and how everyone else is supposed to see it. She's obsessed with image."

Karl left the house feeling as if he'd just been sentenced to the guillotine. She had lied. She had *lied*. She had created an elaborate ruse. And he, the schmuck, had fallen for it.

You probably know how it ended, or at least how the middle part went: Ashley denied everything. She never apologized. She had nothing to apologize for.

"She has no ability to say, 'I lied,'" said Karl, his voice catching. "She will go to her grave not admitting fault. She was playing a role—she was one character with me, another with her husband. She can't bridge her two lives together."

Karl sent her more than thirty emails over the course of two months—some pleading, some wrathful, all demanding an explanation. Ashley ignored them. She quit her job and unfriended all of their colleagues on Facebook, who felt equally betrayed: they, too, had thought she was divorcing her husband to be with Karl. They hadn't seen her wear a wedding ring in years, and she and Karl were always together.

"I had empathy for her during what I thought was the divorce," said Rebecca Richards, a work colleague and friend of both Karl and Ashley. "She knew Karl would talk to me. I'd say to him, 'She needs more time.' I get it—I'm married to a man who's divorced. I know how a broken family interacts. Ashley knew that. I'd say, 'I get why she doesn't want to go to Florida with you yet. It's too soon for her girls.' Now, it annoys the shit out of me."[3]

Rebecca was stunned: "It's so fucking crazy to talk about it like I'm talking about a movie, and then I have to remember how hurtful and awful it was for Karl," she said. "Those were dark and terrible days. She did ruin his life temporarily. I was completely blindsided that she was leading a double life. She and her kids would go on vacation with Karl! Never in a million years did I think someone would be that blatant with their kids. I didn't know that kind of crazy existed, other than in *Gone Girl*."

Rebecca was so worried about Karl after the Ashley horror that she and some friends formed a suicide watch, checking in on him every so often to make sure he wasn't about to do anything rash.

Rebecca swore like a truck driver when she was angry, and like a sailor when she wasn't. When she said "fuck," and she said it often, it was with a mellifluous southern drawl that made it sound like she was singing it: "Fuuuuucck!" She was furious with Ashley, who freaked her out in more ways than one. It wasn't just what she did to Karl, but that Ashley, as finance manager, had access to everyone's personal information. Social Security numbers, bank accounts. Rebecca had nightmares about what Ashley could do with that data.

The other thing was that Ashley and Rebecca knew each other socially. Rebecca's best friend from college, Randi, had a daughter who was best friends with Ashley's daughter (got that?). Ashley taught Randi's kids Bible study; she was active in the PTA. So they were in each other's orbit. Yet

Ashley didn't seem to worry that Rebecca could expose her lies in two seconds. Everyone at work knew about her relationship with Karl. It wasn't an open secret; it was just open. Rebecca could easily have told her husband. But apparently that didn't faze Ashley at all.

"I always thought it was interesting that Karl would talk about what an idiot Ashley's husband was, and I'd say—'She did it to you both! She played you both the exact same way. He's as much a victim as you are, if not more.'"

After the truth unspooled, Karl lost twenty pounds. He got a prescription for Lexapro. He told his twelve-year-old daughter that Ashley had "tricked" them both. That was the worst part—telling his child that the woman she'd thought of as a mother was a fraud.

"It was like being in love with a nickel," he said of the seven years he'd spent with Ashley. "She's two sides, and you can't split that. I loved the head side. I only saw the head side. I didn't want to see the mean, selfish, my-best-friend-saying-everything-right side of the coin."

Only later did he discover the lengths to which Ashley had gone to hide her deceit. She had recorded airport sounds—flight announcements, take-offs, the squeal of luggage dragged on linoleum—to play as background noise. That way, she could call Karl and tell him she was on a business trip, when she was really with her husband.

"Somewhere in there Ashley had decided she couldn't lose me, but she couldn't lose her family, either," he said. "So, instead of letting me leave her, she lied to keep me in the relationship. I've been in purgatory since I found out it was fake. I'm like this ship drifting into sea with no navigational tools."

ASHLEY WAS NO anomaly. You can find plenty of examples of female fraudsters in the news. Sarma Melngailis, the owner of a ritzy vegan restaurant in Manhattan, fled town without paying her employees. She was apprehended when she and her boyfriend were caught ordering pizza (with cheese!) from their Tennessee hotel.[4] Alexis Wright ran a brothel out of a Zumba studio in Kennebunkport, Maine.[5] Rita Crundwell, the comptroller of the small town of Dixon, Illinois, embezzled more than $53 million—reportedly becoming the largest perpetrator of municipal fraud in US history.[6]

Then there was Elizabeth Mulder, who was accused of appropriating $1.5 million from multiple businesses in Laguna Beach, California, and using the money for plastic surgery, renovating a rental home, and buying cattle and horse equipment.[7]

A report from Javelin Strategy & Research, of Greenwich, Connecticut, found that in 2017, more than one million children were victims of identity fraud. Over 60 percent of the victims knew the perpetrators.[8]

Axton Betz-Hamilton was a college sophomore in 2001 when she discovered that her identity had been stolen. The electric company was requesting a $100 deposit because of her credit score. She thought the issue was that she didn't have much of a credit score because she was so young.

She ordered her credit information and received ten pages of accounts and debts that had been sent to collection agencies, going all the way back to 1993. But none of them were hers.

It took Betz-Hamilton eight years to clean up her report, and she did everything in her power to find the source of the breach. In 2013, not long after her mother died, Betz-Hamilton discovered who the culprit really was. Buried among her mother's effects was an overdue credit-card statement with Betz-Hamilton's name on it, along with other forged accounts. Not only had she assumed her daughter's identity, but also her husband's—all the while pointing at others as possible suspects.

"My mother created reasons why we should suspect other relatives and friends as being the identity thieves," said Betz-Hamilton. "Dad and I believed it and we had not spoken to many of those relatives and friends for twenty years. We were taught to suspect everyone as a potential identity thief."

Betz-Hamilton is now a child-identity-theft researcher and college professor.[9]

THE PSYCHOLOGIST PAUL EKMAN believes that there's no difference in men's and women's respective abilities to lie. Social scientist and lying expert Bella DePaulo found the same thing in her research.

But studies have shown that women are more honest than men (except when it comes to investigating people behind their backs. In that case, women are stupendous snoopers).[10] A study of Italian men found that men were more likely to dodge bus fares than women,[11] while in an Israeli study, women were more likely to return excess change at a restaurant.[12]

It's theorized that women shy away from cheating more than men because they're better able to put themselves in someone else's shoes (theory of mind, again).[13] Women are usually more empathetic.

"Men are more likely to approve of questionable bargaining tactics, including promising future concessions that they will not carry through, guaranteeing to uphold an agreement while believing it will later be violated, or misrepresenting the progress of a negotiation to improve their position," said Harvard professor Eugene Soltes, author of *Why They Do It: Inside the Mind of the White Collar Criminal*. "And even when presented with choices that are not illicit or even necessarily deceitful, women feel a stronger desire to be transparent in disclosure. As an example, when given the opportunity to buy a dream property from a couple who doesn't want to sell to anyone planning to tear down the existing house, women feel, on average, a greater duty to disclose their intentions to build a new house. From fraudulent behavior to deceptive negotiating, men consistently have the greater predilection to engage in the more questionable choice presented to them."[14]

A 2008 study from the Stockholm School of Economics found that 38 percent of women were willing to lie to receive a big payout, compared with 55 percent of men. But a 2012 study reported in the journal *Economics Letters* found that, though women were more averse to lying than men when there was only a small financial benefit, this gap disappeared when there were larger amounts at stake.[15]

Jordan Grafman, the Northwestern University professor, suspects it's easier for men to lie because they tend to be less comfortable being vulnerable. So they mask their insecurities with bluster, which is just a half-step away from full-blown deception.

"It's probably also fair to say that men, from complex causes, are more aggressive than women, more predatory in general," said Grafman. "The more one's mentality is, 'I want that, and I'll do whatever I need to do to go get it,' this will sanction, or rationalize, lying. . . . I'd suggest that men possess this mentality more, and at more aggressive levels, than women do. I think this destigmatizes lying for men more than for women."[16]

A 2010 poll commissioned by the Science Museum of London corroborated Grafman's observations, finding that men tell about three lies per day, or about 1,092 per year, whereas women fib twice a day (about 730 times annually).[17]

But the subject matter differs along gender lines. Everyone lies about sex, but men exaggerate their number of sexual partners, while women lower that figure. Of course, social pressure plays a significant role in that example: men are called studs for bedding a slew of people; women are called sluts for the same behavior.

Among men's top ten lies: "I didn't have that much to drink," "Nothing's wrong, I'm fine," and, at number 7, "No, your butt doesn't look big in that" (men who employ that last one are very smart). For women? "Nothing's wrong, I'm fine," "I don't know where it is," and "It wasn't that expensive." Interestingly, while women tend to feel guiltier than men after telling an untruth, 71 percent of both sexes said it's okay if it's done to spare someone's feelings.[18]

Women are also more likely to tell accommodating fibs, or white lies: "Love the dress," or "You're such a great lover." Men, for their part, tell more bragging, self-serving lies.[19] (It reminds me of the old joke: A woman tries on a pair of pants and they're too tight. "Oh!" she says. "I've gained weight!" Whereas a man would say, "Oh! My pants shrunk!")

But it matters who else is around. Women may tell one another more kindhearted lies, but bring a dude on the scene—whether it's men lying to men, men lying to women, or women lying to men—and the self-serving lies kick in, up to eight times as often.[20]

"It's hard to overestimate how competitive men are," said Ralph Keyes, author of *The Post-Truth Era: Dishonesty and Deception in Contemporary Life.* "Men are incredibly competitive in ways that we don't always appreciate— for the attention of women, to be the biggest, to have the most hair, to get the best job, to do the best at work. If they think they can get an edge by being a little deceptive, or more than a little deceptive, and they think they can get away with it, why not? It has to do a lot with the hyper-competitiveness of men."[21]

Hmm. Sound like anyone you know?

Men and women usually have different perspectives on being duped, too. For women, being lied to is a major transgression: "It's not the sex, it's the lies," as the adage goes. Most of the women I talked to said that emotional betrayal was more disturbing than having their partner sleep with someone else. They were not thrilled about the physical infidelity, but they didn't think it was as bad as becoming emotionally involved. Whereas every (straight) man I know cringes at the idea of his partner bedding another man.

Women also tend to feel the wounds of betrayal far more deeply than men do, because we typically take our interpersonal relationships more seriously than men do. A betrayal by someone we're close to smashes us in our teeth.[22]

NONE OF THIS means that women don't deceive.

Ask any man if he's been conned, and he'll mention all the scheming, manipulative, Jezebels he's encountered. After his experience with Ashley, Karl will be leading the pack.

Of course women deceive! One study found that women have been betrayed by their female friends nearly as often as they've been betrayed by their spouses.[23] History and literature are filled with secret wives and silver-tongued seductresses. Today, people test their genomes and discover that their great-great-great-grandma was impregnated by someone other than dear old great-great-great-grandpop.

Some people don't have to go that far back in the family tree. Lacey Schwartz grew up the only child in a Jewish household in Woodstock, New York. Despite her dark complexion and kinky hair, she never doubted that she was Caucasian, though outsiders often questioned her lineage. Family lore had it that she had inherited her looks from her dark-skinned Sicilian grandfather. But Schwartz, a filmmaker, later learned that she was the product of an affair her mother had with an African American man.

"I believe everyone in my family was in denial," said Schwartz, who made a documentary, *Little White Lie*, about her experience. "You can convince yourself to believe what you want to believe. Often, you lie to yourself more than to others."[24]

As her mother says in the film: "It wasn't because I was lying. I mean, I didn't see it, really. And then, maybe once I started seeing it, I chose to ignore it."[25] (Yes. Self-deception. Again.)

It's a different ball game during ovulation. Because when women are ovulating, they feel less attracted to their partners, and become more prone to fantasizing about sex with someone else.

"There's an irony because we have pretty good evidence that women are at their most attractive at the time of ovulation," said evolutionary biologist and sociobiologist Robert Trivers. "Their waist-to-hip ratios are slightly smaller, so they are more curvaceous. They are somewhat more symmetrical and the coloration of their face is better. The time at which she is most attractive to you is the time at which she's least attracted to you. And the men are impervious to this."[26]

WOMEN LIE IN the corporate world, too.[27] In 2010, nearly two-thirds of those charged with stealing over $100,000—behavior that involves deception— were women.[28]

Regardless of the size of their transgressions, women justify their behaviors in different ways than men, and have different motivations for committing crimes.[29] The thinking is that men and women "neutralize" feelings differently—meaning they have different ways of shutting off uncomfortable thoughts, feelings, and values that would normally prevent them from behaving badly.[30]

In 1981, Dorothy Zietz interviewed female embezzlers in a California prison and concluded that they had stolen, lied, and cheated for what they considered a higher purpose—say, to provide for their families, or to send their kids to summer camp.[31] They were noble thieves.

Another study found that men typically stole because they needed money to overcome a problem of their own making, whereas women focused on the needs of their families.[32]

Kelly Paxton, a certified fraud examiner in Portland, Oregon, believes the reason more women aren't committing crimes is what's known as the "pink ghetto." (The term "pink-collar crime" was coined in the late 1980s by Kathleen Daly, a professor of criminology and criminal justice at Griffith University in Brisbane, Australia.[33]) It's not that women are so honest, it's just that they haven't been given the same chances to commit fraud as men have.

"They've always made ends meet either through prostitution or shoplifting," she said. "There's no chromosome that's the honesty chromosome. I want there to be a Bernice Madoff!"[34]

Paxton might get her wish. Back in 1975, criminologist Freda Adler forecast that women's crime rates would soar as a result of the feminist movement. When their opportunities increased, so would their ability to commit crime, a topic she wrote about in her groundbreaking book *Sisters in Crime: The Rise of the Female Criminal.*[35]

One thing that's clear is that the world is much more forgiving of male liars than female ones. Maybe it's because we expect more from women—they're mothers, caregivers. They're not supposed to deceive.

"Society is more accepting of men committing crimes and atoning for their sins than women," said Kelly Richmond Pope, a forensic accountant in Chicago and the director and producer of *All the Queen's Horses*, a documentary about Rita Crundwell. "I don't think it's expected for a woman to embezzle or engage in a Ponzi scheme or to have another family in another town. We accept, allow, and excuse it of men. I think it goes back to the historical role we allow men to play, like *Leave It to Beaver*. We still have this idea that the man goes to work and earns the money and the woman stays home. Because of the pressure and stress of their job, we excuse the men's problems. We're conditioned to do that."[36]

Besides society, who else can we blame for this? Parents.

In a February 2016 study, researchers found that parents usually lie less when kids are around (the dreaded telemarketer aside). But check this out: they act more dishonestly around their *sons* than their *daughters*.[37]

"It's possible that parents lie less in front of girls because they don't want to teach the girls that lying is okay, but they don't feel so bad teaching boys that lying is okay," said Anya Samek, an associate professor of economics at the University of Southern California.[38]

Why would that be? Maybe it's because lying is considered unbecoming and unfeminine. That's also why the slight may feel that much greater when a woman is caught lying: good girls don't do *that*.

BUT THEY DO. Diane Collins learned this the hard way.[39]

Now sixty-five, Diane lives with her wife on Cape Cod, in a two-story white clapboard house. Diane founded a hospice consulting firm along with a company that provides online education for hospice and palliative care programs and professionals. Gray-haired with light green eyes, she has an open, honest face. She is the person you want holding your hand while you transition from this life to the next.

And that's where her story begins, actually.

In 1985, when she was twenty-seven, Diane moved from Oyster Bay, Long Island, to New York City. She had just completed a master's degree in religious education at Fordham University, and was teaching religion at a Catholic high school on the Upper East Side. She loved it, but what she enjoyed most was the counseling part, spending time with kids and talking to them. So she went back to school for another master's, this one in counseling psychology at NYU.

At the time, she was grappling with her sexual identity. It was a different world then—lots of shame and internalized homophobia. She "sort of" knew she was a lesbian, but she didn't know how to deal with it.

Diane met another female teacher and they became lovers. Her girlfriend exposed her to a world of female academics with doctoral degrees—professional, smart, fun women. "I saw that you could be a lesbian in this world and not be an old dyke," she said. These women became her community, her world—it was the first time she'd ever had a group like that.

Diane was living in a railroad apartment in the Bronx, next to Fordham. Her roommate was moving out, and she needed a new one. One of the women in her circle had a friend who had just gotten a job teaching special education teachers at a university in New York. Her name was Amanda.

"I met her at a party and she was really nice, really fun, and everyone felt terrible because she had chronic myeloid leukemia," Diane recalled. Since the end of her life was so near, people assumed she had a certain insight. She was viewed as a wise old sage.

Diane had had a religious conversion some time before that, and she wanted to help Amanda. So she invited her to live in the extra bedroom, and set up a support network with her group of friends. Whatever Amanda needed, someone would be there for her.

Amanda was grateful for all their help. And she was a terrific roommate, vibrant and funny, always paying rent on time. She and Diane became close. They even shared a bed sometimes, though not in a sexual way.

"It was more like sisters," said Diane. "But it may have meant more to her. I don't know."

This was one of the best periods in Diane's life, full of camaraderie and connection. It was also exhausting. Since they were living together, the bulk of the caretaking responsibilities fell on Diane's shoulders, and it was a lot to handle.

For example, there was never any hot water in the flat, and Amanda frequently needed to take hot baths. So Diane would boil pans of water on the stove and pour them one by one into the tub.

She'd also chauffeur Amanda to and from Sloan Kettering for her chemotherapy treatments. She'd drop her off at the front door and pick her up eight hours later in the exact same place. She never went in; she would just watch Amanda shuffle through the big glass doors with all the other patients.

Except the other patients had lost their hair, and Amanda had long, flowing locks. She was apparently one of the lucky ones who didn't have side effects from chemo.

Their friends gave Diane serious recognition for being so kind to Amanda. "That was real good for me," she said.

But Amanda wasn't always sick. Sometimes she would be stable for a month or so, and at those times you'd never know she was ill. Then there would be flare-ups when she would be sick to her stomach. Diane was always bringing Amanda buckets to throw up in.

"I would be thinking, shit, she's going to die," she said. They had long discussions about the afterlife, and what kind of music she wanted at her funeral. She kept her illness secret from her family—she didn't want them to worry—so she instructed Diane on how to explain her death.

"She wanted to protect her parents," said Diane. "I was like, fine for them but what about me? Because she had enough empathy for her family, not wanting them to be worried about her?"

Diane vaguely wondered why she never saw Amanda actually throw up. She brought her pans, but Amanda always washed them herself. She also never saw Amanda naked, which was slightly odd. She'd prepare baths for her, but she never helped her into the tub. "We're two women. Lesbians!" said Diane. "She saw me naked all the time, but I never once saw her."

And Amanda was never hospitalized. But Diane thought they were lucky that Amanda didn't have to go in for extended treatments.

AROUND YEAR FIVE of their cohabitation, Diane became serious with a woman named Martha who didn't like Amanda one bit. Something about her just didn't sit right with Martha. Diane wasn't sure what the problem was; she thought Martha might be jealous of their friendship. Whatever was going on, it caused tension in their relationship.

Diane had finally finished her second degree and had taken a job as a chaplain on the overnight shift at a Bronx hospice center for end-stage cancer patients with less than three months to live.

Death was all around her: she was also teaching a high school course on death and dying, mainly because of Amanda. "I was living with someone I thought was dying, and so I wanted to understand it," she said. She had even done her master's thesis on grief and grieving.

"I thought I'd be really grieving once she died so I figured, well, if I know everything there is to know about grief, I could sort of preempt it, or circumvent it somehow," she said.

But she couldn't have anticipated, preempted, or circumvented what came next.

Diane applied to Boston University for a PhD program in psychology and philosophy. The program only accepted two students each year, and

Diane was one of them. She was elated and planned to relocate to Boston. She felt bad about leaving Amanda behind in New York, but she had seemed stable for a while. It was time for Diane to move.

Diane told Amanda that she'd have to find a new roommate. Suddenly, Amanda's illness came back violently—she couldn't even get out of bed. Diane decided to postpone her admission. There was no way she could go to Boston with Death looming so close.

"I've been with Amanda for five years, I can't just leave her," she told Martha.

Martha's eyes narrowed. "Don't you think it's interesting that as soon as you're getting on with your life and taking care of yourself, all of a sudden her disease gets out of control after it's been calm for however long?"

Diane nodded silently. Martha gave her an ultimatum: *either you go to BU, or I'm dumping you.*

Diane didn't know what to do. She loved Martha. But how could she abandon Amanda?

While Amanda was on a two-week vacation with her family, Diane started doing some sleuthing. First she looked through Amanda's taxes, in a file cabinet in her bedroom.

"I always assumed she would have a lot of medical deductions," she said. But she found none.

Through her work with hospice, Diane had a number of contacts at Sloan Kettering. (This was before HIPAA laws prevented doctors from revealing patient information.) She called them. Amanda was nowhere in the system. She had never been a patient.

"I could not believe it," Diane said, her eyes watering at the memory. "That was the moment where I kind of broke inside, because reality hit. I kept thinking maybe they were wrong, maybe they weren't asking the right person. Maybe they weren't looking in the right database."

She took a bus to Sloan Kettering and walked through the door where she'd dropped off Amanda. "I saw these poor patients who were so sick and I thought, 'How do you do that? How do you go in there and see people who are really dying of cancer and pretend you're one of them?' Unless you're so disassociated from reality, I don't know how you do that."

When Amanda returned from her vacation, she was wearing a full cast from the top of her thigh to her ankle. She had broken her leg and was being treated at a New York University hospital.

Diane waited a few days before pouncing. Amanda was spread out on the living room sofa, her leg elevated on cushions.

They sat in silence for a good five minutes. Finally, Diane spoke up. "For years, I've been praying for you to be healed of your cancer," she said slowly. "But for the last two weeks I've been praying that you do, in fact, have cancer because I have a lot of information that indicates to me that you aren't sick."

Amanda denied it, of course. "I'm dying!" she said.

"Then show me your red patient card from Sloan," said Diane, referring to the admission card every patient received. Amanda flashed a blue card from NYU.

"That's not the right one!" said Diane.

"I lost it," said Amanda.

Diane didn't bite. "Call Dr. Thorndyke," she said, holding the telephone out. "Call your oncologist right now!"

Amanda buried her face in her hands. "It's a lie!" she finally admitted, bawling. "It's all a lie."

Diane started crying, too. Neither one of them spoke; they just sat there in tears. Finally Diane left the apartment to find Martha. The two women walked arm in arm around the Fordham campus, sobbing.

"I realized that it wasn't my problem anymore," she said. "I had my fair share of codependency, too, but a lot of it was being a good Christian. I thought this is what a good Christian does."

Diane called her parents, who had known and liked Amanda. She told their friends, too, who were equally despondent.

"I told Amanda, 'I won't call your boss. I don't need to tell the whole world about this. But if I *ever* have any inkling whatsoever that you are continuing this and that you are duping other people I will call the newspapers.'"

The following day, Diane and Martha got a U-Haul and moved everything except a kitchen table and a chair into Diane's parents' home in Oyster Bay.

Amanda stayed in New York for another year, and then got a job in Indiana. Diane moved to Boston.

THE STORY SHOULD end there, but of course it doesn't.

As part of her doctoral program, Diane had to be in therapy herself. She devoted a lot of sessions to Amanda, and it was grueling. "I needed closure and I needed to understand what motivated her," she said. "She must have really gotten off that I was so sad at the thought of her dying."

She had had no contact with Amanda for more than two years. But then she decided she needed answers to some questions. She planned a trip to Maine and invited Amanda to join her for the weekend.

"You went away with her?" I asked. "You went away with a person who pretended to be dying for *five years*?"

"I was curious," she said, shrugging.

At a friend's cabin in Bar Harbor, Amanda explained that that she had really had a cancer scare years earlier. She had gotten a funky mammogram, and she loved the attention she had received when everyone thought she was sick.

Diane was aghast. "Don't you know that people would have loved you anyway?" she said.

Amanda had no response.

"It was completely unsatisfying," said Diane. Diane couldn't believe a word Amanda said.

Diane swears the experience gave her PTSD. Her immune system was shot; she had a chronic flu that never seemed to get better.

"I was just so shattered on so many levels. You know what was really challenging? What I had to deal with that was so painful was sorting out what of the last five years was true and what was a lie. And trying to hold on to what was good and real and true during that time, and acknowledging and understanding what wasn't true. It was such a mind fuck."

One afternoon a new friend she had made at the school where she was teaching stopped by with a gift of homemade chicken soup. Diane peered through the peephole and saw the woman standing there with the gift in her hands.

"What do you want from me?" she called through the door. The friend set the pot down, turned, and rushed off.

Diane laughed at the memory. "I apologized to her later," she said, adding that they are still friendly. "I told her the story about Amanda, that I was so untrusting of myself in terms of friendships and relationships. I didn't want anybody doing anything for me that would make me be beholden to them in any way. I didn't know if she was doing that because she wanted something from me, and I was so depleted, I had nothing to give. It really took a long time to get over that."

Still, Diane was grateful to Amanda. She owed her career to her, along with the fact that she wrote her dissertation on forgiveness, which was a radical notion back then.

Like me, Diane acknowledged her own complicity. "My basic stance in life is trusting in the goodness of others, without being naïve," she said. "No one could be as critical of me as I was. What was I doing as a twenty-seven-year-old woman, inviting a person with cancer into my home?"

To help her heal, she read M. Scott Peck's *People of the Lie*, from which she learned that evil exists (similar to Hannah Arendt's conclusion in *The Banality of Evil*, which Arendt wrote while covering the Eichmann trial). "There are some really evil people out there, and we don't expect that," Diane said. "Never in a million years would it occur to me that someone would lie for five years about having cancer. Who does that?

"You can take something really shitty that happened to you and it can break you and you can be a victim," she said. "Or it can help you be stronger and you can get something good out of it."

TWENTY-TWO MONTHS AFTER discovering the truth about Ashley, Karl didn't know what good might have come of his relationship with her. He was still unmoored. Every day, he learned new things about her. Like, Ashley once bought both Karl and her husband the exact same shirts and pairs of shoes because she couldn't decide who would look better in them.

"She led a total double life," he told me.

"But so did you," I said.

He looked confused. "I didn't lead a double life."

"Your wife didn't know anything about the world you had with Ashley," I said.

Karl chewed on his lip and didn't say anything for a good two minutes. When he finally did speak, the words came out slowly.

His own duplicity made complete sense to him. (Shades of a modular brain?) "I have a hard time thinking of myself as living a double life," he said carefully. "My deception was because I didn't have a love in my life and all of a sudden I did, so I deceived my current wife until I separated and divorced. To me, I was who I was. I was in a marriage and obviously wasn't in love. Then all of a sudden I was smacked in the face with this friendship with Ashley and a connection that built really quickly. It was the type of relationship we should all be so lucky to find."

Although he hid it from his wife at first, three months into it, he *did* tell her about his feelings for Ashley. "Almost all of my friends knew where I was in life," he said. "Some condemned and judged me and distanced themselves, but others said they wanted to support me."

But with Ashley, only one person had all the information: Ashley. She ran the show. She got to play God and move all the chess pieces.

"Ashley was kind of a spy; she had information that no one else had," he said. "In my case there was a lot of transparency. In Ashley's world only Ashley knew everything. When you're leading a double life you're the leading character in one life and a character in another life and that's two separate lives."[40]

MY HEART ACHED for Karl, and for Diane, too. But how could they not have known what was going on? The signs seemed so obvious—a chemo patient with a lustrous head of hair, a "divorcée" wearing a wedding ring—but the duped always seemed to miss them. Couldn't they have been better at uncovering the truth? Couldn't I have been better at it, too?

NINE

IN GOD WE TRUST—
EVERYONE ELSE, WE
POLYGRAPH

He's lying on purpose! . . . You know how I know how?
Because he constantly says the phrase "believe me."
Nobody says "believe me" unless they are lying.

—Jon Stewart on Donald Trump[1]

I hadn't been to Washington, DC, since the Commander days. Once school ended, I evacuated the area as if it had been hit by a hurricane, and I didn't return for six years. Who wants to live in a swamp in dire need of drainage?

I was never more alone than in the year I spent in DC when I was engaged to be married. I made no real friends, not even with my classmates at Johns Hopkins. It would be easy to say we had nothing in common, but I was at fault, too. What no one realized—what I didn't realize then—was that I was in an abusive relationship. Not physically—there were no bruises or black eyes—but emotionally, for sure. The actual term is "coercive control," and it refers to ongoing behavior used by men (mostly) to manipulate, humiliate, stalk, and/or gaslight their partners, among other things. Physical or sexual abuse sometimes accompanies it. So does lying.[2]

Coercive control is a criminal offense in England and Wales, which have expanded the definition of domestic abuse to include "coercive and controlling behavior in an intimate or family relationship." The behavior carries a maximum sentence of five years over there. But not in the States.[3]

Had the Commander beaten me, I'd have known what to do or where to get help, or at least I'd like to think I would have. But there's no Beltway Center for Mindfucked Women. No wonder I didn't feel like socializing. I didn't trust people. I didn't trust myself.

Six years later, Washington and its environs still made my stomach rumble. But I soldiered on and met up with a lovely dupee in Georgetown. Then I headed south hoping to learn how to nail the next liar who came my way from a company called QVerity.

THE "SPY THE LIE" workshop occupied a nondescript room in QVerity's corporate offices in Williamsburg, Virginia, a short distance from the tourist trap–cum–"living museum" where people in colonial garb reenact the American Revolution—the one historical event in which the Commander did not play an integral role.

About thirty of us, only five female, gathered inside a generic conference room with rows of tables and chairs. It was as if Central Casting had assembled everyone who looked like they might work in law enforcement, special forces, or corporate spying. The women were tough and unfuckwithable. The guys' muscles bulged out of polo shirts tucked neatly into jeans, and they had tidily shorn hair. Nary a man bun in sight.

We introduced ourselves. The two guys on my left, clean, cute, and earnest, worked for the Secret Service investigating the sexual assault of kids as young as three. They weren't smiling much, and can you blame them?

Directly in front of me were three men and a woman from a Swiss corporate intelligence PI firm. The woman explained, "We go through people's trash," which got my attention. I could do that! Why not use my journalism skills in a field that actually pays well? One of the men—a gorgeous specimen with big blue eyes and black hair—conversed in Russian with a heavily tattooed bro named Alex in the row ahead of him. Alex was with another three men and one woman who said they worked for the Department of Defense. Right. Who were they and what did they actually *do*?

When it was my turn, I hesitated. Before signing up for the two-day lie detection class I'd debated whether I should pay the $450 tuition with a friend's credit card using a fake identity and occupation. I didn't want anyone to know I was a journalist, so they would worry that I was going to be doing exactly what I was planning to do: write about them.

But I couldn't settle on a good cover. Kindergarten teacher? Dental hygienist? Why would a dental hygienist care about lie detection? More importantly, was it smart to try to fool people whose specific area of expertise was in *not* being fooled? (As well as knowing how to off someone and make it look like a suicide?)

So I used my real name and paid with my own Amex. In the months leading up to the class, I kept waiting for someone to call and tell me not to come, that it wasn't open to reporters. A similar outfit had said no and ignored my follow-up emails. But no one from QVerity called.

"I'm a writer," I said finally. "I'm interested in lie detection. I'm also working on a project about lying." I didn't say I was working on an article, because technically I wasn't. Nor did I mention a book. I supposed that counted as lying by omission, but I liked to think I was protecting them from unnecessary worry.

Then a silver-haired man of medium build in a suit and tie stood before us: Phil Houston, the Wizard himself, a twenty-five-year veteran of the CIA, a master polygrapher, and the coauthor of two best-sellers, *Spy the Lie* and *Get the Truth*. He's also QVerity's CEO.[4]

In 2001, after leaving "the Agency," he cofounded Business Intelligence Advisors. BIA employed former and current CIA officers with the Agency's approval. Apparently the CIA allowed moonlighting—everyone needs an extra buck now and then, even spies.[5] Hedge funds, law firms, and Fortune 500 companies hired BIA to train investment analysts how to identify deception with their investment targets, and BIA charged them about $25,000 a day.[6]

BIA's agents would sometimes attend investment conferences with their clients where publicly traded companies were presenting. They were kind of like Seeing Eye dogs, trained to determine whether the management teams were answering the analysts' questions truthfully.[7]

BIA chose not to get involved in domestic matters, even though people were always asking Phil to find out if their spouses were cheating on them. That didn't interest him, though by the time I met him it had dawned on him that there was a real need for women to learn how to properly screen their suitors and spouses.

An investment firm named Arcadia Partners acquired BIA in 2003; Phil stayed on until 2009, and then cofounded QVerity, which was similar to BIA, but broader. BIA focused mostly on the investment arena, but QVerity also trained attorneys, government workers, people in law enforcement, and so on.[8] Today's class was one of the only ones open to the public, so dental hygienists like me could learn, too.

Phil was soft-spoken, collegial, and, I imagine, absolutely terrifying when he needed to be. I pictured him taking a pencil and drawing circles around a suspect's open-faced palm, slowly, deliberately, all the while quietly interrogating him, and then finally, when he didn't get the answers he wanted—KERPOW!—jamming the pencil in, and embedding the lead in the suspect's hand.

He could get the pope to confess.

I wondered what it was like being his kid. How could you sneak out of the house in the middle of the night, or half refill the bottle of vodka with water? He'd see right through you in two seconds.

THE SESSION OPENED with a video of a man and a woman sitting at a table with a deck of blue cards. The woman picks a card. Meanwhile, behind the scenes, the filmmakers have changed the duo's T-shirts, the backdrop, and tablecloth. The blue deck is now red.[9] Do any of us notice? Some do. (I'm one of them.) But not all.

"Why do we get sucked in? Because we see what people want us to see," said Phil. We all have big holes in our perception, he was trying to say. It's like the case of the Invisible Gorilla.[10]

In this scenario, six people—three in white shirts, three in black—are videotaped playing a rowdy game of basketball. Viewers are told to count the number of passes the people in white shirts make. Suddenly, a person in a gorilla suit saunters into the group, turns to the camera, thumps its chest like Tarzan, and struts away. The question is: Would you even see the hairy ape?

"Of course I would," you think smugly.

But half of the viewers in the original study didn't. They were too focused on the task at hand. And even if they did see the animal, it might not have fully registered: "Hey! What's up with that? A gorilla just interrupted the game!"

From this, the researchers concluded two things: that we miss a lot of what goes on around us, and that we have no idea how much we're missing.[11]

The QVerity guys agreed with this. But just to drill it home, Phil's coteacher, Don Tennant, a former National Security Agency research analyst, asked us to take a piece of paper and divide it with a straight line.

We all did it dutifully, like elementary school kids in art class. I wondered if there would be crayons or glue sticks.

Everyone split the page in half in two vertical columns—except me. I did it horizontally. And that was Don's point: language is imprecise. So we translate it to fit our needs. "People put their own spin on what they're hearing," he said. "I never specified 'in half.'"

I wish I'd drawn a zigzag.

QVERITY'S METHODOLOGY IS called the REAL Model, an acronym for Response, Evaluate, and Leverage. REAL doesn't rely on polygraphs, functional magnetic resonance imaging machines (fMRI), voice analysis, or any other electronic mode of detection, none of which are 100 percent foolproof. The only necessary instruments are the eyes, ears, and mouth.

Experts say that two-thirds of communication is nonverbal, which might explain why contestants on the $100,000 Pyramid aren't allowed to use their hands in the final round. This means that lie-spotters have to take all kinds of cues into account.

What you really want to look for are *clusters* of actions. On its own, for example, rubbing your eye means nothing; a speck of dust could have camped there. But combine that with crossing and uncrossing your arms, rolling your eyes to the heavens above, clearing your throat, shielding your mouth or eyes, adjusting your clothes or hair, inspecting your nails, or saying the word "yes" while shaking your head "no," and there's a pretty good chance someone's not telling the truth, and it's probably you.

But the clusters must occur in the first five seconds of your interaction, when the liar in question (henceforth known as the LIQ) hasn't yet had time to prepare false statements.

Phil acknowledged that none of this was easy; that's why he made the big bucks. You have to look and listen at the same time, and most people have difficulty doing either one of these things well.

"It's more art than it is science," he said. "*How* you say something is much more important than *what* you say. But it's hard to narrow down human behavior. Humans are so complex."

And something that looks suspicious might turn out to be a rosy red herring. Many people think that failure to make eye contact is a sign of lying. It's not. "Truthful people often have *worse* eye contact than others," said Phil. (The Commander always looked me straight in the eye, unblinking, no matter what he was saying.)

In one experiment, Stanford communications professor Jeff Hancock and his research team paid people to write fake reviews of a hotel in New York. Some of the reviewers had really stayed there; others had never set foot in the place.

The liars, he found, focused on narrative. "They make up a story: *Who? And what happened? And that's what happened here,*" Hancock said in a 2012 Ted Talk. "Our fake reviewers talked about who they were with and what they were doing. They also used the first-person singular, 'I,' way more than the people that actually stayed there. They were inserting themselves into the hotel review, kind of trying to convince you they were there."[12]

Those who really had been at the hotel were more concerned with "spatial information": the size of the bathroom, or how close the hotel was from a shopping center.[13]

What Hancock deduced is that our language changes based on the type of lie we're emitting, and our motivations for telling it. When being questioned in person, for example, liars in Hancock's study tended to use fewer first-person singular words, even though they opted for first-person singular more often in their fake reviews. "Our argument is that it depends on what the liar is trying to accomplish, motivation, and how that affects them psychologically," Hancock told me. "The fake reviewer is inserting the self into their story to make it sound more credible, while the liars in the interview may be distancing themselves from the event in question. This has different effects on first-person singular."[14]

Most people get antsy when they lie. Telling the truth is easy, because the information is already lodged in your head. Lying's another matter: you're crafting an entire story from nothing. Your brain goes into overdrive when you lie, causing "leakage," otherwise known as "tells." You have to remember the details, which takes a lot of mental effort. So lie-spotters must search for signs of the liar's wheels spinning round and round.[15] One way to get people to leak these signs? Ask them to tell their story backward, with nuanced details. Real-life stories usually aren't told exactly in chronological order, so if someone recounts a story in a perfectly logical fashion, chances are that it's contrived.

"In an investigative context, someone who has a perfect story with every detail in place is usually suspicious," said Phil.

This method applies to everyday interactions, too. Early on in any relationship, you need to make sure you're covering all the bases and getting the information you want. Open-ended questions initially allow you to do that, especially if you don't yet know much about the other person. "On a first date, you'd want to ask some open-ended questions. As opposed to diving into the specifics of 'Where do you go for fun?' or 'What do you do for work?' you just say, 'Tell me about yourself,'" said Phil. "If he said, 'Oh, I'm a doctor,' all of a sudden your thought process becomes narrow. You think, 'Oh my god, he's rich!' or 'Oh my god, he's working all the time!' So you need information to work with so you can follow up on it."

(I'd probably say, "Oh my god—run!")

Watch for selective memory: "Not that I can remember" or "To the best of my knowledge" are tells, especially when they're in response to straightforward questions like "Did you rob the bank last week?"

If someone is empathetically "swearing to god," parroting your words, or telling you what a good question you're asking, that usually means they're stalling for time to come up with an acceptable response. They could also be trying to throw you off their scent, distract you, or curry favor by padding your ego.

That's because non-answer statements give someone time to formulate a better answer, or to search for wiggle room to squirm their way out of the question. "People don't realize the distinction between 'I wouldn't do something' versus 'I didn't do something.' It creates a real epiphany for them."

Qualifying words—like "basically," "frankly," "honestly," "fundamentally," "usually," and, of course, "believe me"—Donald Trump's favorites—are red flags. Red blankets! So are qualifying statements like "Trust me," "I'm a good person," and "I'm an honest person."

"Suppose you're talking to a CFO, and the CFO said, 'We're basically on track to meet our numbers this quarter,'" Phil continued. "Do we like that statement? Why not? *Basically.* What does that mean? It tells us there's something that he doesn't want to talk about. Our job is to figure out what that is."

But. But! Don't be combative. Going on the attack makes people retreat, so don't barge in like the Gestapo, as I tend to do when I'm angry. "Don't be accusatory, because people shut down," he said. "You don't want to chastise them."

Avoid negative questions, such as, "You don't have any concerns, do you?"

Or vague questions, such as "What are you thinking?"

Or compound questions: "When was your last foreign travel, and where did you go?"

Or long and involved questions, because "the typical individual is capable of thinking ten times faster than you're talking," as Phil put it. "If your question is three seconds long, how much talk material can they create in that three seconds? Maybe in doing so they can come up with a whole new strategy. They can come up with maybe thirty seconds of things to say to you. That's valuable, right? So keep it as short and simple as you can."

And finally: ask follow-up questions. "Ronald Reagan used to say, 'Trust, but verify.' In the Agency, some of us used to say, 'In God we trust, everyone else we polygraph,'" Phil said. "We can never have enough information. Maybe the two best words you can use are 'What else?'"

If this sounds like a lot to remember, it is. "Not everyone will do it well," said Phil. "We all have different strengths. If you give ten people a golf lesson, some are going to do better than others, even though they all had the same lesson."

ACTUALLY, *MOST* PEOPLE won't do it well, not even proficient lie-spotters.

Our talent for detecting deception, with anyone—friend, foe, lover, family member, or stranger—is no better than a roll of the dice. In fact, the closer you are to someone, the more likely you are to believe them, because your blinders are in place and securely fastened. What's more, there's no slowly growing protuberance that screams "LIAR!"

Pinocchio isn't real.

In a meta-analysis of over two hundred studies, psychologist Charles F. Bond and lying researcher Bella DePaulo concluded that people could only finger a liar 47 percent of the time.[16] Experienced job interviewers didn't fare any better (52 percent) when trying to distinguish between candidates who lied about their career histories and those who didn't.[17]

"So much of lie detection is based on the verbal as well as the non-verbals that one would have to have expertise in psychology, anthropology, sociology, criminology, jurisprudence, sociobiology, neurobiology, psychiatry, anatomy, physiology, communications, zoology, ethnography, primatology, linguistics, language, and grammar, to name a few, to truly understand the depth of what is behind deception and how to detect it," wrote former FBI agent Joe Navarro.[18]

People are more honest online than they are in person, which surprised me. It's so easy to make something up in an email, or respond to a text with a throwaway emoji, that I'd have thought more people lied digitally. Nope. On average, we lie during 14 percent of our emails, compared to 27 percent of the time in person and 37 percent of our phone conversations. If you put it in writing, of course, it lives forever; it can come back to bite you. It's easiest to lie on the phone—provided no one's recording you.[19]

THE QVERITY CLASS is one of a handful of deception detection courses being taught today—not to catch a cheating spouse (though there's a market for that, God knows), but to help Wall Street banks, private equity firms, and Fortune 500 companies figure out whom they can trust.

There's good reason to be suspicious; you really don't know who's under your roof.

A 2017 report from HireRight, a background screening agency, surveyed four thousand employers. Eighty-five percent of them said they'd had job candidates who had padded their résumés with inflated grade point averages or fictitious academic prizes, or created phony degrees altogether. This was up from 66 percent in 2012.[20]

Some embellishers of note: RadioShack's ex-CEO, David Edmondson, who claimed to have two college degrees (he had none).[21] Marilee Jones, dean of admissions at MIT from 1997 to 2007, who said she had three degrees. She never graduated from college.[22] Ditto for Scott Thompson, Yahoo's ex-CEO, who said he held both accounting and computer science degrees, when he only had the former.[23] All three resigned from their posts.

What registered with me the most, though, was that only about half of the employers actually bothered to check the facts. They took things at face value, like most people do.[24]

DECEPTION DETECTION HAS become somewhat trendy, and not just in response to the Trump administration and its proclivity for what the Man himself called "truthful hyperbole."[25] Ever since Richard Nixon shattered America's innocence, trust has slowly been eroding in institutions and among the people who inhabit them. "Trustworthy politician" is an oxymoron.

The financial crisis of 2008 certainly didn't help; neither do daily headlines about beloved coaches/priests/rabbis/doctors/actors doing terrible things at odds with their public personas. So the best way to protect yourself? Learn how to find a liar.

People crave this knowledge. Jeff Hancock's Ted Talk "The Future of Lying" garnered over 1.2 million views; one by Pamela Meyer, "How to Spot a Liar," received over 18 million.[26]

Australian ex-police officer Steve van Aperen (who was "trained by the FBI!" according to his website) sells a series of fifteen instructional videos for $97. Once you complete them, you receive a Master Certificate in Detecting Deception. I'm not sure how worthwhile this credential is, but the website says it's ideal for anyone in "recruitment, HR, marketing, sales, investigations, security, management, the financial and legal sectors or anyone who conducts interviews, negotiations or meetings with clients, staff, stakeholders, customers or anyone who would like the skill sets to determine when people are lying and how to read body language and conduct effective interviews." Van Aperen said that after 2008, his business increased by 43 percent.[27] We have to take his word for it.

But while lie detection may be especially en vogue at the moment, people have been trying to find a way to get at the truth for centuries.

"The Greeks developed a science of physiognomy to assess people's character from their facial features and gestures," said Ken Alder, a history professor at Northwestern. "On the assumption that anxious deceivers generated less saliva, suspected liars in ancient China were asked to chew a bowl of rice and spit it out. Judges in India scanned for curling toes. One Victorian physician suggested that God had endowed human beings with the capacity to blush so as to make their deceptions apparent."[28]

The first lie detector is credited to the Italian doctor and criminologist Cesare Lombroso circa 1895. His device, a hydrosphygmograph, measured physiological changes that occurred in a person's blood pressure and heart rate, which were both associated with lying.[29]

In the 1920s, psychologist William Moulton Marston created a machine that measured variations in both the systolic blood pressure and the respiration cycle, using blood pressure cuffs.[30]

Marston was also the brain behind a certain badass character named Diana Prince—aka Wonder Woman, who wielded the golden Lasso of Truth. Anyone caught with the lariat was unable to lie. Marston also enjoyed a happy ménage with his wife, Elizabeth, and their shared mistress, Olive, which formed the basis for the 2017 film *Professor Marston and the Wonder Women*. It was Elizabeth who was credited with coming up with the idea for his truth-telling machine. She pointed out that "when she got mad or excited, her blood pressure seemed to climb." Marston thought there was something to this.[31]

In 1935, a Berkeley police officer and physiologist, John Larson, and his prodigy Leonarde Keeler devised a technique of interrogation that was considered the nation's first "lie detector" that could be used in the courtroom. The two men eventually became rivals, but their invention remained: by the 1980s, some five thousand to ten thousand polygraph operators were testing two million Americans each year.[32]

The polygraph is commonly called a "lie detector," as in this *People* magazine headline from March 2018: "Stormy Daniels Passed a Lie Detector Test When Asked About Alleged Affair with President Trump."[33] But that's a misnomer. There's no contraption that can truly discern if someone's conveying an untruth. Rather than detecting lies, the polygraph records autonomic responses—heart rate, blood pressure, and respiratory rate. In other words, it measures anxiety and nervousness. But one could be nervous without being a liar, just as a psychopath can lie without feeling anxious.

The polygraph's accuracy is hotly debated. The companies that sell the devices and the people who rely on them, not surprisingly, boast that they have a 90 percent success rate. Others put it much lower. A 2003 report from the National Academy of Sciences concluded that when the contraption was used to investigate a specific situation, its accuracy was "well above chance, though well below perfection."[34]

Almost every polygrapher I interviewed agreed that the test is only as good as the person administering it. "Rates tend to reflect the bias of whoever's doing the study," said Phil. "In the hands of the right person they can be very valuable." The more intimidating the person administering the test is, the more likely the subject is to confess—or, at the very least, to be unnerved.

Today, most examiners use a computerized polygraph system. Breathing rate, blood pressure, and heart rate are all measured by various cords, and electrodes clipped onto the fingertips measure the amount of sweat (or galvanic skin response).

There are three parts of a polygraph test: a pretest phase, when the interrogator explains what to expect, the actual test, and then the analysis of the readings.

Polygraphers use "relevant" and "control" questions. The former are direct and to the point and pertain to the topic under investigation ("Did you stab your husband?"), while the latter are often "known-lie" questions, which refer to broad transgressions that will provoke a reaction in the test subject. A common known-lie question, for example, is, "Have you ever lied to anyone?" The question makes most test subjects squirm, because everyone has lied at some point. Anyone who says no is probably lying, and the response provides information to the polygrapher. (However, the response to a relevant question will be much stronger in a guilty subject.) Another type of control question is the "irrelevant control question," such as, "Is your first name _____?" The response to this type of question allows the polygrapher to compare the subject's responses when lying and not lying.

People who are telling the truth are usually afraid of the relevant questions, which is precisely the point. If there's a greater physiological response to relevant questions than to control questions, the subject is considered "deceptive." A greater response to control questions leads to the opposite conclusion. If there's no difference in the physiological responses to the two types of questions, the test is deemed "inconclusive."[35]

Many innocent people have failed polygraph tests, like Bill Wegerle, of Wichita, Kansas. Wegerle was suspected of killing his wife, Vicki, in 1986. He failed two polygraphs, but was never charged with the crime due to lack of evidence. In March 2004, DNA samples linked her death to Dennis Rader, who was known as the BTK killer (for Bind, Torture, Kill).[36]

STORIES LIKE WEGERLE'S turned Doug Williams from an Oklahoma City cop into an anti-polygraph crusader. Williams, seventy-two, believed that the device was so insidious that he was willing to go to prison if that's what it took to thwart it.

Well, "willing" may not be the right word. But time in prison was what he faced when he was caught in a 2016 undercover sting called "Operation Lie Busters," during which he was teaching undercover agents from the Customs and Border Patrol Internal Affairs Unit how to pass the polygraph. He was charged with two counts of mail fraud and three counts of witness tampering and sentenced to two years in federal prison in Florence, Colorado. That's where he was when I first reached out to him in the spring of 2017. We sent a few emails back and forth, and he sounded miserable. He couldn't believe he was locked up for teaching people to clench their butt cheeks together, but that was pretty much what happened.[37]

We met in person a year later, when he was giving a lecture at a Chicago university. Williams had a goatee, a deep Texas drawl, and shoulder-length blond hair that he routinely flipped behind his ears like he was in a Wella Balsam commercial. His skin was the color of burnished wood—"from riding my Harley for so many years," he said, and I couldn't tell if he was kidding or not.

During the eight years that he was a sergeant on the Oklahoma City police force, he said, he ran over six thousand polygraph exams. He never fully bought into it—he thought the polygraph was a bogus instrument from the start—but he was able to justify its use because it was a good prop for an interrogator, an effective scare tactic. "I was using it on criminals, so I felt that what I was doing was okay," he told me.

He got radicalized in 1979, when he tried to beat the test and realized he could, easily. Williams quit the force and wrote a twenty-page manual called *How to Sting the Polygraph*, which he disseminated for free. In March 1996, he launched Polygraph.com and began selling the manuals for $47.95 each, averaging about $200,000 a year in sales. At least that's what he said—there's no way to verify this. He knows how to pass a polygraph, so that's out.

Williams called his methodology "The Sting Technique." "Your normal reaction to fear is to tighten your anal sphincter so you don't shit yourself," he explained. "If you very slowly tighten up that sphincter and then very slowly relax it, it causes an increase in the blood pressure and pulse rate which shows on the polygraph chart as a rise in the cardio tracing."

This cardio-tracing reaction is accompanied by a rise in the galvanic skin response and in your breathing pattern. But when you relax the anal sphincter muscle, the reaction subsides. "So in order to pass the test you must simply show a reaction on the control questions and relax and show no reaction on the relevant questions," he said.

CIA agent Aldrich Ames passed two tests while working for the KGB. (Ames also failed tests, but the CIA never pursued him.)[38] The polygraph also didn't help catch Gary Ridgway, the "Green River Killer." Ridgway passed a polygraph in 1984 and was set free; twenty years later, DNA evidence proved his guilt.[39] In the interim, he'd killed seven more women.

In 1988, Congress passed the Employee Polygraph Protection Act, which prohibits most private employers from using polygraphs to screen job seekers or workers. (Williams testified in support of the EPPA in 1985.[40]) But the law doesn't apply to certain jobs, such as some employees of security service companies or pharmaceutical manufacturers, distributors, and dispensers. Nor does it cover local, state, federal, or governmental agencies.

This loophole especially stuck in Williams's craw: he believed that decent government workers were being penalized for failing an exam that didn't do what it was supposed to do in the first place. "Imagine you're taking a test," said Williams. "The administrator says, 'Have you ever had unauthorized contacts with a foreign government?' You say to yourself, 'I dunno—I went to France once.' By virtue of the fact that you're worried about it, it's a self-fulfilling prophecy. So you just put your hand on the commode and flush your career down the toilet. You're sunk."

All the big TV shows had him on, including *60 Minutes*, *NBC Nightly News*, and Penn and Teller for their series *Bullshit!*[41] In March 2006, Williams began teaching people how to ace the test in person, charging $1,000 if they went to him and $5,000 if he traveled.

"My dad and granddad were Methodist ministers," Williams said. "The Methodist church has a history of fighting oppression. My dad drilled into me, 'Doug, if you see an oppressive situation and it's within your power to stop it, it's your duty to do it.' I took it to heart. I know people are being hurt and I know I can do something about it."

I asked Williams if he'd polygraph me. I wanted to take it twice: once without his help, and another time with it, just to see if I was a proficient Stinger. Nothing would make him happier than teaching me, he said, but he couldn't. As part of his parole, he wasn't allowed to administer tests anymore. While he was in prison, he filed a motion to have these restrictions removed, but the judge ruled against him, arguing that his activities were a "threat to public safety." (Williams is appealing the decision.) He also wrote a memoir, *False Confessions: The Amazing Story of an Ex-Cop's Crusade Against the Orwellian Polygraph Industry*, which he hopes to bring to Hollywood.

"I used to say, 'Polygraph officers are just assholes with little training,'" he said. "If you're gonna beat the asshole with little training, then you've gotta train your asshole.'"[42]

A bumper sticker if there ever was one.

THERE IS OTHER technology besides polygraphs that also claims to reveal the truth.

A San Diego company called Truthful Brain (formerly No Lie MRI) has been offering brain-scan lie detection services using fMRI since 2006. The company's founder and CEO is Joel Huizenga, who has an interesting pedigree.[43] Joel was brought up around scientists; his father was a well-known nuclear physicist, and Joel has a degree in molecular biology. Joel's brother, Robert Huizenga, was the doctor on *The Biggest Loser*—which was apparently taken off the air in the face of claims that it used deceptive tactics. (Robert Huizenga denied any wrongdoing.)[44]

Joel charges $5,000 to put a person through the machine. Women have been especially eager to be tested. "Women want to be tested so their man stops being jealous and stops mate-guarding them, thus giving them more personal freedom," he said.[45]

Some other machines currently under development can be operated remotely, like a drone. Converus, out of Lehi, Utah, has a product called

Eye Detect, which gauges the level of pupil dilation. (Enlarged pupils signify that your brain is working overtime, which happens when you lie.) It's mostly used to screen job applicants, employees, travelers, and parolees.

Voice-stress analysis, such as the computer-based Vericator, claims to be able to identify certain variations in stress levels in human speech. But does voice analysis work, or is it just another dead end?

One of the skeptics is Mitchell S. Sommers, an associate professor of psychology at Washington University in St. Louis. "All the research that I've seen thus far suggests that it's wishful thinking, at best, to suggest that current voice-stress analysis systems are capable of reliably detecting deception," Sommers told one interviewer.[46]

So maybe good old-fashioned personal judgment is the best way to go after all. One of the methods that's gained popularity in recent years enlists the concept of "micro-expressions," made famous by psychologist Paul Ekman. (The TV drama *Lie to Me* is based on his work.)

Micro-expressions are superfast: they last somewhere between one-fifteenth and one-twentieth of a second. Blink, and you miss them.[47] Ekman estimates that we can make about three thousand different expressions with our faces, and each one is activated when some sort of emotion takes place internally. One famous micro-expression is that of the serial killer Ted Bundy, who everyone thought was convivial and charming until a slow-motion camera caught a glint of his rage.[48]

Ekman has created online training tools on his website, paulekman .com, where you can improve your ability to detect and decipher micro facial expressions—it's a kind of Pin the Tail on the Emotion: Surprise! Anger! Joy! It's fun to see how many you can get. But as Ekman acknowledged, only about 5 percent of people are naturally good at spotting them.

HERE'S THE TRUTH (ha!): the *only* reliable way to detect deception is to have tangible proof: Texts. Emails. Phone records. Bank accounts. Video footage. Your own eyeballs.

Let's imagine that the leader of a major first-world power proclaims that more people showed up to his inauguration than to any other inauguration in the history of presidential elections. If there weren't actual statistics proving otherwise, he could go unchallenged.

I often think about tour guides. We assume they've been properly trained and that all the information they impart is accurate. But who knows? Say I'm in Cambodia and have no idea which temple I'm looking at. The guide could tell me Michelangelo carved it after painting the Sistine Chapel. If I didn't know my history I could believe him.

But hard evidence is not always available. And when that's the case, the next best thing might be our unconscious minds. It's not so farfetched: Scientists maintain that the ability to detect deception has evolved over time.

In a 2013 study, researchers at the University of Mannheim in Germany found that students' ability to detect deception improved if they were given time to think—but only if they thought about something *other* than the problem at hand. If they were allowed to ruminate over the issue, they did no better than chance; when their minds were distracted their accuracy improved significantly.[49]

A year later, researchers from the Haas School of Business at Berkeley asked seventy-two participants to watch a video of people suspected of stealing $100. Half the people had actually taken the money; the other half had not. But everyone had been told to lie. Afterward, the participants were asked if they could identify who had been telling the truth and who had been lying. They could spot the truth-tellers only 48 percent of the time, and the liars only 43 percent.[50]

Later, the students were shown still pictures of the possible criminals alongside "truthful" words like "honest" and "genuine" or lying-related concepts like "deceitful" and "dishonest." They were told to match the words with the faces. The researchers measured their reaction times and found that participants responded faster to deception-related words when they were thinking of people who really were lying, and faster to truthful words when thinking of suspects who were telling the truth.[51]

"When you see a liar's face, the concept of deception is activated in your mind even if you're not consciously aware of it," said lead researcher Leanne ten Brinke. "It's still unclear just how high a percentage of lies our unconscious mind is able to sense accurately, but discrimination is definitely occurring." In other words, we all may have an innate talent for unconscious lie detection.[52]

It's worth noting that not everyone agrees with this conclusion. Volker Franz and Ulrike von Luxburg, from the University of Hamburg, argued that faster reaction times with words don't really predict whether anyone's honest or not.[53]

In general, women are better at reading nonverbal cues, whereas men are better at deciphering verbal messages, whether they are written or oral.[54] And according to a 2017 study, people in positions of power are better liars, but the powerless are better at *detecting* lies.[55]

"When you tell people in positions of power to lie, they show less physiological arousal than the average person," said coauthor Adam Galinsky, chair of the management division of the Columbia Business School. "They feel calmer and less stressed when they lie," he told me, and therefore show fewer physiological signs of stress. That makes it tougher for others to be able to detect when they're lying.

"You can look at that as one of the explanations [for] why women are so much better than men at detecting the emotions of others," Galinsky said. "[It's] not just because they're caregivers. It's that, on average, women have less power in society, and they have to be more sensitive to others so they don't provoke retribution."

The same sort of explanation can shed light on why women are better at detecting lies: the powerless have to be really good at detecting lies, or else they could be taken advantage of.

But, as Galinsky pointed out, it's one thing to be able to detect a lie; it's another to *confront* one. "To tell someone powerful that they're lying—that creates a huge backlash," he said. "That's the whistleblower's dilemma."

Could that help to explain why some disgruntled, disempowered ex-employees go postal? Maybe. "Being lied to makes people feel more powerless," Galinsky said. "It creates an incredible level of anger and impotence if you don't feel you are capable of confronting that lie."[56]

ON THE SECOND and last day of class, I stayed behind to eat lunch with Phil.

He and the Secret Service guys were having an animated discussion about the types of polygraph machines they used, tossing out fancy names that might as well have been R2D2 and C3PO. I felt like a boomer trying to understand Snapchat.

During a lull in the conversation, Phil turned to me. "I'm not going to read about this class in an article, am I?" he asked.

Aha! I wondered how long it would take him to broach the subject. But I was impressed with his subtlety. Not an attack. Not an accusation. The emphasis was on *him*.

"Houston, we have no problem," I wanted to say. But I wasn't sure he'd find it as amusing as I did.

"I knew you were worried about that," I said finally.

"You did? How come?"

"I'm not a moron," I said.

He laughed. "I never thought you were."

I told him the truth, that I was working on a book project but not writing an article. If I did write one, I'd give him a heads-up.

Then I told him I wanted to get polygraphed.

"No you don't," he said. "It's invasive."

"I want to be invaded."

He shook his head. "You can't do a polygraph for the fun of it," he said. "It's not a parlor game."

What he meant was that the stakes weren't high enough. What was I going to lie about—whether I preferred Diet Coke or Diet Pepsi? No one was going to put me in jail for that. Except, maybe, my mother, who'd been yelling at me to get off the stuff for years. A polygraph would be pointless.

WHEN CLASS STARTED back up, I noticed the Secret Service guy next to me repeatedly glancing my way. I'd been recording everything since I'd arrived, and I knew he knew. But I wasn't trying to be coy; I'd have answered honestly if he'd asked what I was doing. But he hadn't.

And anyway, I didn't see it until later, but there was a video camera directly behind me. So the Commander was right: I wasn't subtle enough to be a spy.

At the next break, a guy with a thick Russian accent approached me. He told me his name was Igor and he was a twenty-six-year-old self-employed truck driver from Ukraine. He had gotten interested in lie detection after watching *Lie to Me* and decided to take a course.

Oh, really? Even I wasn't stupid enough to fall for that. Why would a Russian truck driver take a lie detection class? This was long before Robert Mueller's investigation into Russia's participation in the 2016 election. Maybe Igor was behind it.

"Do you want to go back to Ukraine?" I asked.

He looked forlorn. "I want, but I can't," he said.

My ears pricked up.

"Why not?"

"I can't talk about it," he said.

Of course not.

He squinted at me. "Are you really a journalist?"

I shook my head and winked. "No," I said. "But I can't talk about it."

THE NIGHT BEFORE I returned to New York, I stayed with my friends Hilary and Matthew in their Kalorama townhouse. The Commander and I had attended their wedding together, him in full military regalia. He swooned over the attention he received, especially from people thanking him for his "service to the country."

The next day there was a Farmers Market at Dupont Circle and the city felt alive in a way I didn't remember when I lived there. Maybe because when I lived there, I was in the Watergate, where everything was dead, including me.

On the bus ride home, I read a *New York Times* wedding announcement about a couple who met while working in the White House, a story I could have written but would rather have lived. He was a speechwriter for Obama, and she was a researcher; they fell in love in the wee hours of the morning.

Precise and powerful language, proximity to Barack Obama, and romance: Why were they living my life?

The bus was half empty, like that proverbial goddamn glass, and the roads were relatively clear. It was as if the fates, having made their point, wanted to usher me out of Washington as seamlessly as possible. They knew I wasn't coming back unless I had to.

TEN

VERIFY, BUT DON'T TRUST

> I am affected, not because you have lied to me
> but because I can no longer believe you.
>
> —Friedrich Nietzsche, *Beyond Good and Evil*[1]

June 2016. The phone vibrated: it was my brother, Ray, on vacation in Aruba. I was in my apartment in New York, jamming to the *Hamilton* soundtrack and gathering high-level intel (read: doing a Google search) on Alexander Hamilton and his wife, Elizabeth Schuyler Hamilton. I was curious about how she'd handled his affair with the decidedly low-class Maria Reynolds, which he publicly admitted in the eighteenth-century version of a tweet: a ninety-six-page treatise titled *Observations on Certain Documents Contained in No. V & VI of "The History of the United States for the Year 1796," in Which the Charge of Speculation Against Alexander Hamilton, Late Secretary of the Treasury, Is Fully Refuted.*[2] Whew.

Thanks to the "Reynolds Pamphlet," as it came to be known, Eliza discovered that while she and their five kids were summering in Albany, her husband was romantically enmeshed with another woman—*in their marital bed.*

Maria Reynolds's husband, James, had threatened to go public a year earlier, and had blackmailed Alexander in return for staying quiet. For a while Alexander funneled cash his way, but when James got into legal trouble, and Alexander refused to come to his aid, James implicated him in a fraud scheme that *James* was actually involved in. Got it?

This left the scrappy Alexander no choice but to defend his honor. Pussy-grabbing is one thing, but being accused of financial impropriety? *That* was unacceptable—he was the former treasury secretary! His political future would be tarnished. While Alexander did confess to carnally acquainting himself with Maria, he maintained that he was the victim of a scam perpetrated by her husband. *Duped!* James Reynolds went to jail, and Hamilton's career was saved.[3] But the Hamilton marriage was in tatters.

Or maybe it wasn't. No one knows for certain how Eliza dealt with any of this; she "erased herself from the narrative," as Lin-Manuel Miranda put it in his little Broadway show about Alexander.[4] The couple had three more kids together.

Nor does anyone know how Eliza felt about the rumors that her married sister Angelica was cavorting with Alexander. Nothing physical was ever confirmed between them, but based on Angelica and Alexander's affectionate correspondence, they seemed to be carrying on an emotional affair at the very least. Hamilton biographer Ron Chernow noted that "Hamilton's married life was sometimes a curious ménage-a-trois with two sisters who were only a year apart."[5]

This, then, is what I was doing when my brother called with news of his own.

"Guess who just sent me a LinkedIn request?" he asked.

I lowered the music. "Laura Ingalls?"

My brother can name every episode in the *Little House on the Prairie* canon.

"Your ex-fiancé." He sounded confused. "Why would he want to connect with me?"

"The invitation probably went out to his entire address book, and you're in it," I said.

"Well, I don't think I'll accept."

"Why not? Aren't you curious what he wants?"

"Not really. I don't want to be his friend." *Friend.* Funny, that. Such a diluted term these days. What does it even mean anymore?

We hung up and I clicked over to my account. And there, like a hair sprouting from a mole, was my own "invitation to connect" from the Commander.

I enlarged his photo and stared at it for a good five minutes. He looked nerdy and decent, with the same arsenal of capped teeth. His hair was still dark, though there was slightly less of it. Possibly, he was wearing a toupee. He appeared about fifteen pounds heavier than when I'd seen him seven years earlier—maybe because he was no longer using drugs? He was living in DC and running a humanitarian organization; listed among his credentials was his MD from a prestigious university. He didn't mention that he had given up his license, nor was he required to. Once you earn a medical degree the "MD" moniker stays with you for life, like herpes.

I was surprised at how nauseated I felt. Was this request intentional, or, as I'd suggested to my brother, part of a mass mailing?

I worried that he may have seen my story in *Psychology Today*, or heard that I was writing a book in which he featured prominently. Or maybe he'd gotten hold of the statement I'd made about him to NCIS, and was plotting his revenge?

Or maybe he was finally on Step 9 in his "recovery" process and wanted to Make Amends. I hadn't heard one word from him since his arrest, which was a big reason I wondered if his addiction plea had been a stunt. If he'd taken his recovery seriously, wouldn't he have embarked on his Apology Tour earlier on? Sure, there are other models of sobriety—they don't all involve Higher Powers and radical honesty—but I knew that the rehab facility he went to before jail was based on the Twelve Steps. And it certainly would have behooved him to at least *pretend* to take it seriously while he was in the clink. But I never got an apology. Neither did Eileen, the woman he was engaged to when he was engaged to me. Neither did his wife, Kate, or his kids. From what I'd heard, he felt that *he* was a victim.

The thought of a mea culpa brought up other concerns. Like, how would I respond if he *did* want to break bread with me? And how did I feel about second chances in general, and redemption? He'd had every opportunity in the world, and he'd blown them all. I didn't even know what salvation would look like for him.

Eileen thought he should never be allowed to practice medicine again—which he could do if he reapplied in another state. But until 2015, there was no national database of doctors who lost their licenses or had actions taken against them, at least none available for the public. You needed to visit each state individually, and some states kept better records than others.

"I don't think the year and a half in the country club prison was really repaying his debt to society," Eileen said angrily. "If he tried to get his medical license back, I'd go in front of the board and say, 'I've been a board certified internist and a pediatrician for twenty years. I know this man as a human being and he has usurped the power that he has in writing scripts and he should not have a license to practice medicine. Period. The end.' He's a manipulator and will never stop. He's not going to change."

She's right. And yet: I hemmed and hawed and re-hawed about responding.

I fantasized about ambushing him. Here's how it would work: I'd call to tell him about my upcoming book project, convincing him we needed to get together for legal reasons. We'd meet at a quiet diner in DC or LA or Kabul, and then Eileen would appear in a waitress uniform to take our order.

"Can you picture the look on his face?" she said gleefully when I told her my plan.

"He'd probably go straight for the inhaler!" I said.

My mother didn't think any of this was wise. "What do you want to see him for?" she said. She worried that he might get violent and hurt me.

"I'd only meet him in public," I said.

"But there's no *need*."

Well, yes and no. I had no desire to see him for romantic purposes, Lord knows. But the writer in me wanted to complete the story. I wanted an Ending. I wanted to see what, if anything, he had to say for himself.

Had Eileen been game I might have gone for it. But she didn't care. "He's caused enough damage," she said.

And the more I thought about it, the more I realized there was no point, even for literary reasons. What could he tell me? Or, more pointedly, what could he tell me that I'd believe? Nothing. To paraphrase Mary McCarthy's quote about Lillian Hellman, every word that came out of his mouth would be a lie, including "and," "the," "hello," and "goodbye."[6]

I didn't need him to complete the narrative. My narrative had nothing to do with him. Maybe I had learned something, after all: not everything is copy.

AVOIDING THE ENTRAPMENT dinner might have been one of my healthier moves, but I still had lingering torment. I wondered if I'd ever be in another relationship. I hadn't met anyone interesting in years, and I didn't expect to. Some of my most horrendous agonies have been because of love: the longing for it, the chasing of it, the absence of it, the failure of it. It's easier in so many ways to navigate the world on your own. Lonelier, perhaps, but easier. Half of my friends were splitting up and the other half were struggling in their marriages; they didn't look like they were having a good time at all. I had actually been quite content since opting out of romance; a huge chunk of me isn't interested in that nonsense. And yet—that nonsense makes the world go round.

Would I ever be able to make myself vulnerable? And how could I guarantee that I wouldn't attract the same sort of person again?

A friend suggested I reach out to Sandra Brown, who had written a book called *Women Who Love Psychopaths*. Brown holds a master's degree in counseling and is the director of The Institute for Relational Harm Reduction and Public Pathology Education, which holds retreats for women recovering from pathological men. She specializes in helping women who have been involved in pathological relationships with "Cluster Bs"—the antisocial, borderline, narcissistic, and psychopathic personality folks.[7]

Brown defines trauma as exposure to something that makes you feel powerless in a way you can't quite make sense of. It's all about the brain. "We know that the amygdala, where trauma is received, doesn't do a good job making sense of things," she said. "When someone gaslights you and you can't make sense of the stories they tell you, you're helpless."

The institute's research focuses on "supertraits," the Big Five personality characteristics that almost all of us possess, including neuroticism, extroversion, openness, agreeableness, and conscientiousness (also called the Five Factor Model).[8] As with nearly everything, there's a continuum; we vary in how much or how little we have of any given trait.

In 2014, the Institute, along with researchers at Purdue University, interviewed six hundred women who had self-identified as having been in a pathological relationship. Almost all of them were smart and accomplished; most had master's degrees and impressive careers. Additonally, more than 60 percent of them hadn't grown up in abusive households, or with alcoholic parents, or had experienced some kind of early trauma. "Everybody assumes the reason women get in these relationships is because they have untreated trauma and it's like trauma replay," she said. "They assume these are traumatized women repeating their patterns. They're not."

So why did they stay in a bad situation? Because they had high levels of conscientiousness, which made them dependable, achievement oriented, self-disciplined, and deliberate. They were also very agreeable, which means they were straightforward, cooperative, humble, empathic, and loyal.

"One of the traits under agreeableness is always believing the best in human nature," said Brown. "That's a really good trait to have. That's what empathy is based on, putting ourselves in someone else's shoes. But too much empathy or optimism in human nature makes you overlook things."

Brown pointed me in the direction of Jennifer Young, a certified clinical trauma professional who did one-on-one phone counseling. Young sent me a questionnaire and told me to rate myself on each trait, from 1 (extremely low) to 5 (extremely high). I scored highest on conscientiousness, openness, and extroversion.[9]

Then she sent me a list of traits psychopaths and narcissists possess and had me mark the behaviors I'd seen in the Commander. Among them: Deceitfulness. Manipulativeness. Failure to conform to lawful social norms. Insincerity. Grandiosity. Pathological lying. Egocentricity.

Check. Check. Check check check check check.

But so what? What did it all add up to?

Lots, actually. Because my personality led me to miss danger cues. Even though I was able to extricate myself from bad scenarios relatively quickly, "I'm hesitant to say you're low risk to a predator," she said. "What makes you at risk is your conscientiousness and openness. You're warm and approachable. They love that." Extroverts are more likely to engage in social settings, and that's what psychopaths look for. Introverts typically don't tolerate engagement from strangers.

It's a twisted symbiotic relationship.

So did this mean I was doomed to either stay alone, to "settle" for people who really didn't interest me, or to fall for another whacko? No. But it *did* mean I needed to be vigilant, sort of the way diabetics have to monitor their sugar consumption lest they fall into a coma.

Young told me to create a "red flag bucket" and a "that's okay" bucket when meeting someone new. (I wondered about nuances: Could there be a pink flag bucket?)

"Some behaviors go in one bucket, some in the other," she said. "You can't just rely on one behavior or another to tell you who is good or bad. You have to wait to see a pattern develop. That's why we beg people to move slowly in new relationships—to manage the pace. This allows you to see what patterns of behavior develop over time. Your responsibility is to go super slow and watch for patterns. Don't push, don't rush. Stay back and watch."

Some people know this instinctively. My friend Wendy met a charismatic filmmaker at her temple who made frequent references to breaking up with his girlfriend. He flirted with Wendy, even asked her out, but never followed through with plans. He was "smart and cute and creative and sexy," so she was willing to give his flakiness a pass. Then she learned that his girlfriend was actually his wife, even though he'd never used the words "married" or "separated" in conversation.

Once Wendy discovered the truth, she was outta there. "Rudeness and disrespect I kind of accepted," she said. "But that level of lying ended my infatuation instantly."

Another woman I knew had a second husband who turned out to be a mini-Madoff. She didn't beat herself up when he went to jail. She didn't have the problem; *he* did.

"I was mortified, but what got me through was realizing that he wasn't real," she said. She was in her early seventies when his crimes came to light.

"How can you love someone who's not who they're appearing to be? Somehow it registered in me—'If he wasn't real, then that wasn't love,' and I didn't get attached."

All the experts I spoke with said it's better to go into relationships with trust rather than suspicion. Paul Ekman was unequivocal: "You can choose to be suspicious and run the risk of disbelieving a truthful person. Or you could choose to be believing and run the risk [of being lied to again]. My advice is—be trusting. You'll live longer. You'll have better relationships."[10]

Okay, fine. But, *how*? How do you learn to trust again, and go forward with the right balance of openness and discernment?

It's a process, and it means doing things differently. "Some people try to put their lives back together exactly as they were," said psychology professor Stephen Joseph, author of *What Doesn't Kill Us: The New Psychology of Post-traumatic Growth*. "But like a vase which is held together by glue and sticky tape they remain fractured and vulnerable. In contrast, those who accept the breakage and build themselves anew become more resilient and open to new ways of living."[11]

I liked the positivity of that message. It was hopeful, even if the vase shards did puncture a vein. But knowing something in theory and actually *implementing* it are radically different things. The biggest takeaway for me was something Jordan Grafman, the Northwestern professor, had told me: "The opportunity arising from a wounding betrayal is less to learn to *mistrust others* than to learn to *trust ourselves* increasingly, as we show great courage in our eventual willingness to resume our search, after a deep, perhaps traumatic betrayal, for experiences that do us justice."

Hearing it that way did make it a little clearer to me how to proceed: I was in search of experiences that did me justice.

I DON'T BELIEVE in happy endings, but I'd like to. I keep hoping that one of these days Lucy will let Charlie Brown get one good solid kick in before yanking the football out from under him. But she probably won't change, so Charlie needs to be prepared.

I believe that the best way to protect ourselves is by listening to our instincts. The challenge is distinguishing those who deserve the benefit of the doubt from those who don't.

Obviously, each of us has to figure out what we can live with. Every relationship requires small deceptions from both parties, and technology is only going to continue to evolve—it's going to get that much easier to obfuscate. You have to know how much you can tolerate and forgive.

Diane Collins hasn't seen Amanda, the roommate who pretended to have cancer, for nearly twenty years. But she forgives her, whatever that means to her.

"My forgiving Amanda for what she did to me might be really different than what it means for you to forgive the person who hurt you," she said. "I learned a lot about how you can truly forgive someone, but that doesn't mean you need to reestablish the relationship. It doesn't mean that it's okay what they did. What Amanda did is totally not okay and never would be under any circumstances. But my life can go on and be fine without her."

Another woman I know said her husband, a novelist, "embellishes," "elaborates," and "takes liberty with" various facts and details in real life. She never knows if he's telling the truth, but she doesn't care. That's who he is, and she accepts it.

That wouldn't work for me, or for Eileen Morrison, who prefers to remain alone. The Commander was the fourth man to leave her; she said she's done with love for good. She has her work at the hospital, has her three sons, and is hoping to have a grandchild or two in the near future. She doesn't want to deal with any more romantic disappointments.

Neither does White-Collar Wife Lisa Lawler, whose husband stole over $2 million. "Can I ever trust again? The down-and-dirty answer to that question is no," she said. "I cannot ever trust again. I've been through too many mind fucks and have come to know the same from countless others who have been lied and cheated on. So do good guys cheat on their wives? No, they don't. Is every guy a cheater? No, they're not. It's just that life is too short at this point for me to waste precious time trying to find a needle in a haystack."

(For what it's worth, Bella DePaulo, the lying expert, has since turned to the study of chronic singleness. Could there be a link between her deep understanding of deception and her desire to fly solo? Just sayin'.)

Karl Robinson is in a new relationship with someone he "trusts completely," but he still thinks about Ashley, his girlfriend of seven years who pretended to be leaving her husband for him. Not long ago, Karl sent me a detailed email about a trip he and Ashley had taken in Cabo San Lucas in 2014. Karl was already divorced, and Ashley had supposedly just told her family she was getting separated; they went out to dinner to celebrate. A solo guitarist strolled from table to table, serenading the guests.

"Ashley said, 'I hope he doesn't come over here,'" Karl recalled. This surprised him—she usually loved to be the center of attention.

Eventually the musician made his way over to their table in the middle of the restaurant, and in halting English said he had the "perfect song" for them. He strummed a few chords and began his rendition.

"It lasted forever," said Karl. "We were chuckling at how long it lasted. I think he sang the 7-minute version. Other people started laughing, too. He sang in Spanish and English. I guess he really liked the song. Or better yet, he was trying to get his point across. He had a sixth sense and was trying to tell me something."

The song was The Eagles' "Lyin' Eyes," which seemed to be picked especially for Ashley. "I listened and smiled," Karl recalled ruefully. "Ashley looked really uncomfortable. Maybe the irony of the song wasn't lost on her. But it was on me."

I'VE STAYED IN touch with the Commander's ex-wife, Kate; we'll grab lunch sometimes when I'm in LA. Her own mother, who calls him "The Felon," did some serious Internet stalking and in late 2016 found him on Match .com. There were a bunch of photos and a disquisition about his do-gooder efforts. He sought a "best friend." He said he was sixty-one. He was really sixty-four.

In June 2017, he filed for bankruptcy.

Since they had two kids together, Kate had no choice but to be in contact with him; she was envious that I didn't have to speak to him again. Their oldest was in college and doing well, but he was very sensitive about being lied to. "If he feels someone's messing with the truth he gets really upset," she said. His relationship with his father, his former idol, is cordial—"like the eccentric uncle you have to put up with once a year."

The Commander was trying to establish a connection with his daughter, who was now eleven years old. Kate wasn't sure why he was so interested now. He hadn't seemed to care about her when she was younger.

Kate would only allow him to see her in the presence of a therapist, so every three months he'd buzz into Los Angeles and the three of them would go to a counselor's office to talk. Or, rather, he'd yammer about his world-saving endeavors while his daughter rolled her eyes.

In November 2017, he had to break an appointment because he was heading out of town.

"I'm going to Libya for work," he told Kate.

She didn't have the heart to tell him that the US Department of State had issued a warning about Americans in Libya, suggesting they avoid going there or, if they were already there, to leave immediately because of the excessive violence.[12]

It wouldn't have fazed the Commander anyway. He was the exception to every rule.

As of May 2018, he hadn't seen his daughter in six months.

LIKE I SAID, I don't believe in happy endings. But that has as much to do with endings as happiness. I could have moved to Bali and fallen in love with a Brazilian heartthrob. Would that be an ending?

But I did meet a Brazilian—not on a tiny island in Southeast Asia, but in Brazil. It was February 2017, and I was in the country for my annual Winter Avoidance, crashing with friends and writing. I was in search of a mellow village on the water with cheap rooms and hammocks, and I'd heard that Praia do Rosa, in the south, was *it*. So I flew from São Paulo and rented a room in a little *pousada* about an eight-minute walk from the ocean.

On my second day in town I stopped by a convenience store to buy an açaí. The guy behind the counter had closely cropped red hair and bright blue eyes and a sinewy surfer's body. His name was Pedro Gustavo.

"Tell me about Rosa," I said. "Where are the best beaches?"

He spread out a colorful map of the town and its surroundings. "You have time?" he asked tentatively.

Yes, I had time.

He pointed out the best hiking trails and where to catch "good waves." I can't surf; I can't even rollerblade. Gustavo offered to teach me. We made a date for the following afternoon at a little *lagoa*, or lagoon, where the water was warm and tranquil.

I never did get up on the board. But Gustavo and I became buddies, and then more. I understood a bit of Portuguese but didn't speak it well, so we communicated in basic English and Portañol, a hybrid of Spanish and Portuguese. When you don't share a language, you can't get into interminable exchanges about your deep depressions and existential angst and deceptive fiancé. Since we couldn't talk about these things, they didn't exist. Our conversations were simple, and my thoughts were simple. It was frustrating at times, but also exhilarating. Freeing.

Oh. Did I mention he was fifteen years younger? Sometimes, I really am my own hero.

Soon I moved into his tiny one-bedroom cottage, which he shared with his childhood pal Marcel and Nela, an Argentinian schoolteacher who was taking a year's sabbatical. At night Marcel would strum his guitar and the neighbors would drop by. We'd drink *caipirinhas* and sing. There was always a party. It was just what I needed: not long lasting, but meaningful.

Gustavo was totally Brazilian, which meant that he was very serious about his fun. Sometimes he let out a joyous whoop—*uhuuuuuuuuu*—for no reason. He woke up humming. He'd nudge me to watch the sunrise, and then he'd grab his board and race to the beach. He felt about surfing the way I feel about traveling: his soul craved it.

He didn't care about academic degrees or social position. He didn't mind the age difference between us. I'd write during the day, when he was at the store. We'd meet later and stroll arm in arm through town, him barefoot and shirtless, me hauling my laptop in my nylon pack. He always asked if my work had gone well, if the thoughts had come easily, but he didn't know what I was writing about, and I liked that. For those few weeks, it didn't matter who was telling the truth, or who was lying, or how the story ended. It didn't have an ending. It was just happy.

ACKNOWLEDGMENTS

For someone who dabbles in recreational misanthropy, I know some pretty spectacular people. Some were around before the Commander fiasco, others came along much later. But they've all indulged my relentless fascination with duplicity and double lives, and helped make the writing of this book that much more bearable.

Let's begin with my agent, Daniel Greenberg, of Levine Greenberg Rostan. Dan is patient and diligent and kind and not afraid to tell me when I'm not quite getting it. He responds to email almost immediately—and he's fun at a party! Tim Wojcik, whose last name I still can't pronounce, supported this project from day one while graciously fielding my many emails and inquiries. The brilliant, encouraging, patient, and *calming* Wylie O'Sullivan was with me from the get-go. Without her I have no doubt that this thing would still be in a folder marked "Ideas, Vague."

PublicAffairs is the classiest operation in New York City, and that's a testament to Peter Osnos. Peter, Clive Priddle, and Benjamin Adams sat in a room with me and listened intently as I explained my obsession with this subject. They understood exactly what I wanted to do and how I wanted to do it. Everyone should have an editor like Ben: smart, funny, earnest, irreverent when necessary, and a Red Sox fan. Plus, he now knows all about Wella Balsam shampoo.

PR goddess Jamie Leifer strategized with me months ahead of the game and was willing to hop on the phone anytime I wanted to. And she's so nice! My copy editor, Katherine Streckfus, caught grammatical errors and fact-checky things that I clearly had not. Sandra Beris shepherded this manuscript into production and didn't get (too?) annoyed when I was late turning in the acknowledgments page. If I had a firstborn I would bequeath it to designer Amy Quinn, who fixed my many goofs and never complained (at least not to my face). Emily Arbis, of Little, Brown UK, has been so kind.

I've had the privilege of contributing to the *New York Times* for more than two decades; I'm still not sure I exist unless I see my name there. Major shout outs to my editors and former editors: Toby Bilanow, Jane Bornemeier, Alexandra Jacobs, Tara Parker-Pope, and Bob Woletz. Jim Schachter handed me that long ago biz column. Catherine Saint Louis has become a friend. Brent Bowers throws the best yacht soirees. You're all right, Tnerb. Don't let anyone tell you otherwise, unless it's me.

Hara Marano, my magnificent editor at *Psychology Today*, has been championing me for years. She and editor-in-chief Kaja Perina published my cover story on deception, which was the basis for this book. Working with you is a joy and a treat. Ditto for Riza Cruz at *Marie Claire*.

So many people shared their personal experiences with me. Since not everyone wanted their real names used I won't list them all, but I know who you are. Thanks to Elise Ballard, Heidi Brandt, Melissa Chambers, Lanora Franck, Stephen Greenspan, Hanna Halper, Libby Henry, Christine Johnstone, Susan Kim, Judith King, Lisa Lawler, Colette Loll, Melissa Moore, Kevin Nelson, Pamela Simmons, Valerie Smaldone, Hillary Wagner, Jen Waite, Heather Wilson, and the Commander's ex-wives. Peter Young— thank you for reaching out to me, and for letting me run with your tale.

Thanks to everyone who took time to talk dupeage with me: Nobuhito Abe, PhD; Frank Ahearn; Donna Andersen; Dan Ariely, PhD; Amber Ault, PhD; Roy Baumeister, PhD; Kathryn Bowers; Louann Brizendine, MD; Sarah Brokaw; Sandra Brown, MA; David M. Buss, PhD; Ed Caffrey; Colette Davison, Phd; Paul DePompo, PsyD; Jack Devine; Kurt T. Dirks, PhD; Paul Ekman, PhD; Barry A. Farber, PhD; Anna Fels, MD; Frank Figliuzzi; Helen Fisher, PhD; Lisa Aronson Fontes, PhD; Rhonda Freeman, PhD; Adam Galinsky, PhD; Neil Garrett, PhD; Carrie Goldberg, JD; Jordan Grafman PhD; Elizabeth Greenwood; Bob and Debbie Hamer; Jeff Hancock, PhD; Matthew Hornsey, PhD; Joel Huizenga; Peter Janney, PhD;

Vikram Jaswal, PhD; Sue Johnson, PhD; Ralph Keyes; Maria Konnikova, PhD; Robert Kurzban, PhD; Jay Kwawer, PhD; Jack Levin, PhD; Timothy Levine, PhD; Daniel Levitin, PhD; Timothy Luke, PhD; Pamela Meyer; David Modic, PhD; Kelly Paxton; Kelly Richmond Pope, PhD; George K. Simon, PhD; Malcom Slavin, PhD; Sandra L. Robinson, PhD; Heather Mann, PhD; Joe Navarro; LaRae Quy; Edward Reynolds, PhD; Jed Rubenfeld, JD; Jeanne Safer, PhD; Anya Samek, PhD; Ronald Schouten, MD, JD; Jeffrey M. Schwartz, MD; Michael Shermer, PhD; Joyce Short; Jonathan Slavin, PhD; Malcom Slavin, PhD; David Livingstone Smith, PhD; Eugene Soltes, PhD; Susan Stoller; Don Tennant; Jim Taylor, PhD; Robert Thompson, PhD; Jack Trimarco; Paul van Lange, PhD; Kathleen Vohs, PhD; Bernd Weber, MD; Joel Weinberger, PhD; Alissa Wilkinson; Doug Williams; and Jennifer Young.

Phil Houston—you are the opposite of scary.

When you don't have a spouse or kids of your own, your friends become even more important to you. Luckily, I've chosen well. Jill Diamond has been by my side ever since I walked into her Murray Hill apartment with a cardboard Streisand in tow. She and her husband, Neo Baiao, have shown me parts of Brazil I'd have never found on my own. For that, and for taking care of me at various exotic locales (except, maybe, Playa del Carmen), I'm forever grateful.

Darren Scala may be the only person besides Jill and me who knows the entire *Yentl* soundtrack by heart. That alone is reason to keep him around, despite the exhaustion. Neelu Miglani is my fashion consultant, iced-tea maker, and favorite *I*. Nothing makes me happier than knowing that James Alexander Bond, my housemate of six years, is almost as old as I am.

Edith Friedheim—theater pal, travel buddy, music encourager, *Words with Friends* friend, guru—has taught me how to live no matter what age I am. While only some of my pencils don't have erasers, none of hers do. And that's because she truly doesn't need them.

Deannie Thompson spent hours with me on the phone as I discovered crazier things about the Commander. She has only had my best interest in mind since the day we first met. The world is a much less lonely place with her in it.

Among many other things, Wendy Paris has nurtured my later-life love affair with canines by introducing me to Marshmellow. Thank you for sharing your home, your son, your dog, your friends, and the Santa Monica Stairs, and for always looking at the bright side of life. Someone has to. To that end, David Callahan offered his Los Angeles flat to me, while Alexander Parrs-Callahan made me remember the I can still climb trees.

Sarah Rodman. Sarah Rodman! For putting me up, forgiving me for accidentally omitting you from my last book, and introducing me to James Taylor.

Heather Carlucci, Deborah Kerner, Leslie Lefkowitz, and Virginia Roberts all had the pleasure of meeting the Commander. Mike Finkel would have, had he not been in Montana with his wife, Jill Barker Finkel, the brilliant tactician. Mary Bolster and Ann Laschever talked to the Commander on the phone; Larry Smith and Piper Kerman endured a meal with him. (And Jeff Kerman—you nailed it!) David Wallis and Penny Blatt: Thank you for letting me be your platonic Sister Wife, and for acquiring "one of those" named Milo.

Not only is Benita Gold one of the funniest people I know, she's also one of the most honest. She proofed this entire book at record speed, and when something didn't work for her I knew it really didn't work. For that, and for bringing Mateo into my life, you are my hero. Benita, Lenore Neier, and David Terrio were with me on that fateful New Year's Eve. Together we survived the chemical attack in our water glasses.

In addition to hooking me up with my above-mentioned agent, Hillary Black has sent me work, given me a place to stay in DC, and always tells me I look thin. I was fifteen when I met Alex Hahn at the Best. Party. Ever. I'm not sure if Julia Slotnik Sturm was at that bash (if not, you missed a good one), but she has been a steady source of support, humor, and magazine clippings since her mother sent her my way. She, Marc, Alec, and Léo Sturm generously let me crash on their couch during the World Cup. Thank God France won.

As for Eleni Paniccio? LYMY. (And tell Jack to move his piece.)

Bobby, Laura, Katie, and John "Willis" Harrell are among my favorite Smushballs. (But I still think the goal of *Fortnite* should be to hug more people than your opponent.) Rachel Lehmann-Haupt met the Commander, read some pages, and gave invaluable edits. And no one makes a meal of sand like Alexander Lehmann-Haupt.

Muitos beijos to my Brazilian peeps: Kelly Maurice, John O'Brien, and Bridget, Bria, and Michael Maurice O'Brien in São Paulo. To Pedro Gustavo Silva, Nela Alfonso, and Marcel Teramae in Praia do Rosa: *obrigadíssima* for general excellence.

Dave Burton and Jose Nunez always had my back, even when they weren't helping me zip up my dresses.

Barbara Adams shepherded my writing career, such that it is, along with Pamela Painter. I think of you, Pam, every time I give myself a "gift" to reuse at a later time. Aidan Quigley and Miranda Pennington, two fine writers, made sense of endless transcripts. Maya Kukes, Marcy Lovitch, Catherine Mcgeoch, and Jensen Wheeler Wolfe checked facts and reworked endnotes. God's work, and you did it.

I met some highly impressive people at the Johns Hopkins School of Advanced International Studies, but no one wowed me as much as Brigadier General Paula G. Thornhill. I commuted once a week just to take her American Defense Policy class, and I'd do it again in a heartbeat.

Sam Ryan: I wish I'd known you when I was living in Washington. Everything would have been different, and better.

I am a proud member of the Invisible Institute, a group of amazing writers and even more amazing individuals. Special thanks to Annie Murphy Paul for organizing, and Susan Cain, Ada Calhoun, Ben Dattner, Christine Kenneally, Jessica Potts Lahey, Ron Lieber, Katherine Lanpher, Katie Orenstein, Mary Pilon, Josh Prager, Elizabeth DeVita-Raeburn, Paul Raeburn, Deborah Siegel, Katherine Stewart, Debbie Stier, Bob Sullivan, Stacy Sullivan, Harriet Washington, and Tom Zoellner. Gretchen Rubin got behind this idea the second I mentioned it. Rebecca Skloot shared her own tales from the front. Sheri Fink survived a July Fourth with the Commander. Lauren Sandler, Maia Szalavitz, and Alissa Quart looked over various chapters and gave superb suggestions. Judith Matloff is my social and HR director. Randi Hutter Epstein considered every single comma, and even enlisted some of her students to help with my research. Who does that? Randi.

Andy Morris and Pete Holmberg, my Boys of Slumber, have provided me with shelter from many storms. I cherish our Camp Andy weekends on Bell Island, as well as my thrice-yearly birthday dinners with Linda Lipman and Judy Twersky.

Serena Jost keeps me sane with cellistic cellisticity. Elena Rahona, Magdalena Garbalinska, and the New York Late Starters Orchestra have given me a place to play. My neighbors might not appreciate it, but I do.

Big thanks to Mark Abramovich, Scott Allen, Josh Gosfield, Matt Kaufman, George Peng, Jessica Rock, Jessica Siegel, Ed ("Secret lives, secret sex!") Strosser, Camille Sweeney, and Stephanie Tuck for friendship and encouragement. Ari Rajsbaum and my Dude, Rick Feingold, plied me with expert insights and interview subjects. Steve Reynolds offered detective services. Thanks to Dave and Sherry Lovett and The Wildacres Retreat in Little Switzerland, North Carolina. Those Blue Ridge Mountains are divine, even if I can't navigate them at night.

My parents, Barbara and Seymour Ellin, and my brother, Ray, the *Little House* savant, have been with me my whole life. I may be overly flippant, but without you I'd be running around in bigger circles than I already am. Thanks also to Arthur Golden, who inspired my writing.

The Commander once told me that he longed for a romance where he was thanked in the liner notes. While I'm not dedicating this to him, I would like to thank him for the material. I was looking for a story, and I got one. It might not have been the story I wanted, but it was a story nonetheless.

NOTES

One: Gaslit: A Love Story

1. It seems fitting to begin a book on deception with a quotation of uncertain origin. This one has been attributed to everyone from Gloria Steinem to Bill Cosby to Erin Brockovich. Some variation of it has been in existence for many years. For more on this go to Quote Investigator, https://quoteinvestigator.com/2014/09/04 /truth-free.

2. I wrote this in "The Drama of Deception," *Psychology Today*, June 30, 2015, https://www.psychologytoday.com /us/articles/201506/the-drama-deception.

3. H.R. 258, Stolen Valor Act of 2013, https://www.congress.gov/bill/113th -congress/house-bill/258 and https://www.congress.gov/113/plaws/publ12/PLAW -113publ12.pdf.

Two: The Secret Lives of Almost Everyone

1. "Novelist John le Carré Reflects on His Own 'Legacy' of Spying," NPR, Author Interviews, September 5, 2017, https://www.npr.org/templates/transcript /transcript.php?storyId=548632065.

2. Graham Bowley, "Bill Cosby Criminal Case: A Timeline from Accusation to Verdict," *New York Times*, April 25, 2018, https://www.nytimes.com /2018/04/25/arts/television/bill-cosby-sexual-assault-allegations-timeline.html; Carly Mallenbaum, Patrick Ryan, and Maria Puente, "A Complete List of the 60 Bill Cosby Accusers and Their Reactions to the Guilty Verdict," *USA Today*, April 27, 2018, https://www.usatoday.com/story/life/people/2018/04/27/bill -cosby-full-list-accusers/555144002.

3. Rob Evans, "Police Apologise to Women Who Had Relationships with Undercover Cops," *The Guardian*, November 20, 2015, www.theguardian .com/uk-news/2015/nov/20/met-police-apologise-women-had-relationships-with -undercover-officers

4. Yudhijit Bhattacharjee, "The Mind of a Con Man," *New York Times Magazine*, April 26, 2013, https://www.nytimes.com/2013/04/28/magazine/diederik -stapels-audacious-academic-fraud.html.

5. Denny Borsboom and Eric Jan Wagenmakers, "Derailed: The Rise and Fall of Diederik Stapel," Association for Psychological Science, December 27, 2012, https://www.psychologicalscience.org/observer/derailed-the-rise-and-fall-of-diederik-stapel.

6. Bhattacharjee, "Mind of a Con Man."

7. Mario Ledwith, "Two Secret Families Just Ten Miles Apart: Supermarket Boss Kept Two 'Wives' and 12 Children Hidden from Each Other for Two Decades and Killed Himself When They Found Out," *Daily Mail*, June 2, 2012, www.dailymail.co.uk/news/article-2163298/Andrew-Ingham-hanged-secret-double-life-2-wives-12-children-exposed.html.

8. Jane E. Brody, "When a Partner Cheats," *New York Times*, January 22, 2018, https://www.nytimes.com/2018/01/22/well/marriage-cheating-infidelity.html.

9. Mark A. Bellis, Karen Hughes, Sara Hughes, and John R. Ashton, "Measuring Paternal Discrepancy and Its Public Health Consequences," *Journal of Epidemiology and Community Health* 59, no. 9 (2005): 749–754, https://doi.org/10.1136/jech.2005.036517.

10. Bruce Weber, "Arthur Miller Takes a Poke at Devil with 2 Lives," *New York Times*, April 10, 2000, https://www.nytimes.com/2000/04/10/theater/theater-review-arthur-miller-takes-a-poke-at-a-devil-with-2-lives.html.

11. Trevor Aaronson, "The FBI Gives Itself Lots of Rope to Pull in Informants," *The Intercept*, January 31, 2017, https://theintercept.com/2017/01/31/the-fbi-gives-itself-lots-of-rope-to-pull-in-informants.

12. Patrick Radden Keefe, "Assets and Liabilities," *New Yorker*, September 21, 2015, https://www.newyorker.com/magazine/2015/09/21/assets-and-liabilities.

13. "2016: Spokeo's Year in Review," Spokeo, January 4, 2017, https://www.spokeo.com/compass/2016-spokeos-year-in-review.

14. Glen Fleishman, "Cartoon Captures Spirit of the Internet," *New York Times*, December 14, 2000, https://www.nytimes.com/2000/12/14/technology/cartoon-captures-spirit-of-the-internet.html.

15. Julie Fitness, "Betrayal, Rejection, Revenge, and Forgiveness: An Interpersonal Script Approach," in Mark R. Leary, ed., *Interpersonal Rejection* (Oxford: Oxford University Press, 2006), https://doi.org/10.1093/acprof:oso/9780195130157.003.0004.

16. "Melania Trumps Speech Took 6 Percent of Words from Michelle Obama: Text Analysis Company," NBC Bay Area, July 19, 2016, https://www.nbcbayarea.com/news/local/6-percent-michelle-obama-meliana-trumpOakland-Company-Turnitin-plagiarism-387503341.html.

17. Po Bronson and Ashley Merryman, *NurtureShock: New Thinking About Children* (New York: Hachette, 2009), 88.

18. Erin Geiger Smith, "Spitzer Speaking at Harvard Law's Ethics Center, *Business Insider*, November 12, 2009, www.businessinsider.com/spitzer-speaking-at-harvard-law-ethics-center-2009-11.

19. Stephanie Webber, "Lance Armstrong Is Engaged to Girlfriend Anna Hansen: See Her Ring!," *Us Weekly*, May 24, 2017, https://www.usmagazine.com/celebrity-news/news/lance-armstrong-is-engaged-to-girlfriend-anna-hansen-see-her-ring-w483954.

20. ESPN.com News Service, "Lance Armstrong to Pay $5 Mil to Settle U.S. Government Fraud Lawsuit," ABC, April 18, 2018, https://abcnews.go.com/Sports /lance-armstrong-pay-5m-settle-us-government-fraud/story?id=54597187.

21. *Keeping Up with the Kardashians*, "All Grown Up," Season 11, episode 4, December 6, 2015.

22. Bruce Watson, "Catch Us If You Can," *Nautilus*, November 17, 2016, http://nautil.us/issue/42/fakes/catch-us-if-you-can.

23. Chris Rock, *Bigger and Blacker* (HBO, 1999).

24. Jane Mayer and Ronan Farrow, "Four Women Accuse New York's Attorney General of Physical Abuse," *New Yorker*, May 17, 2008, https://www.newyorker.com /news/news-desk/four-women-accuse-new-yorks-attorney-general-of-physical -abuse.

25. The National Women's History Museum, www.womenshistory.org /education-resources/biographies/deborah-sampson

26. "Oxford Dictionaries Word of the Year 2016 Is . . . Post-Truth," Oxford Dictionaries, November 16, 2016, https://www.oxforddictionaries.com/press/news /2016/12/11/WOTY-16.

Three: Who *Are* the People in Your Neighborhood?

1. Cheryl Strayed, "Richard Ford's Masterly Memoir of His Parents," review of *Between Them: Remembering My Parents*, by Richard Ford, *New York Times*, May 1, 2017, https://www.nytimes.com/2017/05/01/books/review/richard-ford-between -them.html.

2. Charlotte Philby, "The Spy Who Loved Me: Charlotte Philby Returns to Moscow in Search of Her Grandfather Kim Philby," *Independent*, March 6, 2010, https://www.independent.co.uk/news/world/europe/the-spy-who-loved-me -charlotte-philby-returns-to-moscow-in-search-of-her-grandfather-kim-philby -1915508.html.

3. Ben Macintyre, "Five Best: Ben Macintyre on the Cambridge Spies," *Wall Street Journal*, August 15, 2014, https://www.wsj.com/articles/five-best-ben -macintyre-on-the-cambridge-spies-1408126920.

4. Neil Tweedie, "Kim Philby: Father, Husband, Traitor, Spy," *The Telegraph*, January 23, 2013, https://www.telegraph.co.uk/history/9818727/Kim-Philby -Father-husband-traitor-spy.html.

5. Philby, "The Spy Who Loved Me."

6. Ibid.

7. Ibid.

8. Rufina Philby, with Hayden Peake and Mikhail Lyubimov, *The Private Life of Kim Philby: The Moscow Years* (New York: Little, Brown, 2003).

9. Unless otherwise noted, the entire Peter Young section is based on in-person and telephone interviews with the author.

10. Arielle Castillo, "Author Erick Lyle Talks Miami's Punk Past and Present; Reading at Sweat Tomorrow Night," *Miami New Times*, December 21, 2010, www .miaminewtimes.com/arts/author-erick-lyle-talks-miamis-punk-past-and-present -reading-at-sweat-tomorrow-night-6507950.

11. Eric E. Magnuson. "What Becomes of Animal Rights Activists After the

Action Is Over?," *Seattle Weekly*, October 4, 2017, www.seattleweekly.com/news/what-becomes-of-animal-rights-activists-after-the-action-is-over.

12. "Farmhouse Conf 3 Fugitives Have More Fun: Confessions of a Wanted Eco-Terrorist by Peter Young," November 3, 2012, YouTube, posted by Confreaks, April 23, 2013, https://www.youtube.com/watch?v=JZaaYu3wSPo.

13. Daniel M. Wegner, Julie D. Lane, and Sara Dimitri, "The Allure of Secret Relationships," *Journal of Personality and Social Psychology* 66, no. 2 (1994): 287–300, https://dx.doi.org/10.1037/0022-3514.66.2.287.

14. Oscar Wilde, *The Picture of Dorian Gray*, Robert Mighal, ed., Penguin Classics (New York: Penguin, 2006), 8.

15. Benedict Carey, "The Secret Lives of Just About Everybody," *New York Times*, January 11, 2005, https://www.nytimes.com/2005/01/11/health/psychology/the-secret-lives-of-just-about-everybody.html.

16. Bella DePaulo, "The Many Faces of Lies," in A. G. Miller, ed., *The Social Psychology of Good and Evil* (New York: Guilford Press, 2004), 303–326, http://smg.media.mit.edu/library/DePaulo.ManyFacesOfLies.pdf.

17. "UMass Amherst Researcher Finds Most People Lie in Everyday Conversation," UMass Amherst, News Archive, June 10, 2002, https://www.umass.edu/newsoffice/article/umass-amherst-researcher-finds-most-people-lie-everyday-conversation.

18. Aviya Kushner, "What Do the Talmud and Torah Say About Trump's Lies?," *The Forward*, May 14, 2017, https://forward.com/culture/371521/talmud-and-torah-and-trumps-lies.

19. "Link Between Lying and Popularity Found by Researcher at UMass Amherst," UMass Amherst, News Archive, December 14, 1999, https://www.umass.edu/newsoffice/article/link-between-lying-and-popularity-found-researcher-umass-amherst.

20. Nobuhito Abe, Toshikatsu Fujii, Kazumi Hirayama, Atsushi Takeda, Yoshiyuki Hosokai, Toshiyuki Ishioka, Yoshiyuki Nishio, et al., "Do Parkinsonian Patients Have Trouble Telling Lies? The Neurological Basis of Deceptive Behavior," *Brain* 132, no. 5 (May 2009): 1386–1395, https://doi.org/10.1093/brain/awp052.

21. Bella DePaulo, "I Study Liars. I've Never Seen One Like President Trump," *Washington Post*, December 8, 2017, https://www.washingtonpost.com/outlook/i-study-liars-ive-never-seen-one-like-president-trump/2017/12/07/4e529efe-da3f-11e7-a841-2066faf731ef_story.html?utm_term=.7996dd1eea2d.

22. Telephone interview with author.

23. In-person interview with author.

24. Michael Shermer, "The Truth About White Lies," *Salon*, April 8, 2014, https://www.salon.com/2014/04/08/the_truth_about_little_white_lies_why_theyre_actually_more_dangerous_than_you_think_partner/?source=newsletter.

25. David Nyberg, *The Varnished Truth: Truth Telling and Deceiving in Ordinary Life* (Chicago: University of Chicago Press, 1995), 10.

26. In-person interview with author.

27. Natalie Zutter, "The Affair and the History of Television Multiverses," *Den of Geek*, November 2, 2015, www.denofgeek.com/us/tv/the-affair/250178/the-affair-and-the-history-of-television-multiverses.

28. Hanna Rosin, "Why We Cheat," *Slate*, March 27, 2014, www.slate.com /articles/double_x/doublex/2014/03/esther_perel_on_affairs_spouses_in_happy _marriages_cheat_and_americans_don.html.

29. Lillian Ross, "Our Secret Selves," *Independent*, October 17, 1998, https:// www.independent.co.uk/arts-entertainment/our-secret-selves-1179087.html.

30. "Lindbergh's Double Life," DW, n.d., https://www.dw.com/en/lindberghs -double-life/a-1620936-1.

31. Ibid.

32. Telephone interview with author.

33. Matthew Hornsey, "Imposters: The Psychology of Pretending to Be Some-one You're Not: Matthew Hornsey at TEDxUQ," YouTube, posted by TEDx Talks, May 22, 2013, https://www.youtube.com/watch?v=vSjlCJaEwZE.

34. Bruce Watson, "Catch Us If You Can," *Nautilus*, November 17, 2016, http://nautil.us/issue/42/fakes/catch-us-if-you-can.

35. Email interview with author.

36. Ibid.

37. Doreen Carvajal, "Disputed Holocaust Memoir Withdrawn," *New York Times*, October 14, 1999, https://www.nytimes.com/1999/10/14/arts/disputed -holocaust-memoir-withdrawn.html.

38. "Rachel Dolezal's Parents React to Daughter's Race Identity Com-ments," YouTube, posted by ABC News, June 17, 2015, https://www.youtube.com /watch?v=7146sy0AZdE.

39. Eun Kyung Kim, "Rachel Dolezal Breaks Her Silence: 'I Identify as Black,'" *Today*, June 26, 2015, https://www.today.com/video/rachel-dolezal-breaks -her-silence-i-identify-as-black-465269315945.

40. Watson, "Catch Us If You Can."

41. Ronald E. Riggio, "Are You a Skilled Social Actor or a Social Chameleon," *Psychology Today*, January 11, 2012, https://www.psychologytoday.com/us/blog /cutting-edge-leadership/201201/are-you-skilled-social-actor-or-social-chameleon.

42. Carey, "Secret Lives of Just About Everybody."

43. Telephone interview with author.

Four: The Joy of Lying

1. Seth Meyers, on *Late Night with Seth Meyers*, November 9, 2016, quoted at Michael Schneider, "Seth Meyers on Trump's Victory: 'I've Been Wrong About Him at Every Turn,'" IndieWire, November 9, 2016, https://www.indiewire .com/2016/11/seth-meyers-donald-trump-president-elected-late-night-1201745049.

2. Robert Crichton, *The Great Impostor* (New York: Random House, 1959), available at https://archive.org/details/greatimpostor010210mbp.

3. "Top 10 Impostors. Faking It: Ferdinand Demara," *Time*, May 26, 2009, http://content.time.com/time/specials/packages/article/0,28804,1900621_1900618 _1900605,00.html.

4. Brothers of Christian Instruction in the United States of America, www .ficbrothers.org; "Brief History of the FIC: The FIC in the World," Internet Ar-chive, WayBackMachine, https://web.archive.org/web/20090625133257/http:// www.slgafi.org/home/en/history_ficworld.asp.

5. Joseph Pilcher, "The Great Impostor Was Surgeon, Teacher, Warden—But Now He's the Real Chaplain Demara," *People*, September 19, 1977, http://people.com/archive/the-great-impostor-was-surgeon-teacher-warden-but-now-hes-the-real-chaplain-demara-vol-8-no-12.

6. Joe McCarthy, "The Master Impostor: An Incredible Tale," *Life*, January 28, 1952, https://bit.ly/2J3DkxC.

7. Telephone interview with author.

8. Ibid.

9. McCarthy, "Master Impostor."

10. Ibid.

11. Ibid.

12. Jan Hoffman, "'Everyday Sadists' Among Us," *New York Times*, September 16, 2013, https://well.blogs.nytimes.com/2013/09/16/everyday-sadists-among-us; Lucy Jones, "How Did Evil Evolve, and Why Did It Persist?," BBC, April 4, 2016, www.bbc.com/earth/story/20160401-how-did-evil-evolve-and-why-did-it-persist.

13. William Hirstein, "What Is a Psychopath?" *Psychology Today*, January 30, 2013, https://www.psychologytoday.com/blog/mindmelding/201301/what-is-psychopath-0.

14. Bruce Weber, "Chris Costner Sizemore, Patient Behind 'The Three Faces of Eve,' Dies at 89," *New York Times*, August 5, 2016, https://www.nytimes.com/2016/08/06/us/chris-costner-sizemore-the-real-patient-behind-the-three-faces-of-eve-dies-at-89.html.

15. Victor Lipman, "The Disturbing Link Between Psychopathy and Leadership," *Forbes*, April 25, 2013, https://www.forbes.com/sites/victorlipman/2013/04/25/the-disturbing-link-between-psychopathy-and-leadership/#49e8841d4104.

16. "Personality Disorders," National Institute of Mental Health, 2017, https://www.nimh.nih.gov/health/statistics/personality-disorders.shtml.

17. Rolf Wynn, Marita H. Høiseth, and Gunn Pettersen, "Psychopathy in Women: Theoretical and Clinical Perspectives," *International Journal of Women's Health* 4 (2012): 257–263, https://doi.org/10.2147/IJWH.S25518.

18. Hirstein, "What Is a Psychopath?"

19. B. H. King and C. V. Ford, "Pseudologia Fantastica," *Acta Psychiatrica Scandinavica* 77, no. 1 (1988): 1–6, https://www.ncbi.nlm.nih.gov/pubmed/3279719.

20. Chris Josefowicz, "Understanding Compulsive Liars," *Psychology Today*, October 1, 2003, https://www.psychologytoday.com/articles/200310/understanding-compulsive-liars.

21. Paul Ekman, "Lying and Nonverbal Behavior: Theoretical Issues and New Findings," *Journal of Nonverbal Behavior* 12, no. 3 (1988): 163–175, https://doi.org/10.1007/BF00987486.

22. This entire section is based on interviews and conversations with the author.

23. Seth Ferranti, "The Drug-Dealing Puerto Rican James Bond," *Ozy*, November 21, 2016, https://www.ozy.com/flashback/the-drug-dealing-puerto-rican-james-bond/72433.

24. Telephone interview with author.

25. Ibid.

26. Ibid.

27. Abigail Zuger, "Shade of Psychopathy and Ambitions Run Amok," *New York Times*, June 25, 2012, https://www.nytimes.com/2012/06/26/health/views /shades-of-psychopathy-and-nobel-ambitions-run-amok.html.

28. Victoria Talwar and A. Crossman, "Little White Lies to Filthy Liars: The Evolution of Honesty and Deception in Young Children," *Advances in Child Development and Behavior* 40 (2011): 139–170, https://www.ncbi.nlm.nih.gov /pubmed/21887961.

29. Evelyne Debey, Maarten De Schryver, Gordon D. Logan, Kristina Suchotzki, and Bruno Verschuere, "From Junior to Senior Pinocchio: A Cross-Sectional Lifespan Investigation of Deception," *Acta Psychologica* 160 (September 2015): 58–68, https://doi.org/10.1016/j.actpsy.2015.06.007.

30. Michael Lewis, Catherine Stanger, and Margaret W. Sullivan, "Deception in 3-Year Olds," *Developmental Psychology* 25, no. 3 (1989): 439–443, https://www .ecu.edu/cs-cas/psyc/upload/Lewis-Stanger-Sullivan-1989.pdf.

31. Po Bronson and Ashley Merryman, *NurtureShock: New Thinking About Children* (New York: Hachette, 2009), 84.

32. Interview with author.

33. In-person interview with author.

34. Nadia Drake, "Bugs and Spiders Disguised as Poop, Leaves, and Each Other," *Wired*, December 5, 2013, https://www.wired.com/2013/12/insect-and -spider-mimicry.

35. Telephone interview with author. He is referring to the article cited above in *Wired*.

36. Jane Brody, "Designing Birds Impress Their Mates with Fancy Décor," *New York Times*, March 5, 1991, https://www.nytimes.com/1991/03/05/science /designing-birds-impress-their-mates-with-fancy-decor.html.

37. "Brown-Headed Cowbird: Life History," Cornell Lab of Ornithology, All About Birds, https://www.allaboutbirds.org/guide/Brown-headed_Cowbird /lifehistory.

38. "Kirtland's Warbler (*Setophaga kirtlandii*)," US Fish and Wildlife Service, Endangered Species, https://www.fws.gov/midwest/Endangered/birds/Kirtland /index.html.

39. Patricia Edmonds, "Why He Minds the Nest While She Takes More Mates," *National Geographic*, May 2017, https://www.nationalgeographic.com /magazine/2017/05/basic-instincts-wattled-jacana.

40. Erik Eckholm, "Deceit Found Pervasive in the Natural World," *New York Times*, January 14, 1986, https://www.nytimes.com/1986/01/14/science/deceit -found-pervasive-in-the-natural-world.html.

41. Brigit Katz, "Chantek, an Orangutan Who Knew Sign Language, Has Died at 39," *Smithsonian*, August 8, 2017, https://www.smithsonianmag.com /smart-news/chantek-orangutan-who-knew-sign-language-has-died-39-180964390.

42. Charles Mudede, "Part One: Deception in the Animal Kingdom," *The Stranger*, May 24, 2010, http://slog.thestranger.com/slog/archives/2010/05/24 /part-one-deception-in-the-animal-kingdom.

43. Neil Garrett, Stephanie C. Lazzaro, Dan Ariely, and Tali Sharot, "The

Brain Adapts to Dishonesty," *Nature Neuroscience* 19 (2016): 1727–1732, https://doi.org/10.1038/nn.4426.

44. Melissa Dahl, "The Truth About the Ways People Lie," *New York*, The Cut, May 18, 2015, https://www.thecut.com/2015/05/8-true-things-about-the-ways-people-lie.html.

45. Tara Parker Pope, "Does Facebook Turn People into Narcissists," *New York Times*, May 17, 2012, https://well.blogs.nytimes.com/2012/05/17/does-facebook-turn-people-into-narcissists.

46. Telephone interview with author.

47. Claire Harman, *Myself and the Other Fellow* (New York: HarperPerennial, 2005); "Robert Louis Stevenson's Split Personality," NPR, Author Interviews, November 27, 2005, https://www.npr.org/templates/story/story.php?storyId=5028500.

48. Bruce C McKinley, Lynn Kelly, and Robert L. Duran, "Narcissism or Openness? College Students' Use of Facebook and Twitter," *Communication Research Reports*, April 2012, 108–118, https://doi.org/10.1080/08824096.2012.666919.

49. Bruce Watson, "Catch Us If You Can," *Nautilus*, November 17, 2016, www.nautil.us/issue/42/fakes/catch-us-if-you-can.

50. Benedict Carey, "The Secret Lives of Just About Everybody," *New York Times*, January 11, 2005, https://www.nytimes.com/2005/01/11/health/psychology/the-secret-lives-of-just-about-everybody.html.

51. Ibid.

52. Seth Stephens-Davidowitz, "Don't Let Facebook Make You Miserable," *New York Times*, June 5, 2017, https://www.nytimes.com/2017/05/06/opinion/sunday/dont-let-facebook-make-you-miserable.html.

53. "Robert Louis Stevenson's Split Personality," NPR, November 27, 2005, https://www.npr.org/templates/story/story.php?storyId=5028500; "Doppelgangers and the Mythology of Spirit Doubles," 2012: The Awakening, July 6, 2014, https://ascendingstarseed.wordpress.com/2014/07/08/doppelgangers-and-the-mythology-of-spirit-doubles.

54. Milica Živković, "The Double as the 'Unseen' of Culture: Toward a Definition of Doppelganger," *Facta Universitatis* 2, no. 7 (November 1, 2000): 121–128, http://facta.junis.ni.ac.rs/lal/lal2000/lal2000-05.pdf.

55. Jennifer Senior, review of *Labyrinths: Emma and Carl Jung's Complex Marriage*, *New York Times*, November 7, 2016, https://www.nytimes.com/2016/11/07/books/review-labryinths-emma-and-carl-jungs-complex-marriage.html.

Five: A Life Divided

1. Letter from Thomas Jefferson to Peter Carr, August 19, 1785, Yale Law School, Lillian Goldman Law Library, Avalon Project, http://avalon.law.yale.edu/18th_century/let31.asp.

2. Jeff Hancock, "The Future of Lying," Ted Talk, September 2012, https://www.ted.com/talks/jeff_hancock_3_types_of_digital_lies.

3. Jeffrey T. Hancock, Catalina Toma, and Nicole Ellison, "The Truth About Lying in Online Dating Profiles," in *Proceedings of Computer/Human Interaction* (2007): 449–452.

4. Boris Kachka, "Proust Wasn't a Neuroscientist. Neither Was Jonah

Lehrer," *New York*, October 28, 2012, http://nymag.com/news/features/jonah-lehrer -2012-11; "The Science of Lying: Why the Truth Really Can Hurt," *Independent*, July 5, 2010, https://www.independent.co.uk/news/science/the-science-of-lying -why-the-truth-really-can-hurt-2018293.html.

5. "What Is Security Culture?," CrimethInc., November 1, 2004, https:// crimethinc.com/2004/11/01/what-is-security-culture.

6. Jesse Bering, "18 Attributes of Highly Effective Liars," *Scientific American*, July 7, 2011, https://blogs.scientificamerican.com/bering-in-mind/18-attributes -of-highly-effective-liars.

7. Robert Crichton, *The Great Impostor* (New York: Random House, 1959).

8. Steven Erlanger, "Kim Philby, Lecturing in East Berlin in '81, Bragged of How Easy It Was to Fool MI6," *New York Times*, April 4, 2016, https://www .nytimes.com/2016/04/05/world/europe/kim-philby-bbc-lecture.html.

9. Amy Davidson Sorkin, "Lance Armstrong's Flawed Confession," *New Yorker*, January 18, 2013, https://www.newyorker.com/news/amy-davidson/lance -armstrongs-flawed-confession.

10. Sarah Lyall, "Spies Like Us: A Conversation with John le Carré and Ben Macintyre," *New York Times*, August 25, 2017, https://www.nytimes.com /2017/08/25/books/review/john-le-carre-ben-macintyre-british-spy-thrillers.html.

11. Brent W. Roberts and Wendy F. DelVecchio, "The Rank Order Consistency of Personality Traits from Childhood to Old Age, a Quantitative Review of Longitudinal Studies," *Psychological Bulletin* 126, no. 1 (2000): 3–25, http:// psycnet.apa.org/record/2000-03445-001.

12. Telephone interview with author.

13. Ibid.

14. Tanith Carey, "Anne Darwin, 'Canoe Widow': Deceiving My Sons Was Unforgiveable," *The Guardian*, October 10, 2016, https://www.theguardian.com/uk /canoe.

15. "500K (pounds) Recovered from Wife of Canoe Fraudster John Darwin," *Mirror*, February 14, 2012, https://www.mirror.co.uk/news/uk-news /500k-recovered-wife-canoe-fraudster-684683.

16. Carey, "Anne Darwin."

17. Email interview with author.

18. Damien Gale, "Kim Philby: I Got Away with Treachery Because I Was Upper Class," *The Guardian*, April 4, 2016, https://www.theguardian.com/world /2016/apr/04/kim-philbys-stasi-tape-reveals-secrets-of-his-success-as-cold-war-spy.

19. The Hamer section is based entirely on a telephone interview with the author.

20. Raj Persaud and David Canter, "Sleeping with the Enemy? The Reporting of Undercover Sex and the Police Neglects the Psychology of the Predicament," *Huffington Post*, April 3, 2013, https://www.huffingtonpost.co.uk/dr-raj-persaud /undercover-police-psychology_b_2806029.html.

21. Michel Girodo, Trevor Deck, and Melanie Morrison, "Dissociative-Type Identity Disturbances in Undercover Agents: Socio-Cognitive Factors Behind False Identity Appearances and Reenactments," *Social Behavior and Personality* 30, no. 7 (November 2002): 631–644, https://doi.org/10.2224/sbp.2002.30.7.631.

22. M. R. Pogrebin and E. D. Poole, "Vice Isn't Nice: A Look at the Effects of Working Undercover," *Journal of Criminal Justice* 21, no. 4 (1993): 383–394, https://www.ncjrs.gov/App/Publications/abstract.aspx?ID=145650.

23. Tom Keyser, "Leonard Nimoy's 'Secret Selves' Exhibit Opens at Mass Moca," *Times Union*, July 29, 2010, https://blog.timesunion.com/localarts /leonard-nimoys-secret-selves-exhibit-opens-at-mass-moca/6291.

24. "Secret Selves," *The Morning News*, August 9, 2010, https://themorninnews .org/gallery/secret-selves.

25. James Helfin, "Nimoy's Lens," *Valley Advocate*, August 19, 2010, http:// valleyadvocate.com/2010/08/19/nimoys-lens.

26. Mark Leary, "John Edwards' Modular Mind," *Connections*, Society of Personality and Social Connections, May 3, 2012, https://spsptalks.wordpress .com/2012/05/03/john-edwards-modular-mind.

27. Tennessee Williams, *The Rose Tattoo*, 1951, Act 3.

28. Haley M. Dillon and Rachael A. Carmen, "Struggling with Our Own Hypocrisy: Modularity of the Human Brain," a review of *Why Everyone (Else) Is a Hypocrite: Evolution and the Modular Mind*, by Robert Kurzban, *Journal of Social, Evolutionary, and Cultural Psychology* (2011), http://psycnet.apa.org/journals /ebs/5/3/208.html.

29. Sharon Begley, "Our Brains Are Wired for Hypocrisy, *Newsweek*, October 19, 2009; Maryam Kouchaki and Francesca Gino, "Memories of Unethical Actions Become Obfuscated over Time," in *Proceedings of the National Academy of Sciences of the United States of America*, May 2016. See also Dr. Paul J. Werbos, "Hypocrisy as a Force in Human History," Werbos, n.d., www.werbos.com/pi/Hypocrisy.htm.

30. See Masha Green, "In Praise of Hypocrisy," *New York Times*, February 18, 2017, https://nytimes.com/2017/02/18/opinion/sunday/in-praise-of-hypocrisy.html; Dean Burnett, "It's Only Wrong When YOU Do It! The Psychology of Hypocrisy," *The Guardian*, November 17, 2016, https://www.theguardian.com/science /brain-flapping/2016/nov/17/its-only-wrong-when-you-do-it-the-psychology-of -hypocrisy; Jillian Jordan, Roseanna Sommers, and David Rand, "The Real Problem with Hypocrisy," *New York Times*, January 13, 2017, https://www.nytimes .com/2017/01/13/opinion/sunday/the-real-problem-with-hypocrisy.html.

31. Dillon and Carmen, "Struggling with Our Own Hypocrisy."

32. Leary, "John Edwards' Modular Mind."

33. Ibid.

34. Robert Trivers, "The Elements of Scientific Theory of Self-Deception," *Annals of the New York Academy of Sciences* 907, no. 1 (2000): 114–131, https:// doi.org/10.1111/j.1749-6632.2000.tb06619.xl; W. von Hippel and R. Trivers, "The Evolution and Psychology of Self-Deception," *Behavioral and Brain Sciences* 34, no. 1 (2011): 1–16, 16–56, https://doi.org/10.1017/S0140525X10001354.

35. "Ignorance Is Genetic Bliss," n.d., http://roberttrivers.com/Robert_Trivers /Print_Interviews_files/ProjectMunich.pdf.

36. Leary, "John Edwards' Modular Mind."

37. Caroline Knapp, *Drinking: A Love Story* (New York: Dial Press, 1997).

38. Sam Allis, "Cold War Pen Pals: Red Spy Kim Philby, Graham Greene," *Baltimore Sun*, April 17, 1999, http://articles.baltimoresun.com/1999-04-17

/news/9904170347_1_kim-philby-graham-greene-spy-kim.

39. James F. Lomont, "Repressors and Sensitizers as Described by Themselves and Their Peers," *Journal of Personality* (June 1996), https://doi.org/10.1111/j.1467-6494.1966.tb01710.x.

40. Adrian Furnham, *50 Psychology Ideas You Really Need to Know* (New York: Quercus, 2009).

41. John Edwards, R. Scott Tindale, Linda Heath, and Emil J. Posavac, *Social Influences: Processes and Prevention* (Boston: Springer, 1990).

42. Benedict Carey, "The Secret Lives of Just About Everybody," *New York Times*, January 11, 2005, https://www.nytimes.com/2005/01/11/health/psychology/the-secret-lives-of-just-about-everybody.html.

43. Ibid.

44. Tim Weiner, "Why I Spied: Aldrich Ames," *New York Times Magazine*, July 31, 1994, https://www.nytimes.com/1994/07/31/magazine/why-i-spied-aldrich-ames.html.

45. Skype interview with author.

Six: Post-Deception Stress Disorder

1. Adrienne Rich, *On Lies, Secrets, and Silence: Selected Prose 1966–1978*, rev. ed. (New York: W. W. Norton, 1995), quoted Maria Popova, "Adrienne Rich on Lying, What 'Truth' Really Means, and the Alchemy of Human Possibility," Brain Pickings, n.d., https://www.brainpickings.org/2014/11/13/adrienne-rich-women-honor-lying.

2. The entire Eileen Morrison section is based on telephone and in-person interviews conducted by the author.

3. Julie Fitness, "Betrayal, Rejection, Revenge, and Forgiveness: An Interpersonal Script Approach," in Mark R. Leary, ed., *Interpersonal Rejection* (Oxford: Oxford University Press, 2006), 95.

4. Robert O. Hansson, Warren H. Jones, and Wesla L. Fletcher, "Troubled Relationships in Later Life: Implications for Support," *Journal of Social and Personal Relationship* 7 (1990): 451–463, https://doi.org/10.1177/0265407590074003.

5. Telephone interview with author.

6. Anna Fels, "Great Betrayals," *New York Times*, October 5, 2013, https://www.nytimes.com/2013/10/06/opinion/sunday/great-betrayals.html.

7. All of the Ault quotes come from a telephone interview with the author.

8. American Psychological Association, *Clinical Practice Guideline for the Treatment of PTSD*, February 2017, https://www.apa.org/ptsd-guideline/ptsd.pdf.

9. Audrey Freshman, "Financial Disaster as a Risk Factor for Posttraumatic Stress Disorder: Internet Survey of Trauma in Victims of the Madoff Ponzi Scheme," *Health and Social Work* 37, no. 1 (2012): 39–48, https://www.ncbi.nlm.nih.gov/pubmed/22908480; US Department of Veterans Affairs, National Center for PTSD, "PTSD Checklist for DSM-5 (PCL-5)," https://www.ptsd.va.gov/professional/assessment/adult-sr/ptsd-checklist.asp.

10. Viatcheslav Wlassoff, "How Does Post-Traumatic Stress Disorder Change the Brain?" *BrainBlogger*, January 24, 2015, http://brainblogger.com/2015/01/24/how-does-post-traumatic-stress-disorder-change-the-brain.

11. Dario Dieguez Jr., "The Neuroscience of Fear and Loathing," *BrainBlogger*, January 19, 2011, http://brainblogger.com/2011/01/19/the-neuroscience-of-fear-and-loathing; Wlassoff, "How Does Post-Traumatic Stress Disorder Change the Brain?"

12. Wlassoff, "How Does Post-Traumatic Stress Disorder Change the Brain?"

13. Telephone interview with author.

14. Joyce Short, "Classic Example of Sex Fraud Mentality," Consent Awareness, March 26, 2015, https://consentawareness.net/author/shortjm/page/10; telephone interviews with author.

15. The American Law Institute, Model Penal Code, https://www.ali.org/publications/show/model-penal-code; "Model Penal Code: Sexual Assault and Related Offenses," The Ali Adviser, n.d., www.thealiadviser.org/sexual-assault.

16. Tony Rizzo, "Raymore Man's Arrest Puts Rape by Fraud Issue in the Spotlight," *Kansas City Star*, October 27, 2016, https://www.kansascity.com/news/local/crime/article110787327.html.

17. "Tennessee Rape and Sexual Assault Laws," FindLaw, n.d., https://statelaws.findlaw.com/tennessee-law/tennessee-rape-and-sexual-assault-laws.html; "Rape by Fraud: Don't Say I Love You Unless You Mean It," Horst Law, December 4, 2014, https://www.criminalattorneysnashville.com/2014/12/04/rape-fraud-dont-say-love-unless-mean.

18. Patrick McGreevy, "Brown Signs Bill Closing Loophole in Rape Law," *Los Angeles Times*, September 9, 2013, http://articles.latimes.com/2013/sep/09/local/la-me-brown-bills-20130910; Robert J. Lopez, "Man Gets Prison in Rape Impersonation Case That Sparked New State Law," *Los Angeles Times*, May 8, 2014, www.latimes.com/local/lanow/la-me-ln-man-gets-prison-rape-impersonation-case-20140508-story.html.

19. Email interview with author.

20. "Alabama Code Title 13A. Criminal Code § 13A-6-65," FindLaw, n.d., https://codes.findlaw.com/al/title-13a-criminal-code/al-code-sect-13a-6-65.html.

21. Eric Levenson, "Larry Nassar Sentenced to Up to 175 Years in Prison for Decades of Sexual Abuse," CNN, January 24, 2018, https://www.cnn.com/2018/01/24/us/larry-nassar-sentencing/index.html.

22. Kim Shayo Buchanan, "When Is HIV a Crime? Sexuality, Gender and Consent," *Minnesota Law Review* 99, no. 4 (2014): 1231–1342, www.minnesotalawreview.org/wp-content/uploads/2015/05/Buchanan_pdf.pdf; Neil MacArthur, "Is Lying to Get Laid a Form of Sexual Assault?," *Vice*, September 4, 2016, https://www.vice.com/en_us/article/4w5w7g/is-lying-to-get-laid-a-form-of-sexual-assault; Mark Theoharis, "Transmitting an STD: Criminal Laws & Penalties," *Criminal Defense Lawyer*, n.d., https://www.criminaldefenselawyer.com/resources/transmitting-std-criminal-laws-penalties.htm.

23. Tony Rizzo, "Next Act for Man Who Used Porn 'Audition' to Con Two Dozen Women into Sex: Prison," *Kansas City Star*, September 13, 2017, https://www.kansascity.com/news/local/crime/article173061946.html.

24. Rizzo, "Raymore Man's Arrest Puts Rape by Fraud Issue in the Spotlight."

25. Ibid.

26. "Sean O'Neill Sentenced to 90 Days in Jail by Colorado Judge," February

16, 1996, www.qrd.org/qrd/trans/1996/oneill.sentenced-02.16.96; Alex Sharpe, "The Dark Truth Behind the Convictions for 'Gender Fraud,'" *New Statesman*, December 16, 2015, https://www.newstatesman.com/politics/feminism/2015/12 /dark-truth-behind-convictions-gender-fraud.

27. "Woman Who Pretended to Be Man to Trick Friend into Sex Jailed for Eight Years," *The Guardian*, November 12, 2015, https://www.theguardian .com/uk-news/2015/nov/12/gayle-newland-sentenced-eight-years-prison -duping-friend-having-sex.

28. Dina Newman, "Unravelling the Israeli Arab 'Rape by Deception' Case," BBC, September 17, 2010, https://www.bbc.com/news/world-middle-east -11329429; Tomer Zarchin, "Jurists Say Arab's Rape Conviction Sets Dangerous Precedent," *Haaretz*, July 21, 2010, https://www.haaretz.com/1.5151268.

29. Zarchin, "Jurists Say Arab's Rape Conviction Sets Dangerous Precedent."

30. Telephone interview with author.

31. Joe Reid, "'Will & Grace' Guest Star Watch: Harry Connick, Jr.," *The Decider*, October 13, 2017, https://decider.com/2017/10/13/will-grace-guest -star-watch-harry-connick-jr.

Seven: "I Knew but I Didn't Know"

1. "Ruth: I Feel Betrayed and Confused," *New York Post*, June 30, 2009, https://nypost.com/2009/06/30/ruth-i-feel-betrayed-and-confused.

2. "Kant's Moral Philosophy," *Stanford Encyclopedia of Philosophy*, https://plato .stanford.edu/entries/kant-moral; Christine Korsgaard, "The Right to Lie: Kant on Dealing with Evil," *Philosophy and Public Affairs* 15, no. 4 (1986): 325–349, https:// dash.harvard.edu/handle/1/3200670.

3. Telephone interview with author.

4. Catherine A. Cottrell, Steven L. Neuberg, and Norman P. Li, "What Do People Desire in Others? A Sociofunctional Perspective on the Importance of Different Valued Characteristics," *Journal of Personality and Social Psychology* 92, no. 2 (2007): 208–231, https://doi.org/10.1037/0022-3514.92.2.208.

5. Jack Schafer, "Truth Bias," *Psychology Today*, June 26, 2013, https://www .psychologytoday.com/us/blog/let-their-words-do-the-talking/201306/truth -bias.

6. Melissa Dahl, "6 Facts on the Thin Line Between Trust and Gullibility," *New York*, The Cut, April 1, 2015, https://www.thecut.com/2015/04/6-facts-on -trust-and-gullibility.html.

7. Telephone interview with author.

8. Email interview with author.

9. Telephone interview with author.

10. John K. Rempel, John G. Holmes, and Mark P. Zanna, "Trust in Close Relationships," *Journal of Personality and Social Psychology* 49, no. 1 (1985): 95–112, https://doi.org/10.1037/0022-3514.49.1.95.

11. Salomon Israel, Einav Hart, and Eyal Winter, "Oxytocin Decreases Accuracy in the Perception of Social Deception," *Psychological Science* 25, no. 1 (2013): 293–295, http://journals.sagepub.com/doi/abs/10.1177/0956797613500794; Michaela Pfundmair, Wiebke Erk, and Annika Reinelt, "'Lie to Me'": Oxytocin

Impairs Lie Detection Between Sexes," *Psychoneuroendocrinology* 84 (July 2017), https://doi.org/10.1016/j.psyneuen.2017.07.001.

12. Pfundmair et al., "'Lie to Me.'"

13. A. Aron, H. Fisher, D. Mashek, G. Strong, H. Li, and L. L. Brown, "Reward, Motivation and Emotional Systems Associated with Early-Stage Intense Romantic Love," *Journal of Neurophysiology* 94 (2005): 327–337, https://doi.org/10.1152/jn.00838.2004.

14. Telephone interview with author.

15. Alice Park, "We Trust Strangers, Even When It Doesn't Make Sense to Do So," *Time*, May 16, 2014, http://time.com/103396/we-trust-strangers-even-when-it-doesnt-make-sense-to-do-so.

16. Ibid.

17. Ibid.

18. Peg Streep, "The Trouble with Trust," *Psychology Today*, March 25, 2014, https://www.psychologytoday.com/us/blog/tech-support/201403/the-trouble-trust.

19. Telephone interview with author.

20. L. Festinger, *A Theory of Cognitive Dissonance* (Stanford: Stanford University Press, 1957).

21. Leon Festinger, Henry W. Riecken, and Stanley Schachter, *When Prophecy Fails: A Social and Psychological Study of a Modern Group That Predicted the Destruction of the World* (Minneapolis: University of Minnesota Press, 1956).

22. Ibid., 3.

23. Thea Buckley, "What Happens to the Brain During Cognitive Dissonance?," *Scientific American*, n.d., https://www.scientificamerican.com/article/what-happens-to-the-brain-during-cognitive-dissonance1.

24. Jonathan Ellis, "Motivated Reasoning: A Philosopher on Confirmation Bias," interview with Michel Martin, NPR, *All Things Considered*, January 28, 2017, https://www.npr.org/2017/01/28/512199352/confirmation-bias; Julie Beck, "This Article Won't Change Your Mind: The Facts on Why Facts Alone Can't Fight False Beliefs," *The Atlantic*, March 13, 2017, https://www.theatlantic.com/science/archive/2017/03/this-article-wont-change-your-mind/519093.

25. Telephone interview with author.

26. Ibid.

27. Ibid.

28. Ibid.

29. Ibid.; Abby Ellin, "The Drama of Deception," *Psychology Today*, June 30, 2015, https://www.psychologytoday.com/us/articles/201506/the-drama-deception.

30. David Modic, "Willing to Be Scammed: How Self-Control Impacts Internet Scam Compliance" (PhD diss., University of Exeter, 2013), https://ore.exeter.ac.uk/repository/handle/10871/8044.

31. Telephone interview with author.

32. Telephone interview with author.

33. Joyce Wadler, "The True Story of M. Butterfly: The Spy Who Fell in Love with a Shadow," *New York Times*, August 15, 1993, https://www.nytimes.com/1993/08/15/magazine/the-true-story-of-m-butterfly-the-spy-who-fell-in-love-with-a

-shadow.html.

34. Dinitia Smith, "One False Note in a Musician's Life: Billy Tipton Is Remembered with Love, Even by Those Who Were Deceived," *New York Times*, June 2, 1998, https://www.nytimes.com/1998/06/02/arts/one-false-note-musician-s-life-billy-tipton-remembered-with-love-even-those-who.html.

35. Marshall Sella, "Anthony Weiner vs. *The New York Times*," *GQ*, October 29, 2013, https://www.gq.com/story/anthony-weiner-vs-the-new-york-times.

36. In-person interview with author.

37. Telephone interview with author.

38. Geoffrey Fattah, "Utah County Is Hotbed for White-Collar Crimes," *Deseret News*, December 6, 2001, https://www.deseretnews.com/article/878209/Utah-County-is-hotbed-for-white-collar-crimes.html.

39. Bourree Lam, "Why Is Utah the First State to Have a White-Collar Crime Registry?," *The Atlantic*, March 29, 2016, https://www.theatlantic.com/business/archive/2016/03/utah-white-collar-crime/475896; Greg Smith and Associates, "Utah No. 5 on FBI List for Ponzi Schemes," https://www.bestutahlawyer.com/Articles/Utah-No-5-on-FBI-List-for-Ponzi-Schemes.

40. Smith and Associates, "Utah No. 5"; State of Utah, "White Collar Crime Offender Registry," https://www.utfraud.com/Home/Registry.

41. Email interview with author.

42. Ibid.

43. Ibid.

44. Ibid.

45. Dahl, "6 Facts on the Thin Line."

46. Telephone interview with author.

47. George K. Simon Jr., *In Sheep's Clothing: Understanding and Dealing with Manipulative People* (Little Rock, AR: Parkhurst Brothers, 2010).

48. Art Markman, "Why We Trust People Who Are Clearly Untrustworthy," *Fast Company*, April 5, 2016, https://www.fastcompany.com/3058573/why-we-trust-people-who-are-clearly-untrustworthy.

49. Maria Popova, "Why We Ignore the Obvious: The Psychology of Willful Blindness," *Brain Pickings*, August 27, 2018, https://www.brainpickings.org/2014/08/27/willful-blindness-margaret-heffernan; "Willful Blindness Law and Legal Definition," USLegal.com, https://definitions.uslegal.com/w/willful-blindness.

50. Telephone interview with author.

51. Ibid.; Ellin, "Drama of Deception."

52. Pamela J. Birrell and Jennifer J. Freyd, "Betrayal Blindness: How and Why We 'Whoosh' Away Knowledge of Betrayal in Relationships," *Huffington Post*, April 26, 2013, https://www.huffingtonpost.com/pamela-j-birrell-and-jennifer-j-freyd/betrayal-blindness-how-an_b_3146159.html.

53. Ruben C. Gur and Harold A. Sackeim, "Self-Deception: A Concept in Search of a Phenomenon," *Journal of Personality and Social Psychology* 37, no. 2 (1979): 147–169.

54. Jad Abumrad and Robert Krulwich, *Deception: Lying to Ourselves*, podcast, Season 4, episode 2, February 29, 2008, Radiolab, produced by WNYC, MP3 audio, https://www.radiolab.org/story/91618-lying-to-ourselves.

55. Self-Deception Questionnaire, http://bigfatgenius.com/3180/Self_Deception_Questionnaire.pdf.

56. Abumrad and Krulwich, *Deception: Lying to Ourselves*, Season 4, episode 2.

57. Erin Falconer, "Achieve Happiness by Creating a Life Lie," *PickThe Brain*, February 28, 2007, https://www.pickthebrain.com/blog/achieve-happiness-by-creating-a-life-lie.

58. Joanna E. Starek and Caroline F. Keating, "Self-Deception and Its Relationship to Success in Competition," *Basic and Applied Social Psychology* 12, no. 2 (1991): 145–155, https://doi.org/10.1207/s15324834basp1202_2.

59. Ibid.

60. Abumrad and Krulwich, *Deception: Lying to Ourselves*, Season 4, episode 2.

61. Robert F. Hurley, "The Decision to Trust," *Harvard Business Review*, September 2006, https://hbr.org/2006/09/the-decision-to-trust.

62. J. P. Wiseman and S. Duck, "Having and Managing Enemies: A Very Challenging Relationship," in S. Duck and J. T. Wood, eds., *Understanding Relationship Processes*, vol. 5, *Confronting Relationship Challenges* (Thousand Oaks, CA: Sage Publications, 1995), 43–72.

63. M. Argyle, M. Henderson, and A. Furnham, "The Rules of Social Relationships," *British Journal of Social Psychology* 24, no. 2 (1985): 125–139; Lauryn L. Wilson, Michael E. Roloff, and Colleen M. Carey, "Boundary Rules: Factors That Inhibit Expressing Concerns About Another's Romantic Relationship," *Communication Research* 25, no. 6 (1998): 618–640.

Eight: Little Pink Lies

1. Oscar Wilde, *The Picture of Dorian Gray*, Robert Mighal, ed., Penguin Classics (New York: Penguin, 2006), 8.

2. This entire section is based on telephone, in-person, and email interviews with Karl Robinson.

3. Telephone interview with author.

4. Alan Salkin, "How Sarma Melngailis, Queen of Vegan Cuisine, Became a Runaway Fugitive," *Vanity Fair*, December 2016, www.vanityfair.com/style/2016/11/how-sarma-melngailis-became-a-runaway-fugitive.

5. Bethany McLean, "Town of Whispers," *Vanity Fair*, February 2013, www.vanityfair.com/culture/2013/02/zumba-alexis-wright-prostitution.

6. FBI press release, "Former Dixon Comptroller Rita Crundwell Pleads Guilty to Federal Fraud Charge, Admits Stealing $53 Million from City," November 14, 2012, https://archives.fbi.gov/archives/chicago/press-releases/2012/former-dixon-comptroller-rita-crundwell-pleads-guilty-to-federal-fraud-charge-admits-stealing-53-million-from-city.

7. Erika I. Ritchie, "Laguna Beach Woman Accused of Embezzling $1.5 Million and Using Money to Get Plastic Surgery and Buy Cattle," *Orange County Register*, June 9, 2017, https://www.ocregister.com/2017/06/09/laguna-beach-woman-accused-of-embezzling-1-5-million-and-using-money-to-get-plastic-surgery-and-buy-cattle.

8. Al Pascual and Kyle Marchini, "2018 Child Identity Fraud Study," Javelin, April 24, 2018, https://www.javelinstrategy.com/coverage-area/2018

-child-identity-fraud-study.

9. Quentin Fotrell, "My Mother Stole My Identity and Racked Up $500,000 in Debt," *MarketWatch*, October 8, 2016, https://www.marketwatch.com/story /my-mother-was-a-psychopath-who-stole-my-identity-and-racked-up-500000-in -debt-2016-10-04; "Researcher Profile: An Interview with Axton Betz Hamilton," *Journal of Financial Therapy*, July 2015, http://newprairiepress.org/cgi/viewcontent .cgi?article=1097&context=jft.

10. Asuman Buyukcan-Tetik, Catrin Finkenauer, Sofie Kuppens, and Kathleen D. Vohs, "Both Trust and Self-Control Are Necessary to Prevent Intrusive Behaviors: Evidence from a Longitudinal Study of Married Couples," *Journal of Family Psychology* 27, no. 4 (2013): 671–676, https://pdfs.semanticscholar.org /a341/9ef0cc75f9f796c7328c4c611877de47e50e.pdf.

11. Alessandro Bucciol, Fabio Landini, and Marco Piovesan, "Unethical Behavior in the Field: Demographic Characteristics and Beliefs of the Cheater," *Journal of Economic Behavior and Organization* 93 (2013): 248–257, https://econpapers .repec.org/article/eeejeborg/v_3a93_3ay_3a2013_3ai_3ac_3ap_3a248-257.htm.

12. Ofer H. Azar, Shira Yosef, and Michael Bar-Eli, "Do Customers Return Excessive Change in a Restaurant? A Field Experiment on Dishonesty," *Journal of Economic Behavior and Organization* 93 (2013): 219–226, http://houdekpetr.cz /!data/public_html/papers/Azar%20et%20al%202013.pdf.

13. Toke Reinholt Fosgaard, Lars Gårn Hansen, and Marco Piovesan, "Separating Will from Grace: An Experiment on Conformity and Awareness in Cheating," *Journal of Economic Behavior and Organization* 93 (2013): 279–284, https:// doi.org.10.1016/j.jebo.2013.03.027.

14. Telephone interview with author.

15. Jason Childs, "Gender Differences in Lying," *Economics Letters* 114, no. 2 (2012): 147–149, https://doi.org/10.1016/j.econlet.2011.10.006.

16. Telephone interview with author.

17. "Men Are Bigger Liars Than Women, Says Poll," BBC News, May 18, 2010, http://news.bbc.co.uk/2/hi/health/8689010.stm.

18. Ibid.

19. Bella DePaulo, "Who Lies?" *Psychology Today*, September 6, 2011, https:// www.psychologytoday.com/us/blog/living-single/201109/who-lies.

20. Ibid.

21. Telephone interview with author.

22. Gerold Mikula, "Perspective Related Differences in Interpretations of Injustice by Victims and Victimizers," in M. J. Lerner and G. Mikula, eds., *Entitlement and Affectional Bond: Critical Issues in Social Justice* (Boston: Springer, 1994), 175–203, https://link.springer.com/chapter/10.1007/978-1-4899-0984-8_8.

23. W. H. Jones and M. P. Burdette, "Betrayal in Relationships," in A. L. Weber and J. H. Harvey, eds., *Perspectives on Close Relationships* (Needham Heights, MA: Allyn and Bacon, 1994), 243–262, http://psycnet.apa.org/record/1994-98284-012.

24. Telephone interview with author; quoted in Abby Ellin, "The Drama of Deception," *Psychology Today*, June 30, 2015, https://www.psychologytoday.com /us/articles/201506/the-drama-deception.

25. *Little White Lie*, directed by Lacey Schwartz (Sundance, 2014).

26. Thomas Rogers, "The Evolution of Deceit," *Salon*, November 5, 2011, https://www.salon.com/2011/11/05/the_evolution_of_deceit; Meg Sullivan, "When She Says, 'It's Not You, It's Me,' It Really Might Be You, UCLA Study Suggests," October 24, 2012, http://newsroom.ucla.edu/releases/i-love-him-i-love-him-not-239857.

27. Jennifer Schwartz and Darrell Steffensmeier, "The Nature of Female Offending: Patterns and Explanation," in Ruth T. Zaplin, ed., *Female Offenders: Critical Perspectives and Effective Interventions,* 2nd ed. (Boston: Jones and Bartlett, 2008), 43–75; Kathleen Daly, "Gender and Varieties of White-Collar Crime," *Criminology* 27, no. 4 (1989): 769–794, https://doi.org/10.1111/j.1745-9125.1989 .tb01054.x; Darrell Steffensmeier, Michael Roche, and Jennifer Schwartz, "Gender and Twenty-First-Century Corporate Crime: Female Involvement and the Gender Gap in Enron-Era Corporate Frauds," *American Sociological Review* 78, no. 3 (2013): 448–476, https://doi.org/10.1177/0003122413484150.

28. Linda M. Grounds, "Forensic Psychological Evaluations of Women Who Embezzle," n.d., www.drlindagrounds.com/2011/forensic-psychological -evaluations-women-embezzle.

29. James William Coleman, *The Criminal Elite: Understanding White-Collar Crime*, 6th ed. (New York: Worth Publishers, 2005).

30. Paul M. Klenowski, "Learning the Good with the Bad," *Criminal Justice Review* 37, no. 4 (November 20, 2012): 461–477, http://journals.sagepub.com/doi /abs/10.1177/0734016812465874.

31. Dorothy Zietz, *Women Who Embezzle or Defraud* (New York: Praeger, 1981); Gilbert Geis, *White-Collar and Corporate Crime: A Documentary and Reference Guide* (Santa Barbara, CA: ABC-CLIO, 2011), 127.

32. Paul M. Klenowski, Heith Copes, and Christopher W. Mullins, "Gender, Identity, and Accounts: How White Collar Offenders Do Gender When Making Sense of Their Crimes," *Justice Quarterly* 28 (2011): 46–69, https://doi.org/10.1080 /07418825.2010.482536.

33. Kelly Paxton, "Catch Her If You Can," *Fraud Magazine*, November/December 2016, www.fraud-magazine.com/article.aspx?id=4294994705.

34. Telephone interview with author.

35. Paxton, "Catch Her If You Can."

36. In-person interview with author.

37. Daniel Houser, John A. List, Marco Piovesan, Anya Samek, and Joachim-Winter, "Dishonesty: From Parents to Children," *European Economic Review* 82 (February 2016): 242–254, https://doi.org/10.1016/j.euroecorev.2015.11.003.

38. Telephone interview with author.

39. This section is based entirely on an in-person interview with the author.

40. Telephone interview with author.

Nine: In God We Trust—Everyone Else, We Polygraph

1. Tod Perry, "Jon Stewart Points Out the Two Words Donald Trump Always Uses When He Lies," *Good*, February 28, 2017, https://www.good.is/articles /jon-stewart-points-out-trumps-lies.

2. Abby Ellin, "With Coercive Control, the Abuse Is Psychological," *New York Times*, July 11, 2016, https://well.blogs.nytimes.com/2016/07/11/with

-coercive-control-the-abuse-is-psychological.

3. Ibid.

4. Everything in this section comes from in-person interviews, class attendance, and follow-up telephone interviews with Phil Houston.

5. Eamon Javers, *Broker, Trader, Lawyer, Spy: The Secret World of Corporate Espionage* (New York: HarperBusiness, 2010), 179.

6. Ibid., 192; telephone interview with Phil Houston.

7. Javers, *Broker, Trader, Lawyer, Spy*, 195; telephone interview with Phil Houston.

8. Javers, *Broker, Trader, Lawyer, Spy*, 185.

9. Richard Wiseman, "Colour Changing Card Trick," Quirkology Psychology Videos, https://sellfy.com/p/Jp6S.

10. Christopher Chabris and Daniel Simons, The Invisible Gorilla, www .theinvisiblegorilla.com/gorilla_experiment.html.

11. Ibid.

12. Jeff Hancock, "The Future of Lying," Ted Talk, September 2012, https:// www.ted.com/talks/jeff_hancock_3_types_of_digital_lies.

13. Jeffrey T. Hancock, Laure E. Curry, Saurabh Goorha, and Michael Woodworth, "On Lying and Being Lied To: A Linguistic Analysis of Deception in Computer-Mediated Communication," *Discourse Processes* 45 (2008): 1–23, https://doi.org/10.1080/01638530701739181; Ted Radio Hour, "Does Technology Make Us More Honest?," NPR, June 20, 2014, https://www.npr.org/templates /transcript/transcript.php?storyId=322536435.

14. Telephone interview with author.

15. Javers, *Broker, Trader, Lawyer, Spy*, 182.

16. Charles F. Bond Jr. and Bella DePaulo, "Accuracy of Deception Judgments," *Personality and Social Psychology Review* 10, no. 3 (2006): 214–234, http://www.communicationcache.com/uploads/1/0/8/8/10887248/accuracy_of _deception_judgments.pdf.

17. Marc-André Reinhard, Martin Scharmach, and Patrick Müller, "It's Not What You Are, It's What You Know: Experience, Beliefs, and the Detection of Deception in Employment Interviews," *Journal of Applied Social Psychology* 43, no. 3 (2013): 467–479, https://onlinelibrary.wiley.com/doi/full /10.1111/j.1559-1816.2013.01011.x.

18. Joe Navarro, "The Truth About Lie Detection," *Psychology Today*, March 15, 2012, https://www.psychologytoday.com/us/blog/spycatcher/201203 /the-truth-about-lie-detection.

19. Jeffrey T. Hancock, Jennifer Thom-Santelli, and Thompson Ritchie, "Deception and Design: The Impact of Communication Technology on Lying Behavior," in Elizabeth Dykstra-Erickson and Manfred Tscheligi, eds., *Proceedings of ACM CHI Conference on Human Factors in Computing Systems* (April 24–19, 2004): 129–134, http://sml.stanford.edu/ml/2004/04/hancock-chi-impact.pdf.

20. "2008 Employment Screening Benchmark Report," https://www.hireright .com/resources/view/2018-employment-screening-benchmark-report.

21. Floyd Norris, "RadioShack Chief Resigns After Lying," *New York Times*, February 21, 2006, https://www.nytimes.com/2006/02/21/business

/radioshack-chief-resigns-after-lying.html.

22. Keith J. Winstein and Daniel Golden, "MIT Admissions Dean Lied on Résumé in 1979, Quits," *Wall Street Journal*, April 27, 2007, https://www.wsj.com /articles/SB117760330348583547.

23. Amir Efrati and Joann S. Lublin, "Thompson Resigns as CEO of Yahoo," *Wall Street Journal*, May 13, 2012, https://www.wsj.com/articles/SB100014240527 02304192704577402224129006022.

24. Roy Maurer, "Verify Degrees and Protect the Company from Resume Fraud," Society for Human Resource Management, June 14, 2017, https://www .shrm.org/resourcesandtools/hr-topics/talent-acquisition/pages/verify-degrees-and -protect-the-company-from-resume-fraud.aspx.

25. Emily Price, "'I Call It Truthful Hyperbole': The Most Popular Quotes from Trump's 'The Art of the Deal,'" *Fast Company*, April 4, 2017, https://www .fastcompany.com/3068552/i-call-it-truthful-hyperbole-the-most-popular-quotes -from-trumps-the-art-of-the-deal.

26. Pamela Meyer, "How to Spot a Liar," Ted Talk, July 2011, https://www .ted.com/talks/pamela_meyer_how_to_spot_a_liar.

27. Steve Van Aperen offers a master's certificate in detecting deception on his website, www.stevevanaperen.com/online-training.

28. Ken Alder, *The Lie Detectors: The History of an American Obsession* (Lincoln: University of Nebraska Press, 2007), xii.

29. Jack Kitaeff, ed., *Handbook of Police Psychology*, 2nd ed. (London: Taylor and Francis, 2018).

30. "William Marston: The Father of Polygraph," Polygraph Museum, www .lie2me.net/thepolygraphmuseum/id17.html.

31. Marguerite Lamb, "Who Was Wonder Woman 1? Long-Ago Law Alumna Elizabeth Marston Was the Muse Who Gave Us a Superheroine," *Bostonia*, no. 3 (Fall 2001): 12–17, https://open.bu.edu/bitstream/handle/2144/20658 /Bostonia2001Fall3_web.pdf?sequence=2.

32. "John Augustus Larson," Revolvy, n.d., https://www.revolvy.com/main /index.php?s=John+Augustus+Larson; Tony Long, "Feb. 2, 1935: You Lie," *Wired*, February 2, 2012, https://www.wired.com/2012/02/0202polygraph -leads-conviction.

33. Alexia Fernandez, "Stormy Daniels Passed a Lie Detector Test When Asked About Alleged Affair with President Trump," *People*, March 20, 2018, https:// people.com/politics/stormy-daniels-passed-lie-detector-alleged-trump-affair.

34. G. T. Monteleone, K. L. Phan, H. C. Nusbaum, D. Fitzgerald, J. S. Irick, S. E. Fienberg, and J. T. Cacioppo, "Detection of Deception Using fMRI: Better Than Chance, but Well Below Perfection," *Society for Neuroscience* 4, no. 6 (2009): 528–538, https://doi.org/10.1080/17470910801903530.

35. "Frequently Asked Questions," American Polygraph Association, https:// www.polygraph.org/polygraph-frequently-asked-questions.

36. Daniel Schorn, "BTK: Out of the Shadows," CBS News, September 29, 2005, https://www.cbsnews.com/news/btk-out-of-the-shadows.

37. This entire section is based on in-person interviews with the author.

38. Ronald Kessler, "Spies, Lies, Averted Eyes," *New York Times*, March 8,

1994, https://www.nytimes.com/1994/03/08/opinion/spies-lies-averted-eyes".html.

39. Sean Robinson, "What Made Ridgway Kill Still a Riddle," *News Tribune*, November 9, 2003, http://archive.is/FWnyS.

40. "Polygraphs in the Workplace: The Use of 'Lie Detectors' in Hiring and Firing," Hearings Before the Subcommittee on Employment Opportunities of the Committee on Education and Labor, House of Representatives, 99th Cong., 1st sess., on H.R. 1524 [and] H.R. 1924, July 30 and September 18, 1985, https://babel.hathitrust.org/cgi/pt?id=pst.000019083421, 279.

41. There is video footage of all of this on Polygraph.com.

42. Telephone interview with author.

43. In-person interview with author; Eli Wolfe, "Catching the Brain in a Lie: Is 'Mind Reading' Deception Detection Sci-Fi—or Science?," *California*, July 22, 2015, https://alumni.berkeley.edu/california-magazine/just-in/2016-02-18/catching-brain-lie-mind-reading-deception-detection-sci-fi-or.

44. Olga Khazan, "Doomed to Be the Biggest Losers?," *The Atlantic*, May 11, 2016, https://www.theatlantic.com/health/archive/2016/05/doomed-to-be-the-biggest-losers/482094.

45. In-person interview with author.

46. Washington University, "Research Casts Doubt on Voice-Stress Lie Detection Technology," *ScienceDaily*, February 11, 2004, https://www.sciencedaily.com/releases/2004/02/040211080041.htm.

47. Maria Konnikova, "How to Tell When Someone Is Lying," *New Yorker*, April 23, 2014, https://www.newyorker.com/science/maria-konnikova/how-to-tell-when-someone-is-lying.

48. Jad Abumrad and Robert Krulwich, *Deception: Lying to Ourselves*, podcast, Season 4, episode 2, February 29, 2008, Radiolab, produced by WNYC, MP3 audio, https://www.radiolab.org/story/91618-lying-to-ourselves.

49. Marc-André Reinhard, Rainer Greifeneder, and Martin Scharmach, "Unconscious Processes Improve Lie Detection," *Journal of Personality and Social Psychology* 105, no. 5 (2013): 721–739, http://psycnet.apa.org/record/2013-37998-001.

50. Konnikova, "How to Tell When Someone Is Lying"; Leanne ten Brinke, Dayna Stimson, and Dana Carey, "Some Evidence for Unconscious Lie Detection," *Psychological Science*, March, 21, 2014, http://journals.sagepub.com/doi/abs/10.1177/0956797614524421.

51. Konnikova, "How to Tell When Someone Is Lying"; ten Brinke et al., "Some Evidence for Unconscious Lie Detection."

52. Ibid.

53. Volker H. Franz and Ulrike von Luxburg, "No Evidence for Unconscious Lie Detection," *Psychological Science*, August 24, 2015, http://journals.sagepub.com/doi/abs/10.1177/0956797615597333?ssource=mfr&rss=1.

54. Audrey Nelson, "How Women and Men Interpret Unspoken Messages," *Psychology Today*, April 25, 2016, https://www.psychologytoday.com/us/blog/he-speaks-she-speaks/201604/how-women-and-men-interpret-unspoken-messages.

55. D. Dubois, N. Nichiporuk, L. ten Brinke, D. D. Rucker, A. D. Galinsky,

and D. R. Carney, "The Deception Equilibrium: The Powerful Are Better Liars but the Powerless Are Better Lie-Detectors," 2013, http://faculty.haas.berkeley.edu /dana_carney/deception.equillibrium.ms.and.ols.pdf.

56. Telephone interview with author.

Ten: Verify, but Don't Trust

1. Friedrich Nietzsche, *Beyond Good and Evil*, Part 4, "Aphorism," no. 183, Project Gutenberg, www.gutenberg.org/files/4363/4363-h/4363-h.htm.

2. Alexander Hamilton, "Observations on Certain Documents Contained in No. V & VI of 'The History of the United States for the Year 1796'" (Philadelphia: John Fenno, 1797), https://books.google.com/books/about/Observations_on _Certain_Documents_Contai.html?id=HX1bAAAAQAAJ.

3. Angela Serratore, "Alexander Hamilton's Adultery and Apology," *Smithsonian*, July 25, 2013, https://www.smithsonianmag.com/history/alexander -hamiltons-adultery-and-apology-18021947.

4. Lin-Manuel Miranda, lyrics to "Burn," *Hamilton: An American Musical* (Atlantic, 2015), available at AZLyrics, https://www.azlyrics.com/lyrics/linmanuel miranda/burn.html.

5. Christian Holub, "Hamilton Historical Facts That Didn't Make the Musical," *Entertainment Weekly*, March 16, 2016, http://ew.com/article/2016/03/16 /hamilton-historical-facts-book-musical.

6. Dick Cavett, "Lillian, Mary and Me," *New Yorker*, December 16, 2002, https://www.newyorker.com/magazine/2002/12/16/lillian-mary-and-me.

7. Telephone interview with author.

8. Bálint Kőszegi, "Five Universal Supertraits of the Human Personality," *Medium*, April 10, 2017, https://medium.com/heraclesport/the-five-universal -supertraits-of-the-human-personality-efbe91090456.

9. Telephone interview with author.

10. Ibid.

11. Stephen Joseph, "The Metaphor of the Shattered Vase," *Psychology Today*, May 21, 2012, https://www.psychologytoday.com/us/blog/what-doesnt -kill-us/201205/the-metaphor-the-shattered-vase.

12. "Travel Warning–Libya," US Embassy in Libya, https://ly.usembassy.gov /travel-warning-libya-3.

INDEX

Abby Ellin is an award-winning journalist and the author of *Teenage Waistland: A Former Fat Kid Weighs in on Living Large, Losing Weight and How Parents Can (and Can't) Help.* For five years she wrote the Preludes column about young people and money for the Sunday Money and Business section of the *New York Times.* She is also a regular contributor to the Health, Style, Business, and Education sections of that newspaper. Her work has been published in the *Wall Street Journal, Psychology Today, Time, New York, The Village Voice,* the *International Herald Tribune, Salon, Marie Claire, Glamour, Cosmopolitan, Good Housekeeping,* and *Redbook.* She holds a master of fine arts degree in creative writing from Emerson College and a master's in international public policy from Johns Hopkins University. As of this writing, her greatest accomplishments are summiting Kilimanjaro (with a broken wrist!) and naming "Karamel Sutra" ice cream for Ben and Jerry's.

PublicAffairs is a publishing house founded in 1997. It is a tribute to the standards, values, and flair of three persons who have served as mentors to countless reporters, writers, editors, and book people of all kinds, including me.

I. F. Stone, proprietor of *I. F. Stone's Weekly*, combined a commitment to the First Amendment with entrepreneurial zeal and reporting skill and became one of the great independent journalists in American history. At the age of eighty, Izzy published *The Trial of Socrates*, which was a national bestseller. He wrote the book after he taught himself ancient Greek.

Benjamin C. Bradlee was for nearly thirty years the charismatic editorial leader of *The Washington Post*. It was Ben who gave the *Post* the range and courage to pursue such historic issues as Watergate. He supported his reporters with a tenacity that made them fearless and it is no accident that so many became authors of influential, best-selling books.

Robert L. Bernstein, the chief executive of Random House for more than a quarter century, guided one of the nation's premier publishing houses. Bob was personally responsible for many books of political dissent and argument that challenged tyranny around the globe. He is also the founder and longtime chair of Human Rights Watch, one of the most respected human rights organizations in the world.

· · ·

For fifty years, the banner of Public Affairs Press was carried by its owner Morris B. Schnapper, who published Gandhi, Nasser, Toynbee, Truman, and about 1,500 other authors. In 1983, Schnapper was described by *The Washington Post* as "a redoubtable gadfly." His legacy will endure in the books to come.

Peter Osnos, *Founder*